T0313847

POVERTY AS SUBSISTENCE

Emerging Frontiers in the Global Economy

EDITOR
J.P. Singh

SERIES BOARD
Arjun Appadurai
Manuel Castells
Tyler Cowen
Christina Davis
Judith Goldstein
Deirdre McCloskey

Poverty as Subsistence

THE WORLD BANK AND PRO-POOR LAND REFORM IN EURASIA

Mihai Varga

STANFORD UNIVERSITY PRESS
Stanford, California

STANFORD UNIVERSITY PRESS
Stanford, California

© 2023 by Mihai Varga. All rights reserved.

Printed and bound by CPI Group (UK) Ltd, Croydon, CR0 4YY

Library of Congress Cataloging-in-Publication Data
Names: Varga, Mihai, author.
Title: Poverty as subsistence : the World Bank and pro-poor land reform in Eurasia / Mihai Varga.
Other titles: Emerging frontiers in the global economy.
Description: Stanford, California : Stanford University Press, 2023. | Series: Emerging frontiers in the global economy | Includes bibliographical references and index.
Identifiers: LCCN 2022015740 (print) | LCCN 2022015741 (ebook) | ISBN 9781503633049 (cloth) | ISBN 9781503634183 (ebook)
Subjects: LCSH: World Bank—Eurasia. | Land reform—Eurasia. | Agriculture and state—Eurasia. | Poverty—Government policy—Eurasia. | Farms, Small—Eurasia. | Subsistence farming—Eurasia. | Land reform—Bukovina (Romania and Ukraine) | Farms, Small—Bukovina (Romania and Ukraine) | Subsistence farming—Bukovina (Romania and Ukraine)
Classification: LCC HD1333.E83 V37 2023 (print) | LCC HD1333.E83 (ebook) | DDC 333.3/15—dc23/eng/20220611
LC record available at https://lccn.loc.gov/2022015740
LC ebook record available at https://lccn.loc.gov/2022015741

Cover design: George Kirkpatrick
Cover photo: Old houses with vegetable gardens in the village of Fedyakovo (Kstovsky District, Nizhny Novgorod Oblast) Wikipedia Commons
Typeset by Newgen North America in 10/14 Galliard

Familiei mele

Contents

Contents

Preface

THE RESEARCH BEHIND THIS book started in 2013 on the European Union's eastern border. Fieldwork often involved crossing the border in one of my respondents' car, a thirty-year-old Soviet-made Lada Zhiguli. When crossing into the EU, the Zhiguli was full of cheap Turkish and Chinese merchandise bought nearby in an informal and very large bazaar. When leaving the EU, the Zhiguli transported medication that Misha, my respondent, had bought in the EU to sell for a profit in his home community. Border guards repeatedly received their "right," a small payment usually waiting in my respondent's passport. Although struggling to combine incomes from several activities, Misha was anything but poor in comparison to other people in his community. Back in his village in Ukraine's Carpathian Mountains, he owned a small shop and an Italian-made, second-hand Fiat and a house with an agricultural land parcel, and he received a rent for his lifelong service for the state. Most importantly, his wife had been working as a cleaner for ten years in Italy, and from the money she regularly sent home and the money he earned from small trade, Misha and his wife supported their several children financially, from helping them build houses to, once the Donbas war erupted in 2014, helping them dodge military service. Misha paid no taxes and did not bother to register any of his commercial activities, except for his small shop.

For official statistics, Misha however was a rural smallholder and—given the extremely small size of his land possessions—a subsistence farmer. Relying on assessments coming from international organizations, his country's government equated small land plots with subsistence farming and poverty and portrayed subsistence as a major developmental problem, responsible for keeping large swaths of rural and peri-urban populations in poverty. If only smallholders could increase land plots—"consolidate" them, as formulated in official documents—they could turn agriculture into a profitable entrepreneurial activity. According to official discourses, local populations were prohibited from doing so because of their specific risk-averse and Soviet-socialized mindsets, because of the survival of former collective farms squeezing them out of commercial activities, and because of "predatory" informal traders, buying up for derisory prices the little production they had.

But Misha and the numerous other respondents I interviewed between 2013 and 2019 had a different story to tell. This was a story about combining various income sources and lucrative activities in complex social settings, in which households could—after decades of working both at home and abroad without holidays, formally but mostly informally—find ways to avoid poverty. Incidentally, what sparked this complex development was not the smallholders' resistance to plans from above to improve their lot but the very land reform enacted in the 1990s, the distribution of land to local populations. While pushing them into "subsistence," it protected their livelihoods by offering them food, one of the few things that they could live on without having to pay for it, next to the family labor that went into working the land. The poor, in my sample, were elsewhere. They were not "subsistence" farmers. The poor were those *forced* to sell their labor and everything they produced to pass the cold winters, those whose households and families had fallen apart and could not diversify income sources, and those who owned little to no land because land reform had failed to include them and were forced into informal day-laborer jobs paying no social contributions.

This book draws attention to subsistence, or a population's self-sustainment capacity, as a critical variable for socioeconomic development. Simply put, it builds on the thesis that development is often about how states engage with that subsistence capacity. This thesis is to be taken as both a positive and a normative statement. First, as a positive description of what "development" at times ends up meaning in practice, it implies that states attempt to reach developmental goals by reducing what they perceive as "underdeveloped" or "backward" sectors and the corresponding population owing its livelihood to such sectors. "Development" then becomes a race to diminish the numbers of people pursuing "subsistence" occupations, be it in agriculture, in handicraft, or more generally in the "informal economy," and a key indicator for "successful" or even "development" per se becomes the dwindling number of people pursuing occupations in agriculture and the informal economy. Second, as a normative statement, the "subsistence thesis" is about how development should work: development interventions recognize the "secure subsistence" need of the poor and design policies accordingly, building on the existing distribution of subsistence-maintaining resources and careful not to reduce them, be they land tenure or occupational or handicraft arrangements. They should avoid promoting "registration offensives," in particular if there is demanding conditionality for the poor to meet in order to benefit from registration.

The specific development intervention that this book focuses on—the "propertizing" land reform advocated by international organizations such as the World Bank foremost —was widely applied throughout the transitioning countries of Eurasia. It found support in a selective reading of China's early 1980s "market-making" reforms, suggesting that even limited land reform, if "individualizing" agricultural producers, translates into massive productivity, output, and income increases. The World Bank had emphasized land reform as a central mechanism for addressing poverty: land *transfers* help turning the poor into smallholders, while land *markets* would ideally help surpass even China's experience by helping turn smallholders more rapidly into *commercial* or entrepreneurial farmers. These reform steps seemingly supported each other and in China appeared indistinguishable, as land transfers to local populations translated into steep production and productivity increases. This apparently implied that achieving even more land reform—not just "transfers" of land but also markets for land—would bring even more positive results and possibly outdo developments in China. Yet post-communist Eastern Europe, Transcaucasia (the South Caucasus), and Central Asia defied this expectation. Land transfers and commercialization did not support each other but ended up in increasing tension. Even in the countries that introduced markets for land, smallholders were still characterized by what the World Bank refers to as subsistence: low productivity, avoidance of markets, self-consumption, and poverty. As argued throughout this book's chapters, this tension pushed governments and World Bank to forsake poverty reduction for commercialization.

International organizations, including the World Bank, widely acknowledge the limitations of land reform in spurring productivity increases and entrepreneurship on a large scale among the rural poor, with the notable exceptions of China and Vietnam. The World Bank has explained this failure by claiming that other countries have been unwilling or incapable to adopt reforms resembling China's. In contrast, this book argues that it is precisely because other countries adopted a limited version of Chinese reform components that the outcome of reforms was an increase rather than a decrease in subsistence. This outcome of increased subsistence is hardly negative, as it provided tens of millions of families in transitioning countries with a safety net in the context of difficult reforms and recurring economic crises. But reforms in post-communist countries failed to approximate the results in China and Vietnam, two countries achieving productivity increases without rural depopulation and labor shedding.

At first sight, land reform in post-communist countries featured many pro-poor ingredients: it expanded the subsistence-maintaining stock of resources at the disposal of local populations, and while involving registration, it did not link it to conditionality. However, the land reform program also had its failings. In particular, while it featured many subsistence-increasing elements, it had little in place to limit subsistence and spur the sort of officially sanctioned, taxable commercialization that reformers favored. Reform proponents soon became unsettled by the sheer increase in "subsistence"—that is, by the local populations' preference for self-consuming its agricultural production and selling surplus informally instead of commercializing it on official markets. The World Bank and other international organizations increasingly problematized subsistence, turning it into a major indicator of underdevelopment. They blamed subsistence not on the reform but on features of the smallholders' environment, in particular the survival of former collective farms. As a consequence, the reform program shifted dramatically from showing little interest in limiting subsistence to declaring the need to reduce subsistence as the reform's most important goal, forsaking original goals of reducing poverty through land transfers. The relationship between subsistence and poverty was simplified down to the level of claiming that reductions in subsistence equal reductions in poverty. Against this background, the book argues that subsistence in the sense of low productivity will be the outcome wherever reforms focus only on the transfer of property rights while ignoring or even seeking to contain the smallholders' immediate environment—that is, the changing social structure of actors and institutions determining whether smallholders survive and even grow in their respective environments: larger farms, informal traders, intermediaries, and secondhand machinery and fresh product markets.

The chapters to follow will first trace the land reform program to a selective reading by international organizations of Chinese rural reforms, which became a central reference for similar reforms throughout the transitioning countries in Eastern Europe, Transcaucasia, and Central Asia. Through its analysis of China's reforms, the book argues that reforms were far more complex than initially portrayed and took into account the smallholders' immediate environment. The analysis then moves to land reform in post-communist countries in Europe and Central Asia, to show that this element (the smallholders' immediate environment) was largely overlooked or even criticized or derided as "traditional" and "non-market." Rather than advocate support for segments of this immediate environment, the World Bank extended financial support to finance the expansion of international retail chains to post-communist countries. National governments too acted by increasingly trying to contain the informal activities specific for this environment, thus further strengthening the contrast between post-communist countries and China.

The analysis of the land reform program across Eurasia combines with a qualitative research design that compares fieldwork regions with similar outcomes (high subsistence) but different "land reform" approaches to poverty—one seen as approximating the Chinese pattern of fast collective farm dismantlement (Romania), the other one criticized for resembling Russia's pattern of protracted reforms (Ukraine). It confronts the assumptions of the land reform perspective with developments and realities on the ground to show how smallholders grow out of subsistence despite the failings of the land reform program. Thus the book argues that the discursive construction of subsistence prevailing in the World Bank's expert network is based on a limited and arbitrary understanding of markets. That is, it downplays the extent to which local populations—cast as "subsisting" on agriculture—actually engage in markets, and it dismisses such markets as traditional and informal "non-markets," although much could be gained from approaching them as resources for rather than obstacles to development.

This book took seven years to mature, through yearly fieldwork rounds and a vigorous exchange of ideas at the Institute for East-European Studies (OEI) at the Freie Universität (FU) Berlin and in a wider and international community of scholars. At the OEI I would like to thank in particular Katharina Bluhm for the support, inspiration, and sharp comments she offered me throughout these years and ever since my beginning days at the OEI in 2012. I have also benefitted tremendously at the FU Berlin from the support and friendship of Aron Buzogány, who has encouraged me to keep working on the World Bank's role in land reform and pro-poor reforms. In Amsterdam, Annette Freyberg-Inan and Rüya Gökhan Koçer offered early supportive comments on the first ideas behind this book. Michael Burawoy has offered me excellent reading recommendations and friendly support for my career. Mitchell Orenstein provided the inspiration for this study's first part, encouraging me to work on the production of ideas at the World Bank. Simone Piras confronted me with constructive criticism from the perspective of authors involved in research for the World Bank. Sebastian Hoppe and Tobias Rupprecht read and commented on parts of the book. Diana Mincyte kindly supported me in the process of turning this book into the basis for my post-doctoral degree (*Habilitation*). Ştefan Dorondel, Petr Jehlička, and Oane Visser included me in an international network of scholars passionate about self-provisioning and the resilience of smallholders throughout the world, and they offered excellent comments on parts of my work and the research supporting this book's second part. Thanks are also due to the enthusiastic team at Stanford University Press that has helped improve and finish this manuscript, and in particular to Steve Catalano for his encouragements and feedback and to Barbara Armentrout for her excellent comments and language editing.

Finally, this book would not exist without the openness and continuous support from my fieldwork contacts, many opening to a complete stranger the doors of their homes and the secrets of how they fought for their livelihoods during the terrifying times of a collapsing old world and an emerging, unknown realm of post-communist capitalism. Among them, my greatest thanks goes to Vanya and Sveta, who have allowed and encouraged me to accompany them through the daily undertakings necessary for ensuring their livelihood.

POVERTY AS SUBSISTENCE

Poverty Reduction through Land Transfers

ONE OF THE MOST ENDURING TENETS of World Bank development policy has been that propertizing reforms have pro-poor effects. The World Bank has emphasized since the 1970s the importance for economic development of transferring agricultural land to the rural and peri-urban poor (Chenery et al. 1974; Deininger and Binswanger 1999; World Bank 1975). Following the fall of the Soviet Union and citing the success of land reforms in China and Vietnam, World Bank experts generally advocated the full and *egalitarian* distribution of collectively owned land to local populations in post-communist countries (Csaki, Lerman, and Feder 2002; Deininger and Binswanger 1999; Lipton 2009; Swinnen and Rozelle 2006). Broadly following this logic, the fastest pace of "propertizing" land reforms to date was achieved by countries in Eastern Europe, Transcaucasia, and Central Asia, distributing property titles to 145 million hectares of land throughout the 1990s and early 2000s (Dudwick, Fock, and Sedik 2007; Lerman 2017). The expectation was that secure and transferable rights over farmland would incentivize smallholders to work their land more, spend less on enforcing their rights, and—if allowed to trade property titles—use their land as collateral for obtaining bank loans.

For the World Bank, post-communist countries at first constituted the least problematic region, expecting—in contrast to Latin America—few to no complications in the process of "land titling." If Latin America generally presented the problem of having to redistribute land against the interests of large landowners (De Janvry and Sadoulet 1989; Binswanger, Deininger, and Feder 1995), the post-communist countries of Eurasia were believed to be capable of quickly transferring land to the rural population (Deininger 2003). But while China and Vietnam managed to pull "hundreds of millions of households out of dire poverty" (Swinnen and Rozelle 2006, 1), in Eurasia's post-communist countries the early years of reform were marked by a tremendous fall in output. World Bank economists documented productivity increases in only those countries that massively reduced agricultural employment (Swinnen and Rozelle 2006; see also chapters 2 and 3). The distribution of millions of property titles to former, pre-communist owners and rural populations did not spur the emergence of a stratum of commercial or entrepreneurial farmers, as expected by reformers, but of millions of "subsistence households," producing more for self-consumption than for markets. Private ownership seemed too fragmented to allow production surpluses beyond what rural households would use for self-consumption (Csaki, Lerman, and Feder 2002; Deininger 2003; Lipton 2009; Swinnen and Rozelle 2006).

In the largest post-Soviet countries, reforms failed to dislodge or dismantle former collective farms. In Russia, Kazakhstan, and Ukraine, most smallholder households relied on informal arrangements with former collective farms for receiving inputs and marketing outputs (Amelina 2000; von Cramon-Taubadel and Zorya 2001; Yefimov 2003; Zorya 2003). World Bank experts concluded that reforms in most post-Soviet countries were often only "nominal" and that "subsistence agriculture" and the survival of collective farms characterize those countries that halted or aborted reforms (Csaki, Lerman, and Feder 2002; Lipton 2009; Swinnen and Rozelle 2006). The World Bank had expected that land reform—the egalitarian distribution of agricultural land property titles— would turn the poor into producers selling on markets. As this expectation did not materialize, World Bank experts initially suspected the cause to be the insufficient pursuit of reforms. But as land reform unfolded with subsistence and collective farm survival as unwanted companions, the idea of addressing poverty through land transfers in post-communist Europe and Central Asia lost traction. Instead, the World Bank shifted to perceiving "subsistence" agriculture as the main problem stalling rural development and keeping large swaths of rural and semi-urban populations in poverty or forcing them to migrate.

Subsistence: From Dualism to Symbiosis

Subsistence refers to food production destined for consumption within the producing household or to those producers "who sell less than 50% of their production" (Kostov and Lingard 2002; Mosher 1969). It implies a faulty or incomplete relationship with markets. It can characterize not only what people produce for self-consumption but also what inputs they use in producing: subsistence can indicate a farm that does not procure its inputs on markets. *Subsistence agriculture* implies that a household entirely or largely depends on a form of agriculture for its livelihood that rarely engages with markets and that, because of the low contribution it brings, can at best help the household survive or "subsist," keeping it in a "vicious" circle of poverty. In other words, the term is used not just to measure or describe low to nonexistent levels of market integration but also to measure or describe (low) living standards and poverty (Heidhues and Brüntrup 2003). As argued below and in the next chapters, most World Bank studies on land reform approach subsistence farming as the opposite of commercial farming, referring to farms selling most production on markets. Those forced to "subsist" on their own production are by definition poor.

In the aftermath of the Soviet Union's collapse, Eastern Europe, Transcaucasia, and Central Asia entered post-communism with sizable populations owing their livelihoods to agriculture, be it in rural or peri-urban areas on city outskirts. The 1990s, characterized by manufacturing job losses in the millions due to deindustrialization, stabilized or even increased agricultural occupation, thus interrupting (in Russia and Ukraine) or stopping (in Poland and Romania) the decreasing trend in rural population encouraged by communists, while in Central Asia rural populations continued to increase. This situation not only contrasted with highly urbanized Western Europe but was also characterized by a type of agriculture that went on with little mechanization, little commercialization, small land plots, and low—if any—profit rates. Most international advisors and local reformers saw little future in such "small-scale farming," given its alleged lack of "efficiency" (Sarris, Doucha, and Mathijs 1999). Equated with subsistence, small-scale agriculture seemed a form of "extreme primitivization" (Gaddy and Ickes 2002) that needed to be "overcome," as "subsistence production entails significant misallocations of resources, especially of human time" (von Braun and Lohlein 2003, 47). The surviving former collectively owned farms (*kolkhozy*) were seen as facilitators of subsistence agriculture and also as its beneficiaries. Subsistence farmers were thought to "subsidize" the former collective farms by "allowing" the farms to use their land for a very small lease, often paid in kind, and farms "subsidized" smallholders by paying them a lease that was crucial in allowing small-holders to keep small stocks of animals, without, however, incentivizing them to develop production (Koester and Striewe 1999; von Braun and Lohlein 2003). Smallholders and former collective (now corporate) farms thus engaged in a mutually beneficial arrangement that these studies referred to as "dualism" or "dualization," implying that "entrepreneurial" farmers were squeezed out by the dual structure formed by former collective farms and smallholders. In a line of argumentation that would also appear in World Bank publications and country reports (chapters 2 and 3), the dualist argument emphasized the continuities with the communist past, prompting the comment that land reform was more "imaginary than real" (Yefimov 2003) and was basically derailed by the powerful collective farm "lobby". Despite claiming that little has changed in the arrangements between smallholders and former collective farms since communism, the same literature identifies one area in which there is a break with the communist past: it claims that because of the abuses of collectivization, the local population is reluctant to establish and enter cooperatives or any associative forms using the same "collectivist" terminology (Gardner and Lerman 2006; Lerman and Sedik 2014; Hagedorn 2014). Such reluctance appeared to contribute to the fragmentation of smallholder farming.

Other observers produced a more nuanced take on small-scale farming. Heidhues and Brüntrup (2003, 16–17) argued in favor of understanding subsistence as "the most rational answer to an adverse environment" and underlined that what passes as subsistence should not be discarded as "non-economic mentality."[1] Research on earlier, pre-communist land reforms suggested a different relationship between poverty and subsistence, arguing that it is the poor that are forced to commercialize or sell the little production they can achieve and that an increase in landholdings might spur self-consumption rather than more commercialization (Mitrany 1951). A rich literature explained post-communist "dualist" arrangements as adaptive reactions to the shock produced by initial reforms (Nikulin 2011, 2012; Visser 2009; Wegren 2005). It underlined the "urban bias" of reforms evident in areas such as price liberalization, subsidy reductions, and the state's withdrawal from marketing and questioned whether land reform followed pro-poor goals (Wegren 1998, 2005). Others argued that small-scale farming was far too diverse and fluid to fit under the term *subsistence* easily, and they proposed alternative notions such as "self-provisioning." *Self-provisioning* acknowledged that rather than being a sign of "primitivism," production for one's own consumption can indicate a desirable and sustainable outcome (Jehlička and Smith 2011; Smith and Jehlička 2013), valued positively by farmers (Ries 2009). Instead of "dualist," they described the relationship between former collective farms and smallholders as "symbiotic" (Humphrey 1998; Pallot and Nefedova 2007; Visser 2009; Abrahams 1996). Rather than showing "strong psychological resistance to cooperation" (Gardner and Lerman 2006), smallholders establish or enter even production cooperatives (despite the resemblance to collective farms) *if* expecting efficiency gains and if the state-imposed conditionality is low (Sabates-Wheeler 2002).

This latter perspective stresses continuities with communism too, but it does so not to question the impact of reforms but to show how smallholders matter for food production. Despite forced collectivization, under communism, private agricultural production on small land plots was widespread and outmatched the productivity of collective farms, with 30 percent of agricultural output produced on only 2 percent of the land. Dairy products, eggs, and vegetables often originated in private production (with inputs such as fertilizers often extracted from collective farms), supplementing the incomes of collective farm workers and playing an important part in feeding the cities (Spoor and Visser 2001; Wädekin 1973). The high productivity of small-scale farming relative to larger farms survived communism, with smallholders producing until the 2010s most food (vegetables, milk, and meat) in most post-communist countries, particularly in the largest ones such as Russia, Ukraine, and Romania. Therefore, the role of small-scale farmers appears crucial for these countries' "food sovereignty" (Visser et al. 2015).

Nor was subsistence a good predictor for the fortune of small-scale farms: several authors argued that depending on the geographical location, small-scale farming seemed to be intensifying rather than declining (Kuns 2017; Pallot and Nefedova 2007; Varga 2016), even if the land reforms demanded by the World Bank were postponed (Ukraine) or seen as deficient (Romania). And the corporate farms' interest in "symbiotic" arrangements should not be taken for granted: depending on the institutional context and the role played by authorities, corporate farms in certain regions opted out of "symbiotic" arrangements with smallholders (Kurakin, Nikulin, and Visser 2019). What appears problematic from the self-provisioning and symbiosis perspectives is not smallholder agriculture per se but the role of national and supranational actors in forcefully reducing the diversity of agricultural actors in post-communist countries. Such reduction happens as governments and supranational actors—like the European Union—exclude local forms of food production from the wider spectrum of "legitimate economic actors" (Aistara 2009; Mincyte 2011; Roger 2014; Smith, Kostelecký, and Jehlička 2015).

Monetization and the Smallholders' Internalizing Logic of Action

The symbiosis and self-provisioning arguments contend that subsistence represents a reaction to wide-ranging reforms rather than being a sign of insufficient reform. I take this argument further to suggest that the life-world of smallholders is heavily affected by reforms and that smallholders are anything but living in a world of "imaginary" reform. Reforms mean not only what governments officially identify as such but also the wider changes previously introduced by states, now "normalized" and in most situations already taken for granted—that is, not counting as "reforms" anymore. One of the vastest historical reforms to affect peasantry and rural populations across the globe has been the increasing *monetization* of household needs—that is, the gradual reduction of the "fallback resources" (Scott 1977, 64) available to households and households' ensuing "growing need for money" (Akram-Lodhi and Kay 2010, 186). The increase in monetary needs is an effect of the growing industrialization of agriculture, state-imposed enclosure acts, and forced dispossession, restricting rural populations' access to common land, fields, or forests (Akram-Lodhi and Kay 2010). Furthermore, it also reflects increasing taxation, forcing the adoption of crops and breeds that help households meet their monetary needs. In the words of James C. Scott (1977, 21), referring to colonial governments in Ghana and Nigeria, authorities "did what they could to encourage cash-cropping by imposing hut taxes and other levies that would increase the need for cash production." I will refer to this focus on monetary needs as the "monetization perspective," presented in detail in part 2.

A key implication of this perspective is that commercialization constitutes a reaction to the poverty caused by declining "fallback resources" rather than the cure to or polar opposite of subsistence and poverty.

Poverty forces smallholders to sell whatever they have, including their labor and whatever they can grow on the little land—usually the household plot—they own. From this perspective, one can better understand the reaction of local populations in Eastern Europe to the previous round of propertizing land reform, the pre-communist distribution of land following World War I. In his 1951 study of pre-communist and communist land reforms in Southeastern and Eastern Europe, David Mitrany (1951, 100–101) noted that instead of simply increasing commercialization, post-WWI reforms not only increased subsistence (self-consumption of produce) but also improved the livelihoods of local populations receiving land:

> The real change [brought by land reform] was not from large-scale to small-scale, . . . but rather from farming for the market to farming for subsistence. What distinguished the eastern peasant from the western large farmer or peasant farmer was that to him his land was first and foremost a means of raising food for his family and his animals. His production was accordingly diversified and he took to market only the surplus, or perhaps something more if he were in need of cash. A freer use of their crops or even a larger yield meant first of all a higher consumption among the peasants themselves, who formerly had gone short of food or had been living on poor food. "I used to take my geese to market," was the way a Hungarian peasant put it, "and keep myself on potatoes; now I sell the potatoes and eat the geese."

Like post-WWI reforms in Eastern Europe, the initial land reforms enacted by communist countries in East Asia and post-communist countries in Eastern Europe and Central Asia, to the extent they took the form of land titling, *increased* the amount of "fallback resources" at the local population's disposal. They deeply impacted the livelihoods of those involved but did so in varying ways. In a first group of countries, land reform rapidly dismantled collective farms and distributed land to the population, turning rural and semi-urban dwellers into smallholders. Out of this group, only in China and Vietnam did reforms succeed in turning smallholders into commercial farmers. They lifted them out of subsistence production and poverty by initially keeping a strong state presence in the commercial structures buying up the smallholders' production and by generally supporting the smallholders' immediate environment—that is, the larger set of structures and actors determining whether smallholders survive and grow, such as local markets of suppliers and buyers (see chapter 2). According to international experts and authors of World Bank publications, a few post-communist countries, located in Transcaucasia and the Balkan peninsula, followed a reform path approximating China's fast distribution of land (Lipton 2009, 205; see also Csaki and Lerman 1993; Swinnen 2005). In fact, however, they enacted propertizing land reforms with little concern for the smallholders' immediate environment. Same as roughly seventy years before in Eastern Europe's post-WWI land reform, the outcome was a highly fragmented, "subsistence" agriculture, far from the productivity gains experienced by China and Vietnam.

As argued in the next chapters, the World Bank, on the one hand, praised these countries as best practices of "propertizing" reforms. On the other hand, it criticized them for failing to enact even more reforms, in particular marketizing and cadastral reforms, seeing subsistence as the direct effect of this failure. Propertizing reforms nevertheless had a profound impact, raising the range and amount of fallback options at the disposal of local populations. With little competition from international retailers throughout post-communism's first years, local informal markets proliferated, helping smallholders sell production directly or through intermediaries.

The other large group of countries earned heavy criticism from World Bank experts for pursuing less ambitious reforms. This group of countries, referred to as "Russia-like" (Lipton 2009, 205; Swinnen 2005, 18), avoided or postponed dismantling the collective farms and distributed land through shares in collective farms rather than property titles. The largest post-Soviet countries—Russia, Ukraine, and Kazakhstan—fall under this category. However, as argued in this study, land reform had a profound impact also in this group of countries, as it reorganized the relationship between tenant and owner, which in turn facilitated a pattern of informal commercialization. The owners (smallholders) outnumbered the tenants (farms) in the post-reform context, and the owners owed at least part of their livelihood to the capacity of tenants to pay rents—indeed, the post-communist (re)birth of "symbiosis." Furthermore, tenancy was most often demonetized, as tenants paid for the land not in money but in grain, which owners used as animal fodder. This arrangement limited the cash needs of both owners and tenants: owners (smallholders) received demonetized inputs that fed either them or their animals, while tenants (former collective farms) produced without having to pay rents in cash. In other words, reform was real and lowered the monetary needs in the smallholders' immediate environments. Here too the reform outcome was subsistence *and* a pattern of informal and selective commercialization among smallholders.

In both contexts—which Michael Lipton referred to as "China-like" and "Russia-like"—land reform spurred an increase in subsistence, acknowledged in World Bank discourse and seen as the outcome of insufficient land reform, failing to establish land markets in the China-pattern countries and failing to propertize local populations and establish land markets in the Russia-pattern countries. In response, the World Bank and national governments called for land reform to go beyond propertizing. Instead, reform should establish markets and incentivize smallholders to "trade" their property titles, assuming that this will facilitate the differentiation between smallholders capable of increasing operations and those inclined to leave the sector. Furthermore, authorities and international advisors initiated the registration of larger smallholders as a precondition for disbursing state aid, thus seeking to drive the sector's differentiation further. But land market participation and registration come with increased conditionality and an increase in the monetary burden smallholder households face and, as argued in this book, they are therefore resisted.

The next chapters will focus in detail on the discourse emerging in the World Bank's knowledge network for coming to terms with land reform outcomes in post-communist countries. In doing so, it follows a broader stream of studies dedicated to national and supranational improvement plans that has long emphasized how national states and supranational organizations design interventions that are bereft of political-economic complications. Thus they avoid political questions by turning them into "technical" issues (Ferguson 1990), "objectivizing" (Escobar 1984) or "simplifying" (Scott 1998) highly diverse populations, territories, and economic relationships (something discussed in more detail in the next chapter). In the context described by this study, the World Bank's and national governments' discourse about the outcomes of land reform becomes one about "subsistence" as the result of incomplete reform. Yet this reading, applied to a highly diverse population, operates as a simplification, as it reduces it to one numerical indicator, the size of the land plot, irrespective of whether anyone is actually "subsisting" on agriculture. As a consequence of World Bank and national governments becoming increasingly worried over the high incidence of subsistence, policy goals shifted from pursuing poverty reduction through "propertizing" and "individualizing" the use of land to "consolidation"—that is, overcoming the land fragmentation characterizing subsistence by incentivizing smallholders to increase operations or leave agriculture.

Against this background, this study paints a different picture. Despite or because of the failure to establish land markets, land reform had important demonetizing effects, allowing smallholders to secure control over inputs and allowing an "immediate environment" to emerge that supports smallholders with vital, cheap, in-kind inputs, as well as cash incomes. But this immediate environment and the actors populating it are themselves characterized by fragmentation, informality, and absence of contractual transactions. Consequently, and in contrast to China, the reaction in World Bank discourse and national policies has been to dismiss this environment and call for its containment through "commercialization" and inclusion of smallholder economies into global value chains. In other words, land reform brought two developments that take center stage in this book and that the World Bank had not intended and, therefore, dismissed or condemned: an increase in subsistence, coupled with a pattern of prudent and informal commercialization "from below" among smallholders.

Overview of This Book

The book's first part (chapters 1 to 3) focuses on the World Bank land reform discourse. Chapter 1 analyzes the World Bank's land reform program as encapsulated in key publications appearing in the 1990s. It shows where and how land reform ideas compromised with neoliberalism, arguing, based on World Bank oral history interviews, that the World Bank's land reform proposals constitute a compromise between the neoliberal focus on structural adjustment and critical receptions of World Bank policies following the Green Revolution. The chapter further argues that the impact of neoliberalism was not so much the stress on markets as a reduction of markets to private property, translating into an emphasis on only a very narrow set of institutional reforms. This narrow set of institutional reforms—the land reform program—informed post-communist countries' approach to poverty and transforming agriculture. Before reaching the post-communist countries, the land reform program incorporated one more ingredient: the use of China as reform benchmark for post-communist countries.

Chapter 2 argues that World Bank experts drew support for land reforms in post-communist Eurasia from a selective reading of China's early

1980s "market-making" reforms. The Bank's treatment of Chinese policies reduced them to their land reform component and ignored the state's role as subsidizer and buyer of poor people's production. This simplified version of China's reforms—turning poverty reduction into one institutional "fix" to be settled by introducing property rights—became an important reference for the post-communist countries of Eastern Europe, Transcaucasia, and Central Asia that undertook land reform. The chapter shifts from the key World Bank publications treated in chapter 1 to country-level reports produced by the World Bank about four post-communist countries: Moldova, Romania, Tajikistan, and Ukraine. This change from publications with global reach to country-level reports seeks to check whether and how the Bank's general expectations differ from what reformers find on the ground and whether such findings, if different from expectations, lead to a reformulation of policies. According to the World Bank, the four countries differed in their government's ability and capacity to implement land reforms: the poorer, small former Soviet republics of Moldova and Tajikistan are considered relatively good performers, while Romania and Ukraine earn continuous critique for their levels of subsistence. The World Bank initially emphasized land reform as a central mechanism for addressing rural poverty worldwide: land transfers help to turn the poor into smallholders while land markets help to turn smallholders into commercial or entrepreneurial farmers. While these reform steps seem to support each other, the analysis of twenty-five years of World Bank reports on land reform in the four post-communist countries finds that the two steps—land transfers and commercialization—develop in a tension unacknowledged at the level of more general publications. The analysis shows that by the end of the 2000s, World Bank–inspired policies prioritized commercialization over addressing poverty reduction, and the underlying understanding of poverty had changed from poverty as lack of farmland to poverty as lack of alternatives to farming. Furthermore, even though later seen as a sign of underdevelopment, the subsistence capacity of local populations following land transfers was in earlier reports acknowledged and encouraged. The expectation was that subsistence would support the commercialization of agriculture as price and trade liberalization would incentivize producing for export and relieve welfare systems.

Chapter 3 combines the focus on discourse with an analysis of how outcomes of land reform in post-communist countries fared against each other and against reform outcomes in China and Vietnam. Several points emerge from the comparison. First, some countries switched categories from Russia-like to China-like, increasingly handing out property titles and corresponding land parcels to local populations. Yet this hardly impacted the prevalent pattern of subsistence or helped to reverse dualization. Second, the reforms' impact on poverty was often left out of sight and replaced with a focus on productivity or the extent of individualization of land use or property rights. Finally, there hardly were numerical indicators measuring subsistence at the level of smallholder farms other than the size of the land plot, as productivity measures tended to reflect official total output data. Thus, small farms with land holdings below two hectares were seen as practicing subsistence farming simply based on their land plot size. This strengthened the impression that smallholders generally failed to engage with markets. The problem, therefore, in the World Bank's perspective was not so much the failure of having pro-poor results but the decreasing control over smallholders perceived to have withdrawn from "markets" into "subsistence." Subsistence became an effect of anything but reforms, having little to do with markets. The next chapters offer a contrasting perspective.

Part 2 starts with a detailed description of a fieldwork study of smallholders and subsistence and agricultural value chains pursued in the Ukrainian-Romanian border region of Bukovina (chapter 4). The rationale for selecting the Bukovina region was that this historical region currently belongs to two countries with contrasting approaches to land reform. One is presented as China-like (Romania), the other as Russia-like (Ukraine), with differing speeds of dismantling communist village institutions and propertizing local populations: fast in Romania, slow in Ukraine. Nevertheless, on both sides of the border, the region features very high numbers of smallholders, which authorities characterize as practicing subsistence agriculture. This similarity in outcome allows research to move beyond statements reducing subsistence to lack of land reform and explore the hypothesis that the labelling of informal economic activities as "subsistence" hides important developments treated in detail in chapter 5: the informal commercialization observable among smallholders irrespective of the pattern of land reform enacted and the consolidation through decreasing smallholder numbers from the 2010s on.

Chapter 5 returns to the observation—confirmed by the World Bank and the Food and Agriculture Organization—that in most post-communist countries, smallholders produce some of the most basic food staples and until the mid-2000s were generally the source of most of the food produced in these countries. Since the fall of communism, they have managed to increase production and the land they work, even though their numbers start to decrease in the 2010s. The increasing smallholder production is a puzzling development since smallholders had little to no access to credit markets and formal investment, as most were or still are unregistered and said to practice subsistence production. The chapter contends that the tendency among smallholders is not one of growth toward and through economies of scale but one of self-provisioning, understood as organizing production so as to internalize production steps and demonetize costs and growing to control upstream and downstream links in their respective value chains. It asks what makes such demonetization possible in the fieldwork area and identifies various features of the smallholders' environments, such as a diverse scene of intermediaries supplying smallholders with cash incomes. It draws attention to the mixed-income household (the notion it uses instead of "subsistence" farms) as the numerically dominant presence in the post-communist rural landscape, combining incomes from agriculture (and other forms of informal self-employment) with incomes from welfare transfers and wage work. How such households interact with larger local producers is crucial for the latter, allowing them to increase informally the land at their disposal or enter deals with traders. The research implies that the features of their immediate environments are crucial for the smallholders' growth and survival and should be valued accordingly rather than dismissed in favor of integrating smallholders into the retailer- and supermarket-dominated value chains of the global food economy.

The first two chapters in part 2 centered on issues of resilience—that is, on how smallholders survive and grow in their immediate environment despite authorities treating them as subsistence farmers. But from Central Asia to Eastern Europe, the strong showing of smallholders is a source of embarrassment for national governments. Chapter 6 turns to "resistance," or economic practices and mental attitudes imputed by authorities to smallholders. To curb subsistence farming, the World Bank and authorities call for or promote measures seeking the "commercialization" of smallholder agriculture. Commercialization is about increasing the smallholders' monetary needs rather than facilitating the smallholders' access to markets or acknowledging those markets where they already operate. Markets are not just supposed to help small-scale farmers access investments and credit but are expected to discipline a sector perceived as alien to "business orientation" and owing its existence not to markets but to the surviving structures of the communist past, such as the former collective, now corporate farm, as well as to its "subsistence mentality." The resistance imputed to smallholders and others is their very operation in conditions of informality, the land use patterns they practice, and the rejection of state programs incentivizing them to adopt more profitable crops and animal breeds or to establish and join cooperatives. But the chapter argues that instead of facilitating formal commercialization, state actions fail to reduce the involvement of smallholders and their environments in the informal economy.

The final chapter concludes by noting how international organizations and national governments continue to approach rural and peri-urban populations as caught in subsistence and to devise programs to "pull them out" of it, such as commercialization. It revisits the discussion of land reform in China and post-communist countries by pointing out how the World Bank's narrative about China's reforms completes its broader treatment of East Asia's developmental path. Post-communist countries become further evidence that this developmental path, as the World Bank depicted it, has nothing new to add to its depiction of pro-poor development: namely, that what it mainly takes is an effort to introduce a narrow set of "pro-market" institutions such as property rights over productive assets and markets for property rights. But actual developments in post-communist Eurasia show that there was a lot to learn from the enactment of land reform and its outcomes. The findings of this study show that poverty reduction and the development of entrepreneurship are irreconcilable goals if they involve only the transfer of productive assets. And they further show that land reform, even if falling short of establishing land markets, in fact created several mechanisms that favored the differentiation of commercializing informal producers and traders from smallholders. This differentiation hardly happened at the expense of smallholders and required close interaction between the latter and commercializing actors. Given its informality, this post-reform environment hardly benefits from the protection of authorities and attention of international organizations. Still, its existence holds the key to understanding the resilience of smallholder agriculture.

The Discursive Construction of Pro-poor Land Reform

Part One

The Discursive Construction
of Pro-poor Land Reform

CHAPTER 1
Pro-poor Reforms
The Propertizing Paradigm

THE WORLD BANK'S AND the International Monetary Fund's (IMF) influence over lending countries extends beyond the "conditionality" involved in disbursing loans. These "Bretton Woods twins" can "lend credibility" to countries simply by opening up negotiations (R. Stone 2002), and their country rankings and benchmarks impact investment flows (Broome and Quirk 2015; Appel and Orenstein 2018). Since *willing* governments facilitate the operation of international organizations in lending countries (Woods 2006), international organizations have expanded their involvement in knowledge production and dissemination to increase the willingness of lending countries and prepare the ground for policy advice. The World Bank, in particular, appears as a global "knowledge bank" and a key agent of globalization, the main global disseminator of neoliberal ideas to non-Western countries (Babb and Kentikelenis 2018; Béland and Orenstein 2013; Burns and Giessen 2016; Goldman 2007; Plehwe 2007; Weber 2020). This has invited criticism of the Bank as pursuing "deep neoliberalism" through the pursuit of Western interests in the guise of structural economic change and "epistemic communities" of favorable expert networks (Cammack 2004; Escobar 1995; Ferguson 1990; Goldman 2005; Güven 2012; Rich 1994; Wade 2002).

A different take on international organizations has problematized less their politicized character and more their "pathologies" due to the specificities of "bureaucratic cultures" operating between several fields (Barnett and Finnemore 1999, 2004; Ferguson 1990). Corresponding studies approach the World Bank as a more benign organization, driven not only by a need to align with Western or US economic interests but also by a good-willed intention to "improve" or "fix" the world while downplaying the complexity of the reality it seeks to address. The Bank, however, avoids questioning the position from which it offers advice (Li 2007, 2014; see also Bøås and McNeill 2003; Peet 2009). And even though it is the more "reform-prone of the Bretton-Woods twins" (Woods 2006), the Bank has been the subject of a particular bureaucratic pathology, "organizational hypocrisy." This denotes a pervasive gap between what an international organization says and does (Weaver 2008), or a "self-defeating behavior that undermines the stated goals of the organization" (Barnett and Finnemore 1999, 702). On the one hand, "organized hypocrisy" shields the Bank from unrealistic demands coming from donor countries. On the other hand, if uncovered, it saps its legitimacy (Barros, Rodrigues, and Panhoca 2019; Mundy and Menashy 2014; Shandra, Rademacher, and Coburn 2016; Weaver 2008).

This chapter approaches World Bank policy prescriptions less from a background of the "pervasive gaps" between talk, decisions, and practice (Brunsson 1993) than from a pervasive bias in favor of institutionalist fixes such as "land reform" in the form of large-scale "propertizing" or titling reforms, promising to address poverty through the distribution of property titles over agricultural land. As emphasized in agrarian political economy, World Bank theorists of titling reform provided "the landmark publications key to understanding the main features of the contemporary mainstream land policies" (Borras, Akram-Lodhi, and Kay 2007, 25; Scott 2015). Their work translated into an influential narrative[1] that land reform is a fundamental factor in poverty reduction. Since the World Bank is seen as the primary international "agent" of neoliberalism (Lahiff, Borras, and Kay 2007; Borras 2003; Babb and Kentikelenis 2018), in what follows I present the Bank's land reform program by discussing its relationship to neoliberalism. The next section argues that neoliberals outside the Bank had little to say about land reform and opposed it to the extent that it involved the distribution of agricultural land. Using "landmark publications" and interviews from the World Bank's oral history database,[2] I show how land reform as a narrow institutional fix represents a compromise between neoliberal and other ideas. This narrow vision turned out to be compatible with a reception of Chinese reforms as successful mainly because of the incentives introduced by land reform, and not because of the state's continuous presence in and support for the smallholders' immediate environment. This interpretation of Chinese reforms would turn out to be highly consequential for the transitioning post-communist countries in Europe and Asia.

The Promise of Land Reform

The most representative formulations of the World Bank's land reform narrative were several publications that appeared in the 1990s and early 2000s. They were authored, co-authored, or edited by World Bank Senior Advisor Hans Binswanger, Chief Economist Klaus Deininger, and Gershon Feder, a World Bank economist and division chief throughout the 1980s and the rural development research manager of the World Bank Development Research Group from 1997. They culminated with a 1999 paper in the *World Bank Research Observer* (Deininger and Binswanger 1999) and a 2003 volume authored by Deininger and written "under the supervision" of Feder.[3] These publications form the standard of the World Bank's land reform perspective (Borras 2003). They narrow pro-poor land reform to a short list of "institutional arrangements" and several mechanisms through which they were expected to raise productivity incomes, incentivize investments, and help reduce poverty. The main component is the "provision of secure tenure to land," expected to "improve the welfare of the poor . . . by enhancing the [poor's] asset base," creating "incentives needed for investment." The second component, "facilitation of land exchange," expedites "land access by productive, but land-poor producers," helping them access credit as "financial markets would rely on the use of land as collateral" (Deininger 2003, ix–x).[4]

This land reform perspective appears as an exemplary expression of World Bank neoliberalism (Borras 2003; Wolford 2016), reflecting the general influence of neoliberal ideas on World Bank policies since the 1980s. But the intellectuals and scholars more generally associated with neoliberalism had little interest in land reform and had criticized both international organizations and development aid. To take the case of the Mont Pelerin Society (MPS), the most influential network of neoliberal intellectuals, its members had long opposed development aid and the policies of international organizations, including the "Bretton Woods twins," IMF and the World Bank, using the moralizing arguments that Margaret Somers and Fred Block (2005) called the "perversity thesis"—namely, that any form of aid (and with it, the involvement of international organizations in "Third World" countries) does not solve any "developmental problem," including poverty, but deepens such problems because it creates "perverse" incentives undermining the individuals' willingness to work. This criticism had intensified since the 1970s with the work of MPS member Peter Bauer (1976; 1981), whose arguments travelled beyond the MPS to influence the work of many other economists (e.g., Easterly 2006; Shleifer 2009).

Echoing their skepticism vis-à-vis "development" (Strassmann 1976), neoliberals hardly considered land reform a pressing issue; in fact, to the extent they even took the issue into account, they vehemently rejected it. There are no indications that land reform had been seriously discussed in meetings of the MPS prior to the 1980s, nor did it have to. Land reform was hardly an issue for MPS members even when discussing questions of international development (Plehwe 2015), despite the centrality of property rights for spurring economic growth evident in the works of notable members of the MPS, such as Harold Demsetz (1974 [1967]) and Douglass C. North (1989), and despite the focus on smallholders or peasants in developing countries in the work of Peter Bauer and Theodore W. Schultz (1964).[5] Property rights over land in developing countries featured prominently in the work of Hernando de Soto, who made a strong case for the importance of holding legal titles certifying land ownership in Peru. However, de Soto was skeptical about land reform, criticizing it at length for its radical approach, and he focused on the poverty-reducing effects of land ownership in urban areas rather than in rural areas (de Soto 1989). De Soto stays the best-known neoliberal to develop a propertizing agenda, a well-acknowledged contribution in studies of neoliberalism (de Soto 1989; Mitchell 2005). But, as will be shown below, the World Bank's land reform script goes further or differs from de Soto's propertizing ideas as well as from those of other MPS neoliberals.

A 1986 MPS conference offers a glimpse of neoliberal perspectives on land reform by the time that thinking about land reform was well on the way at the World Bank. Key MPS members such as Milton Friedman, Peter Bauer, Arnold Harberger, and others came together on October 5–8, 1986, in Napa Valley, California, for the International Symposium on Economic, Political, and Civil Freedom.[6] Land reform came up following an incisive comment by the libertarian Walter Block, who, after a paper on Latin America by Ramon Diaz, criticized MPS members (referring to them as "conservatives") for "dismissing" the issue. In contrast, he outlined a "libertarian" approach to land reform: whereas "socialists" would redistribute land from the rich to the poor, "libertarians" would redistribute from "thieves" to "victims"; he admitted that often there is no difference between the two approaches, since in Latin America "the rich are often the thieves" (Walker 1988, 275n6). MPS members strongly objected to this position. Public choice theorist Gordon Tullock stated, "These Indians never owned that land; the Inca owned it. They can't have had anything stolen if they never had it" (Walker 1988, 279). Echoing de Soto's position on the issue, Ramon Diaz—who would a decade later lead the MPS as its president from 1998 to 2000—questioned whether land reform could succeed at all given the high levels of state intervention it entails (Walker 1988, 279). Peter Bauer, the MPS's best-known development expert, called the issue of land reform "overblown and confused," rejecting "the expropriation and redistribution of cultivated land on which effort and money have been spent to make it valuable" (Walker 1988, 280). Finally, as the other libertarian present, Tibor Machan, called for land reform as indispensable for achieving "justice," Milton Friedman intervened by quoting Frank Knight as saying, "What's really going to ruin this world is a search for justice" (Walker 1988, 281). In brief, neoliberals around Milton Friedman objected to seeing land reform as the key to delivering social justice. They doubted that it could address poverty, fearing that it could harm the few better-performing individuals, the large estate-owning farmers.

These positions should not come as a surprise, as they reflect long-held positions inimical to the postcolonial governments' efforts at land reform at the expense of large estate owners (Plehwe 2015; Connell and Dados 2014). The perception of land reform as an "overblown" issue (to cite Bauer) would carry on in the statements of the MPS member to lead the Bank's research department from 1982 to 1987, Anne Krueger,[7] who received considerable support from the Bank's operations director, Ernest Stern. Implicit in Krueger's and Stern's writings and defense of structural adjustment policies was that the best way to help the rural poor was by paying them world prices for their production, based on the belief that such prices are kept artificially low through state subsidies (Stern 1995).

In contrast, the World Bank had already under Robert McNamara posited from the 1970s on the importance of land reform from a self-termed social justice perspective needed to stabilize postcolonial countries. Put differently, MPS neoliberals and World Bank land script authors diverge on the very "master signifier" in their thought constructs. While the ideological discourse of MPS neoliberals is "quilted" (Žižek 1991) into the master signifier of "freedom," the World Bank from the 1970s on established the centrality of "poverty reduction" requiring "justice" through land reform as a means to ensure the pacification and political stability of "Third World" societies. Neoliberals at the World Bank, such as Krueger and Stern, accepted the centrality of poverty reduction but decoupled it from land reform, claiming that poverty alleviation mainly requires price and trade liberalization (Stern 1995; Wolf 2019). Yet throughout the 1980s and culminating with publications in the 1990s and 2000s, World Bank authors hammered home the message that land reform matters not only on justice grounds but also for efficiency, as the productivity of small farms exceeds that of large estate-owning enterprises and individuals. Underlying the debate between neoliberals and land reform proponents is a different understanding of poverty. Neoliberals pointed to the lack of *market incentives* due to state interventions tolerated (at least until the 1980s) by IMF and the World Bank. World Bank land reform proponents echoed Amartya Sen's arguments and criticized instead the lack of *assets* characterizing poor people in developing countries (Lipton 1988).

Take the most succinct formulation of the Bank's pro-poor land reform, encapsulating the following three propositions (Deininger 2003, ix–x; my emphasis):

> (1) provision of secure tenure to land improves the welfare of the poor, particularly by enhancing the asset base of those whose land rights are often neglected, and creates incentives needed for investment, paramount to sustainable economic growth; (2) facilitation of land exchange, and *distribution*, whether as an asset or for current services, at low cost, *through markets, and non-market channels*, will expedite land access by productive, but land-poor producers, so that once economic growth improves, financial markets would rely on the use of land as collateral; and, (3) governments' contribution to the promotion of *socially desirable land allocation*, and utilization.

While the first proposition resembles, on first sight, the stress on "titling" in de Soto's work (1989) and on property rights in North's (1989), the second and third propositions indicate that World Bank authors specifically took into account "non-market channels" for distributing property rights according to "socially desirable" criteria. These channels include

the political redistribution that would take property away from large landowners and distribute it, preferably to tenants—that is, to those already
working the land. This idea not only breaks with the neoliberal perspective shunning state redistribution but also differs from earlier 1980s work
at the Bank, which saw the development of property rights as a response
to land scarcity.

This latter idea—summarized as the "postulate of scarcity" (Xenos
1987)—characterized much of the 1980s literature and still appeared in
work such as Gershon Feder's seminal 1991 article published by the World
Bank. It builds on a long line of contributions claiming that private property rights develop "endogenously" in response to land scarcity, starting with MPS member Harold Demsetz's 1967 article (1974 [1967]) and
continuing with contributions by Binswanger (Binswanger and McIntire
1987; Binswanger and Rosenzweig 1986), David Feeny (1984), and Feder
(1987, 1985). It approaches the development of land rights as paralleling
the societal demand for them, irrespective of political complications and
lacking the political power to press for demands.[8] As pointed out by Jean-
Philippe Platteau, the writings of World Bank authors had assumed that a
"mechanism exists whereby land arrangements tend to evolve in an opti-
mal fashion" and that the role of the government is simply "to supply an
institutional innovation in the form of land titling" (1996, 37).

Landmark publications abandon this "postulate of scarcity" by claiming that the development of property rights is more complicated and
often achieved *only* through policy interventions emerging out of quasi-
revolutionary situations pitting peasants against large landowners. It cannot be deduced from the level of land scarcity (Binswanger, Deininger,
and Feder 1995). Nor, one could add, does it reflect in a Northian vein (as
more generally institutions) the costliness and uncertainties of transactions or the inability to establish institutions conducive to growth (North
1990). Instead, the landmark contributions place the power issue on center stage. They argue that property distributions, as a rule, tend to reflect
power differences between social groups (Binswanger, Deininger, and
Feder 1995), especially in "developing" countries. The 2003 book, an almost verbatim treatment of the 1995 report, also puts in center stage the
disruptive and revolutionary situations that created modern institutional
arrangements (Deininger 2003, 15). What speaks to the distance between
the World Bank's land reform perspective and the neoliberalism of the

MPS is the Bank's insistence on land tenure as a serious social problem rather than a sign of "socialism"; the Bank discusses the completion of land reform as a key ingredient to ending civil wars in Central America (Binswanger, Deininger, and Feder 1995), and not as a sign of "romanticism" and "socialism" characterizing Latin Americans, as in the writings of Ramon Diaz (1986).

Landmark publications of the 1990s and 2003 also differ from neoliberal writings such as those of North (1989, 1990) and other MPS neoliberals in their more complex and nuanced treatment of non-Western settings. Instead of juxtaposing the "Western world" (usually exemplified by the US or the UK) and the "Third World" as major institutionalist economists did, such as Demsetz (1974 [1967]) and North (1990), landmark publications distinguish between different landowner-laborer relationships, from tenancy to salaried work. The difference between Western and non-Western cases nevertheless resurfaces in landmark publications by extrapolating from contrasting Western and Eastern Europe to drawing parallels between Eastern Europe and the rest of the world, from Southeast Asia to Latin America. The gist of the argument is that a monopoly of ownership over land allowed landed elites to stall the development of these world regions.[9] The 2003 World Bank publication (Deininger 2003) does not clarify what eroded this monopoly in Western Europe. Still, earlier writings (Binswanger, Deininger, and Feder 1995) did, relying on Robert Brenner's work on class struggle (1976 and 1977) and, in particular, on the strength of the peasantry for explaining what sapped the power of large estate owners in Western Europe.

In explaining why institutional development reflects power inequalities, World Bank reports and authors avoid the Northian account of institutional development of property rights as simply a contractual arrangement between landowners and tenants (North and Thomas 1973). World Bank authors rely on sources and authors hardly compatible with institutionalist accounts, from Ester Boserup's to Alexander Chayanov's and Amartya Sen's contributions highlighting the existence of an "inverse relationship" between landholding size and farm productivity (Chen, Huffman, and Rozelle 2011; Helfand and Taylor 2020). In fact, the widely cited paper by Binswanger and Rosenzweig (1986) gives further support to the "inverse relationship" thesis by clarifying the mechanisms through which small farms were more productive than larger ones, and in particular, because of their reliance on family labor. Chayanov's thesis had been resurrected by Amartya Sen with research on India in the 1950s and 1960s and by a range of further research on Latin America conducted by Albert Berry and William Cline and published by the International Labour Organization in 1979. Criticized as "populist" or "neo-populist," some of its proponents (largely unaffiliated with the World Bank) adopted the terms *populist* and *neo-populist* and used them to designate support for land reform grounded on the inverse relationship (Griffin, Rahman Khan, and Ickowitz 2004; Lipton 1977; Griffin 1979).

Binswanger and others at the World Bank picked up and further developed research on the inverse relationship. In doing so, they were hardly portraying their theses as refutations of neoliberalism, which would have been difficult to expect since Anne Krueger was already the Bank's vice president (1982–1987).[10] Instead, during the 1980s, Binswanger and Rosenzweig (1986) presented their support for land reform as criticism of "Marxist" endorsement of large-scale mechanized agriculture, while during the 1990s, Binswanger and co-authors would build on Brenner's Marxist argumentation rather than North's to explain differences between Western and Eastern Europe (Binswanger, Deininger, and Feder 1993; 1995).

Ester Boserup's framework is seen as fundamentally different from North and Thomas's because she rejected neo-Malthusianism, showing how population growth drives agricultural change and innovation (Boserup 2014 [1965]; Darity 1980). Yet the World Bank landmark publications use her framework for its ability to globally map different land tenure arrangements rather than claim that there is an evolutionary development toward only one land tenure arrangement—namely, one based on individual property rights.[11] Boserup's theories on subsistence farmers also pit her, as well as the World Bank authors who seconded her on this point, against neoliberals such as Peter Bauer, claiming that the poor can turn into entrepreneurs only if state structures reduce their distortive involvement in the economy, an argument also pursued by Krueger (1986, 61). In contrast, Boserup, like Chayanov earlier, viewed subsistence farmers as fundamentally different from capitalist entrepreneurs, being far more risk averse because of the pressure to maintain the livelihood of their family members and therefore requiring different policies, such as, according to Chayanov, land reform (Chayanov 1966; see also Boserup 2014, 94; Grigg 1979; Turner and Fischer-Kowalski 2010).

Land Reform: The Intellectual Climate at the World Bank

The discovery of the "inverse relationship" and the defense of "smallholders" built on an intellectual climate at the World Bank around the late 1970s and early 1980s that saw the intersection of three different development discourses. First, there was a 1970s discourse shaped by Robert McNamara, Hollis Chenery, Montague Yudelman, and Mahbub ul-Haq. On one hand, this discourse started from the positive reception of the Green Revolution in Asia and agricultural reforms in India and China. In the words of the Agricultural Department's director:

> We were in a period of great growth in agriculture in Asia. It was euphoria. The Green Revolution was taking place, and this was the heart of the Bank's activity. Growth rates were unbelievable, and all of a sudden this terrible fear of famine in Asia seemed to be disappearing. We thought we knew what needed to be done and how to do it. (Yudelman 1986)

On the other hand, this discourse incorporated Amartya Sen's criticism of the Green Revolution focus on technical solutions (mechanization, irrigation, and credit) by redefining the World Bank's mission from a focus on growth to one on poverty alleviation (Kapur, Lewis, and Webb 1997). Through addressing "basic human needs" and "integrated rural development" (IRD), it sought to combine the Green Revolution's focus on technology with an explicit focus on assistance to smallholders and the development of their communities and regions (Yudelman 1986, 1991; Christoffersen 2016).

Second, within the Agricultural Department, there were dissenting voices, skeptical in light of having directly experienced the limits of what they referred to as technical solutions to poverty in Africa (Lele 2005) and Latin America (Binswanger 1991) and increasingly insisting on land reform as a solution to poverty. Meanwhile, even among those staff members in charge and supportive of IRD (Leif Christoffersen, for instance), there was a strengthening perception that more was needed, in particular, structural adjustment, an approach also supported by McNamara by the end of his presidency (Christoffersen 2016; Wapenhans 1991; Eccles 1994).

Third, there was a growing neoliberal presence and acceptance of neoliberal arguments, stressing the importance of "doing less" (that is, doing less or abandoning IRD) and of agricultural price increases to address poverty among producers. Neoliberals were particularly opposed to Chenery's and McNamara's underlying "notion" of poverty as a "massive social problem" (Wapenhans 1991, 24). Strengthening with Krueger's arrival at the Bank in 1982 and supported by operations director Ernest Stern, the neoliberal strand was "not interested"[12] in land reform, seeing the solutions to poverty in spurring growth through trade and price liberalization. Neoliberals around Krueger were especially opposed to the technology, infrastructure, and IRD focus in their predecessors' policies, discontinuing, according to Devesh Kapur, an entire publication series after one author (Kevin Cleaver, in a study of Africa) questioned Krueger's focus on liberalization and "getting the prices right," insisting instead on the importance of infrastructure and credit projects (Gulhati 1991). Furthermore, Krueger praised the work of Uma Lele, a staff member of Yudelman's Agricultural Department, for her criticism of the department's IRD approach and promoted her by inviting her to join the Bank's research department (Binswanger 1991; Lele 2005; Yudelman 1991).

The resulting land reform perspective represents a compromise between the latter two discourses: neoliberals accepted land reform as a solution to poverty, while land reform proponents avoided systemic questions about the possible contradictions between land reform as key to poverty alleviation and other reforms, such as the structural adjustment policies advocated by Krueger and Stern.[13] Worries over such contradictions were still being voiced from within the Bank, for instance, by Yudelman and Shlomo Reutlinger in the 1980s (Binswanger 1991; Reutlinger 1987; Yudelman 1991); they feared that the subsidy cuts promoted under structural adjustment could hurt smallholders and increase poverty. These possible contradictions are absent from later work, especially from the landmark publications of the late 1990s and early 2000s.

Landmark publications explicitly distanced themselves from the Bank's first paper devoted to land reform, the 1975 sectoral paper (World Bank 1975), which came out as Yudelman was leading the Agricultural Department and ideas of integrated rural development were taking shape (Christoffersen 2016; Kapur, Lewis, and Webb 1997). The 1975 paper emphasized coupling land reform to creating or developing "an input supply system to meet the special needs of the beneficiaries of land reform" (World Bank 1975, 11). The landmark publications avoided such a focus, criticizing that paper for failing to establish connections between land reform and wider economic development, for its "almost exclusive focus on formal title," and for its lack of attention to "issues of governance, conflict resolution, and corruption" (Deininger 2003, xlv).

But the landmark publications focused policy interventions on institutional elements and avoided discussions about the potential contradictions between its smallholder focus and the structural adjustment policies advocated under Krueger. They largely stayed silent about the interaction between land reform and other policies or even conditions that make land reform work or not in particular contexts. One of the few conditions getting attention was the type of "manorial estate" targeted by land reform (Binswanger, Deininger, and Feder 1995, 20–22; Deininger 2003, 14–15). Landmark publications expected reform to be successful if land were distributed to beneficiaries already working as farmers, particularly if they were not only a salaried labour force but were also responsible for marketing production (as tenants). The least success was expected where the manorial estate resembled the Junker type, using a labor force of salaried workers rather than tenancy arrangements with farmers, for reasons having to do with the workers' limited resources, including marketing experience and capital. In fact, landmark publications were geared precisely to gauge the fit between manorial estate types and the outcomes of land reform (Binswanger, Deininger, and Feder 1995, 78; Deininger 2003), rather than to explore the broader conditions under which land reform can help tackle poverty.

Conclusions

The World Bank and other international organizations are often approached as agents of neoliberal influence, and one could, in analyzing the Bank's land reform ideas, stress the commonalities between Bank and neoliberals, pointing out that both the MPS's and the World Bank's positions concur on reforms primarily being about setting up institutions supporting Krueger's formula of "getting the prices right" (Wolford 2016). Clear property relations facilitate the pricing of land and the formation of land markets, which in turn facilitate investment (Deininger and Nizalov 2016; Deininger and Binswanger 1999). Furthermore, the compromise with neoliberalism most likely helped not only land reform ideas to survive but also neoliberal ideas to carry on through "mongrelization" (Peck 2010) with other approaches. But in the light of the differences mentioned in this chapter, such a conclusion about the overlap between neoliberal and World Bank positions would hardly be sufficient. While one can find numerous areas in which international organizations have followed the intellectual lead of neoliberals, the case of land reform shows that the survival of other vantage points from which to judge policies was possible within the World Bank even during the heyday of neoliberalism.

Two conclusions stand out. First, even though one can depict land reform as congruent with the focus on prices in Krueger's work, the World Bank's land reform ideas incorporate a different lineage of ideas than that of MPS members such as North, de Soto, or Krueger. They not only defended private property but called for its redistribution from large landowners to smallholders or the landless. They defended private property and smallholders as particularly efficient based on the inverse relationship between farm size and productivity, an idea with a long and non-neoliberal lineage that differs fundamentally from how neoliberals motivated their reform proposals—namely, by insisting that private property is the key to "freedom." Although neoliberals supported the legalization of existing land use patterns to a certain extent, they rejected any redistributive reforms on the grounds of doing injustice to present-day owners.

Second, the survival of such non-neoliberal ideas built critically on a discourse that differs from both neoliberalism and the landmark publications: the interest in mechanization and "technology" (irrigation, seeds, and credit) sparked by the Green Revolution that characterized both McNamara's and Yudelman's plans for the Bank. The thinking behind the landmark publications emerged in response to this discourse while keeping its focus on poverty alleviation. The survival of such non-neoliberal ideas (the inverse relationship or poverty as lack of assets) was therefore facilitated by such neoliberals as Krueger, perceiving these ideas as less problematic than the ideas surrounding the Green Revolution.[14]

Neoliberalism's imprint is an inclination not only to pursue market-oriented policies but also to turn the recipe for successful poverty alleviation into a narrow set of institutional reforms surrounding the redistribution of land. Simply put, the expectations vis-à-vis land reform *alone* addressing poverty were huge. There was little stress on finding out whether and how land reform might need other measures to support it, and the silence over the potential conflict between land reform and the structural adjustment policies encouraged by the World Bank from the

1980s on is a characteristic feature of the discourse surrounding land reform. In other words, what is characteristic is not so much the "market
simplification" (Mitchell 2007; Lahiff, Borras, and Kay 2007) but the institutionalist simplification of reducing complex questions of development
to the adoption of *one* institutional fix while reducing the operation of
markets to the issue of land ownership.

CHAPTER 2
Pro-poor Land Reform in Eurasia

THE WORLD BANK'S LAND REFORM perspective deeply influenced the propertizing policies aiming to reform collectivized agriculture in transitioning countries in Eastern Europe, Transcaucasia, and Central Asia (Lerman 1998). Furthermore, it formed the basis of MLAR, or the "market-led agrarian reform" enacted in Southeast Asia and several countries in Central and Southern America and Africa (Borras 2003; Lahiff, Borras, and Kay 2007). At first sight, the Bank advocated different land tenure reforms in post-communist transitioning countries and developing countries in Latin America and Africa (Swinnen, Vandeplas, and Maertens 2010; De Janvry, 1989; De Janvry and Sadoulet 2010). The key difference is that in the latter case (non-collectivized countries), the main channel of distributing land was market based; it involved the voluntary transfer of land from large landholders to the rural poor. The state's role was to incentivize this transfer process and support the rural poor in acquiring land (Lahiff, Borras, and Kay 2007). In the case of transitioning countries (including China and Vietnam as well as post-communist Eastern Europe and Central Asia), the largest transfer of land was to happen by administrative fiat or decision, simply dividing up the land of former collective farms and transferring it to rural populations.[1] Despite this difference, both variants of land tenure reform, market-led and state-led distribution of property titles, built on the idea that simply transferring land—even if failing to develop land markets—would have a decisive effect on productivity and, therefore, on fighting poverty. State-led distribution was also supposed to culminate with the establishment of markets for land, in turn expected to spur even more poverty reduction, as it would allow the more productive farmers to increase the size of their operations (Nyberg and Rozelle 1999).

Reflecting the compromise between neoliberalism and land reform, the focus on property transfer meant tremendous expectations about institutional reforms doing the job of poverty alleviation. This compromise would show in the Bank's treatment of China. China was a highly consequential case because not only was it the largest communist country to attempt economic reform but also given the World Bank's early involvement in China (Weber 2020), it inspired the advice extended to postcommunist countries in Europe and Asia. Simply put, "in the early 1990s, [China] was the only international benchmark for the reform of collectivized agriculture" (Lerman 1998, 311). Reflecting the thinking behind its landmark publications, the World Bank presented China's successes in poverty alleviation as an outcome of land reform creating market incentives. Reforms appeared as a seamless transition from collective to private usage rights over land: the shift from "collective to private cultivation . . . has been associated with large increases in productivity, as in the case of China" (Deininger 2003, 92). This change from collective to private cultivation is presented as the only factor behind growth in rural China in the other standard World Bank publication on land policy as well: "The household responsibility system in China (which gave 15-year lease rights and at the same time made individuals residual claimants to output) has led to tremendous increases in output and productivity" (Deininger and Binswanger 1999, 259).

These publications identify the experience of China (and to a lesser extent, Vietnam) as the basis for policy prescriptions targeting transitioning countries in Central and Eastern Europe (CEE) as well as the Commonwealth of Independent States (CIS):

> The transition from collective to private models of cultivation has often been associated with large increases in productivity, as in China after the 1978 introduction of the household responsibility system . . . and in Vietnam after the reforms of the early 1980s. . . . Land reform and restructuring of the rural sector have therefore become a key part of the transformation of the rural sector in all CEE and CIS countries. (Deininger 2003, 182–83)

A few such "transitioning" countries were seen as further evidence for the proper workings of Chinese-like "propertizing" reforms; these include Albania (Deininger 2003, 135), Moldova, and Romania, as well as the three Transcaucasian states, at times referred collectively as "China-like" or China-"pattern" cases. They are to be differentiated from "Russia-like" cases (Lipton 2009; Swinnen 2005),[2] countries that have failed to individualize land tenure arrangements. Commonplace assessments read developments in the post-communist world as confirmations of the effectiveness of the Chinese approach, as understood by the World Bank, and stress how eventually, privatizing and liberalizing reforms in transitioning countries led to the same developments as in China: "In Eastern Europe and Central Asia, labor productivity fell during the transition out of collective farming into a market economy, but it was subsequently followed by rapid labor productivity gains and sharp rural poverty reduction" (De Janvry and Sadoulet 2010, 4).

The *World Development Report* (WDR) of 2008 offers a more encompassing presentation of China's reforms, with repeated mentions of "statist" components such as the increases in procurement prices and the subsidies program. Yet in summarizing the pro-poor results of China's reforms, the focus was still on "institutional innovations," the "household responsibility system," and "market liberalization" (World Bank 2007, 26). This construction of the Chinese reforms as successful due to land transfers and the "market incentives" they entailed proved tremendously consequential for post-communist countries in Eurasia. Early on, Zvi Lerman, perhaps the longest-serving World Bank advisor specializing on Eastern European, Transcaucasian, and Central Asian countries, noted:

> The basic Western model focused on land and labor only, ignoring other factors of production. This was dictated primarily by the experience in China and Vietnam, where the level of mechanization and purchased input use was very low and agrarian reform did not have to involve much beyond distributing land to households. (Lerman 1998, 310)

The quote implies that the Western model predominantly focused on land reform in the advice extended to transitioning countries because it read the East Asian cases (China and Vietnam) as mainly being about land reform in the sense of distributing land to local populations. But while Vietnam perhaps indeed featured more marketizing components

(Ravallion and Van De Walle 2008), the Chinese case is more about slowly "growing out of the plan" (Naughton 1995), developing market incentives in a protective state environment in which the state acts as the main or last-resort buyer. As outlined in the next section, the "market incentives" are inseparable from the "statist incentives" in the form of the administrative price increases at the onset of reforms.

In contrast, most transitioning countries embarked on a different path, prioritizing land reform over other reform components and massively reducing the role of the state, especially in procurement, while simultaneously liberalizing foreign trade and thus increasing the competition that slowly developing local producers and markets faced (Swinnen and Rozelle 2006; Varga 2017). China's household responsibility system remained unique, as transitioning countries practiced land reform without a "responsibility system," meaning that there was no systemic support for rural households' role in addressing procurement.

Chinese Reforms—The Lost Statist Components

The reforms enacted in China from 1978 on mark the highest successes in worldwide poverty reduction to date. Lifting close to 700 million people out of poverty, much of the worldwide success in eradicating poverty is due to the drop in China's rural poverty rates (World Bank 2007). This point is largely uncontroversial and so, increasingly, is the point that marketizing reforms, such as most importantly, land reform in the guise of the household responsibility system (HRS), helped bring about this outcome. However, this section reminds us that reforms in China were more complex, particularly if compared with the reforms enacted roughly a decade later in other countries transitioning away from planned economies. China's policies combined land reform with continued state involvement in procurement and subsidizing production. This differed from de-collectivizing reforms elsewhere. While, as outlined in the next section, many subsequent studies framed Chinese reforms as introducing "market incentives" for local producers, in fact reforms worked through the optimizing boost of the HRS and the increase in state procurement prices (hardly representing a "market incentive") and later on increasingly through the constitution and spread of an alternative to state procurement, periodic markets. Table 2.1 gives an overview of these components.

The overview above suggests that reforms in China were not a story of "liberalization," but one of institutional complementarity (Aoki 1997)

TABLE 2.1. Components of Chinese reforms from production planning to price planning. Source: Author's elaboration based on secondary literature (Huang 2012; Lin 1988; Sicular 1988; Lardy 1983; Putterman 1993).

	Before 1978	From 1978 on
Land contracting and procurement	**Unified procurement and "production planning"**; state monopoly on domestic trade, producers could sell only to state procurement stations.	After 1977: change in commercial policies as government promoted "multiple channels" for commerce and substantially increased purchase prices (an average 42% above 1977 levels; **"price planning"**). From 1981: government allowed individuals to establish small-scale businesses in trade (animal products, vegetables, minor crops, and light manufactures such as textiles and clothing). From 1982: restrictions on grain trade eased—individuals, state agencies, enterprises, and collectives allowed to trade in grain both locally and long-distance (after meeting local grain quotas). The periodic market system began to re-emerge. State commercial agencies became players in market trade (**"negotiated" procurement**): the state purchased farm output at below market prices; sales were voluntary. In the early 1980s, farmers could sell certain crops over their quotas to the state at an above-quota bonus price (30–50% higher), could sell to the state at negotiated prices, or could sell to new market entrants at market prices. Land was not privatized; it was **contracted out** to farmers on long-term leases. State firms were not privatized, but entrepreneurs were allowed to start their own businesses.
Subsidies	Keep/increase price subsidies: In 1984 subsidies for oilseeds, grain, and cotton reached 14% of government budgetary revenues (22 million yuan); in 1989, 12% (37 million yuan).	
Security for proprietors rather than property	Cultural Revolution repressed rural markets and proprietors.	1979: The Chinese government returned confiscated assets—bank deposits, bonds, gold, and private homes—to former capitalists and landlords; large numbers of people imprisoned during the Cultural Revolution for engaging in private commerce released from jail.
Off-farm rural employment	Only "Five Small Industries" allowed to operate in rural areas.	Township and village enterprises spurred non-agricultural employment (9% increase per year) and output (from 6% of GDP in 1978 to 26% in 1996).
Credit	Agricultural Bank controlled credit cooperatives.	Mix of - state-owned banks and credit cooperatives with - private free lending and borrowing under bank supervision.

between state and emerging market economy. On one hand, the most famous component of reforms was the introduction of the household responsibility system, later understood in a series of World Bank documents, including the landmark publications, as bringing about a shift from "collective to private cultivation . . . associated with large increases in productivity" (Deininger 2003, 92). But in fact, the HRS's significance was that at least throughout the reforms' first decade, it was rural households, not collective farms, that would fulfil the "responsibility" of meeting state procurement targets. The household responsibility system was thus partly about land reform, as the World Bank claims (see below in this section), transferring land use rights from collective to individual actors, and partly about integrating individual actors in a procurement system in which they supply state actors with their production. Rather than an instance of market liberalization and increasing market incentives to producers, the HRS was about institutional complementarities between individual incentives and systemic demands and support (Ang 2016; for the same argument extended more generally to the broader economy, see Naughton 1995; McMillan 1994; Lardy 1983).

Correspondingly, the reforms' other central elements were that, rather than eliminating planning, state agencies shifted from steering agriculture through "production planning" to "price planning," while continuing to buy as much as half of the grain and most of the cotton and tobacco until well into the 1990s—that is, at least a decade after the "liberalization" of land use. Furthermore, state agencies encouraged the creation and spread of periodic markets as an alternative to state procurement and increased production subsidies to agricultural producers (Sicular 1988, 1995; see also Lardy 1983, 88–92; Hu, Hu, and Chang 2005; Putterman 1993). They thus diversified rural employment opportunities through the creation of state and also increasingly private rural enterprises while strictly controlling migration from rural to urban areas (Huang 2012). As criticized by the World Bank in its reports, state authorities at the village level heavily interfered in the allocation of land (Ravallion and Chen 2004; Ho 2014), staying clear of the World Bank proposals for formal property rights and agricultural land markets (for an example, see Nyberg and Rozelle 1999).

This story of a complex interplay between continuous state involvement in directly buying up the production of smallholders and slowly developing domestic market structures is very different from the advice received by "transitioning" countries, engaging in reforms a decade after

China. Rather than being about the development of rural periodic markets, the advice extended by the World Bank involved a reading of the Chinese case as being about "the initial economic agents of change [being] countless smallholders increasing their output in response to newly unleashed market incentives" and about "external trade liberalisation," as the World Bank's economists Martin Ravallion and David Dollar later summarized (Ravallion 2009; Dollar 2008). These "market incentives" were mainly conceived as the result of land reform (HRS), and the extent to which the state still acted as the most important buyer of smallholder produce was overlooked. Also overlooked was that initially it was the increase of administrative purchase prices rather than the development of markets that translated into the most relevant "incentive" for smallholders (Sicular 1988; Lin 1988). The complexity of the Chinese case was thus reduced to an easily transferable institutional "fix" to poverty (Li 2014), a narrative about land reform, to become the basis of advice to "transitioning" countries. The "land reform" component—in particular, land privatization—was the crux of the approach to poverty in numerous post-communist countries and the most important meter for judging reforms in post-communist countries (Deininger 2003; Lipton 2009; Lerman 2017).

The tendency to ignore statist components and emphasize the propertizing and liberalizing components is present in the Bank's landmark publications (Deininger and Binswanger 1999; Deininger 2003), as well as in the 1999 World Bank report *Accelerating China's Rural Transformation*. The report depicted pro-poor results largely as the effect of "improved incentives for households" (Nyberg and Rozelle 1999, 4) and generally called for further liberalization of agricultural land tenure, including by the introduction of fully tradable property rights. The same perspective is also present in the *World Development Report* of 2008, where much of the WDR's treatment of China comes from the work of then Research Group head Martin Ravallion. Like Ravallion, World Bank China country director David Dollar also attempts to extract from Chinese reforms a transferable "core" of policies in "Are There Lessons for Africa from China's Success against Poverty?" (2008). This core is again the set of "pro-market economic reforms, starting with the household responsibility system and supported by other reforms to liberalize markets for farm outputs and inputs" (Ravallion 2009, 310). There are statements relativizing the marketizing narrative, such as "The pattern of China's growth has not been a purely market-driven process," but the state's involvement is depicted as problematic rather than as facilitating reform (Ravallion 2011, 79–80). There is no mention of the possibility that "pro-market reforms" might have worked because of the state's role in supporting increasing production through its pricing policies, and there are almost no citations of works making such claims and approximating Barry Naughton's (1995) metaphor about China's economy "growing out of the plan" (Lardy 1983; Putterman 1993). Instead, the claim is that reforms worked through an abrupt break with the past.

Also missing from the World Bank's narrative on land reform are mentions of the role of "free," "periodic" or "weekly" rural and urban "markets" in China's anti-poverty program. An important part of China's reforms, this aspect of the smallholders' immediate environment received considerable attention from the authorities after 1979. In the 1960s and 1970s such market activity was—as in most other communist countries—severely limited in order to channel all production toward the state procurement system. Yet by the mid-1980s periodic markets in China had experienced a dynamic development, increasing the product specialization and incomes of smallholders and operating even though their existence complicated state procurement. Authorities initially kept many restrictions in place, allowing smallholders to sell in urban markets only in semi-urban (city outskirts) areas or keeping Maoist-era limitations on sales to products that smallholders could carry by foot or bicycle. They also restricted the development of markets for products such as grain, where the state continued to buy production at submarket prices and distribute it at subsidized prices in the cities. Nevertheless, authorities had lifted by 1983 most of these restrictions, allowing the use of mechanized vehicles for long-distance transport, eliminating restrictions on the destination of private goods, and even allowing wholesale trade in rural markets. The outcome was, in brief, increasing trading volumes that made "a growing proportion of markets no longer traditional nor periodic" and allowed their operation on a daily basis (Lardy 1983; Putterman 1993; Skinner 1985; Sato 2003). In contrast, reports authored by the World Bank's top experts on China, such as Dollar (2007; 2008) and Ravallion (Ravallion and Chen 2004), emphasize external trade liberalization and not the development of local markets prior to it, or they discuss the productivity-enhancing effects of the HRS without mentioning the marketing channels that accompanied it: state procurement and local markets.

Post-communist Eurasia: The Surprise of Subsistence

The World Bank's discursive construction of land reform as conducive to poverty reduction translated into the following expectation. Smallholder agriculture should have pro-poor results if reforms transfer farmland to the poor and turn them into smallholders, and if they incentivize smallholders to become "commercial" or entrepreneurial producers. Yet while these two stages seem to build on each other and were indistinguishable in landmark publications and in the Chinese case, with the HRS directly translating into a massive increase in output (Lin 1992), the post-communist practice in Eastern Europe and Central Asia showed that there is a tension between the two. This tension has been increasingly acknowledged by the World Bank, as illustrated in this chapter with empirical material from World Bank reports on four countries (Moldova, Tajikistan, Ukraine, and Romania). I structure this material into three phases of reflecting land reform and its effects in World Bank publications and increasing realization of the tension between making smallholders and making commercial farmers. As the comparison between landmark publications and World Bank sources more directly concerned with post-communist Eurasia will show, the World Bank solved this tension by supporting the transfer of land assets to rural populations only to the extent this transfer helped with spurring entrepreneurship and reforming former collective farms. Its advice was to prioritize these latter goals at the expense of poverty reduction. Instead of aiming to curb poverty through land transfers, in practice the World Bank returned to ideas of curbing it by encouraging the creation of land markets and deregulating nonagricultural labor markets. This return was facilitated by depicting post-reform populations as "subsistent," reducing the different agricultural production patterns of these populations to one numerical indicator, the size of the land plot, irrespective of whether they actually "subsisted" on agriculture.

This section moves beyond the landmark publications on propertizing land reform discussed in chapter 1 to explore a wider set of documents and trace changes in World Bank prescriptions away from the prescriptions of landmark publications in what was the farthest-reaching enactment of World Bank–inspired land policies, the privatization of land in "transitioning" Eurasia. It approaches these documents as constituting policy narratives (Jones and McBeth 2010) and narratives as "meaning-making systems," helping construct and symbolize "experienced reality at the level of both sensegiving and sensemaking" (Homolar and A. Rodríguez-Merino 2019; Mayer 2014; Selbin 2013). Narratives help in setting the agenda and defining the problem through "the very language that is presented to the public" (Forrester and Fischer 1993, 6). As outlined later in this section, "definitions of policy problems usually have narrative structure" (D. Stone 2002, 138), with "plots" or problem definitions, "characters," and "policy solutions" (Jones and McBeth 2010). The study examines with a narrative policy framework a number of World Bank documents that it calls "stocktaking"—that is, publications that construct narratives around land reform processes in post-communist countries and present these to wider audiences.[3]

The World Bank's experts—lead economists, advisors, and consultants—are part of a broader network that includes not only Bank-employed staff, but also university researchers and research institutes with which the World Bank works or from which it commissions reports. External researchers and institutes enlarge the network by participating in authoring papers and reports also issued by other organizations, such as the Food and Agriculture Organization of the United Nations (FAO) and the Organization for Economic Cooperation and Development (OECD), as well as the European Commission's Joint Research Committee (JRC). Given its expertise on post-communist countries, the prominent institute in this knowledge network is the Leibniz Institute of Agricultural Development in Transition Economies (IAMO) in Halle, Germany. To sum up, "stocktaking" documents include publications issued by the World Bank directly or by its wider knowledge network (most importantly by the IAMO or by World Bank experts writing in academic venues). Stocktaking publications reflect on the state and outcomes of agricultural reforms in the post-communist area (see endnote 3).

The second source of data, to supplement the World Bank stocktaking documents, is the country-specific documentation followed in this study in respect to several countries that differ in how stocktaking publications treat them: as cases of relative success because they followed World Bank advice (such as Moldova), as cases of failure because they ignored that advice (such as Ukraine), or as ambivalent cases (such as Romania and Tajikistan), where despite ambitious initial land reforms and strong World Bank involvement, the results were roughly the same widespread land fragmentation as in less-reform-prone countries.[4] The main documents include Poverty Assessments and Country Assistance or Partnership Strategies. I refer to these documents as "country reports," to distinguish them from the aforementioned stocktaking publications. Where available and relevant, the study also collected data from Structural Adjustment Loans, although most such data remains undisclosed. I further draw on these countries' national and/or rural development strategies, to the extent it could be established that these were written with the assistance of the World Bank. These publications were coded by two main categories: "underlying problem" (or "plot", in the terminology of narrative policy framework) and policy "fix" or solution. The data comes from the country reports listed in table 2.2. I refer to country reports and stocktaking documents collectively as "World Bank publications."

The third data source comes from Romania and Ukraine, two extremes in the stocktaking publications' depiction of transitioning countries as approaching the Chinese standard. For these countries, I studied national-level documentation in detail (chapters 3 and 6) and conducted fieldwork (detailed in part 2). Such documentation includes government agricultural "strategies" or "plans" drawn with World Bank assistance, such as Ukraine's 2015–2020 rural strategy document and the 2007–2013 and 2014–2020 Romanian government's rural development plans.

The phrases "World Bank experts" and "World Bank publications" should not be taken as an implication that the World Bank is a monolithic entity. The research published by development economists (stocktaking publications) serves goals that differ from those of country assistance documents. However, the policy prescriptions in country reports and stocktaking documents are in line with each other, which should not come as a surprise. To recall the work of Diane Stone, the World Bank is directly involved in knowledge production, employs its own "experts" (economists, advisors, and consultants), and expects the knowledge produced by its experts to be reflected in policy prescriptions. Generally, research, country work, and advocacy are closely interrelated, as noted by Banerjee et al. in their study of knowledge production at the World Bank (2006, 54). In Diane Stone's words, "the boundaries between scholarly and policy ecologies constantly move and overlap in new combinations via networks," and for the "World Bank, the creation, management and application of knowledge is crucial to achieving its mission of poverty reduction" (Stone 2012, 246; see also Broad 2006; Wade 1996; Weaver 2007).

TABLE 2.2. Overview of World Bank country documents. Source: Varga 2020.

Country	Poverty assessments and poverty alleviation projects	Country assistance/ partnership strategies	Structural adjustment loans	National development strategies
Moldova	1999, 2004, 2006, 2016	2004, 2013	1997, 2000	2019–22
Tajikistan	1997, 2000, 2002, 2009, 2014	1996, 2005	1998, 2001, 2004	2016–30
Ukraine	1996, 2005, 2017	1996, 2000, 2003, 2007	1999, 2000	2015–19
Romania	1994, 1997, 2003	1997, 2004, 2006	1995, 2001, 2005, 2008	2007–11 2012–16

Phase 1. 1990s—Land Titling: Reduce Poverty through Entrepreneurship

Depending on the underlying problem, stocktaking publications and land reform documentation can be divided into three different phases of thinking about poverty and land reform. A first phase—roughly spanning the 1990s—fits the landmark publications of 1999 and 2003 and firmly posits poverty as a problem of lacking assets, to be addressed by propertizing land reform. Land reform was supposed to work by encouraging entrepreneurship through the distribution of ownership rights over agricultural land (Deininger and Binswanger 1999). This was expected to lift rural populations out of poverty through three mechanisms. First, if receiving more land, the rural population would work the land under its control as efficiently as it produced on the small plots in the vicinity of households. Second, farmland could serve as collateral for bank loans, and loans would provide badly needed investment. Third, by simply being able to transfer land to the most capable individuals, the land reform program was expected to create land markets and "discipline" rural populations, encouraging the most capable individuals to grow and allowing the less capable to exit agriculture. The operation of these mechanisms was prevented according to World Bank documents by "institutional" factors, most importantly by the continued presence of state actors such as the former collective farms of the communist era and their antiquated management structures. Land reform was expected to reach two objectives: transfer assets to the rural poor and weaken the collective farms.

To cite from an early report on Tajikistan that represents a typical Phase 1 analysis of poverty and its remedies:

> The agricultural sector is characterized by two features which aggravate poverty among the rural population. These are: (i) incomplete land reform which does not allow effective use of the land and agricultural production opportunities; and (ii) weaknesses in the current management and operating system of major agricultural subsectors, especially cotton production. More generally, *organizational structures, management systems and government thinking* in agriculture are still far from requirements of a market economy. In addition, *equal access to land, in particular for the rural poor*, is impeded by the high costs and complicated procedures for getting land use certificates, the lack of information on procedures, and the lack of knowledge about land use rights. (Working Group on Poverty Reduction—Tajikistan 2000; emphasis added)

Poverty is largely seen as a rural phenomenon, an effect of lacking access to land and of the low wages paid by unreformed former collective farms to rural workers. In its reports on Moldova, the Bank compares these workers to the few "private farmers" at that time, claiming that the latter have higher incomes and that if the former were to receive more land, they would increase their incomes correspondingly. The assumption was that as in China, "private farmers" and "rural workers" are comparable and that private farmers emerge independently of the former collective farms' leading cadres:

> In 1997, most farms were still unreformed kolkhozi (collective farms) or sovkhozi (State farms). With Soviet input and output channels in disarray, and existing sales mostly in barter, the farms are chronically unable to pay wages to workers, especially in cash. The findings, described earlier in this chapter, about the emergence of a large class of "working poor," are also generated by these workers. The few private farmers (landowners) who had emerged by 1997 were able to respond relatively well to the structural changes in the economy, and were thus better off than their landless compatriots. (World Bank 1999, 41)

In brief, World Bank documents depicted poverty as due to the lack of productive assets such as first and foremost agricultural land (Lipton 1988) and—in post-communist settings—rural households as being kept dependent on the low wages paid by the surviving collective farms. The situation could easily be changed by transferring land from the former collective farm to the rural population. Corresponding land reform, in the form of "titling," or distributing land titles to rural populations, would peak in pace and regional reach in Eurasia: in only ten years, between 1990 and 2000, more than 145 million hectares were privatized in Eastern Europe, Transcaucasia, and Central Asia (Dudwick, Fock, and Sedik 2007; Lerman 2017).

An important question is whether World Bank experts were aware at this stage of the possibility that land titling would entail the fragmentation of ownership and subsistence rather than entrepreneurship and smallholders producing for self-consumption rather than for markets. Early reports on Ukraine show that World Bank experts were well aware of the possibility of subsistence production. They even welcomed it to the extent it allowed eliminating subsidies and increasing prices: rising prices for grain, it was argued in the World Bank competitiveness report in 1996, would incentivize investment in agriculture in order to benefit from high world market prices. The local population, presumably hit by the price increase of its basic food staple (bread), should switch to subsistence production now that it had land:

> Changes in the world prices for Ukraine's exports would also affect future income and growth. For example, agricultural exports will benefit, in the short run, from rising world grain prices. But in order to take advantage of this opportunity domestic prices of bread must be allowed to reflect market conditions, which would imply that many domestic consumers will increasingly substitute other staples (e.g. potatoes and carrots, usually grown on household plots) for bread. (World Bank 1996, 12)

While later, throughout the 2000s, World Bank reports on post-communist countries would depict subsistence as deeply uneconomical, suffice to say that at least in the case of Ukraine, reports in the 1990s regarded the population's "substituting" capacities as important for allowing the export-orientation of the agricultural sector. They facilitate the elimination of subsidies, which in turn allows profitable exports. Early reports on Romania showed a similar stress on simultaneously driving land reform and eliminating subsidies, price controls, and export limitations in the belief that these measures work together in incentivizing smallholders to produce more (World Bank 1994, xiii); what these measures ignore is the possibility that as in Ukraine, increasing prices affect not only production incentives but also the households' consumption patterns.

More generally, while on the one hand, expressing concern over the size of the subsistence phenomenon, World Bank publications at times stressed the merits of "subsistence" in helping people cope with economic shocks (Dudwick, Fock, and Sedik 2007; Lerman 2017). At times they argued that lacking land titles might have beneficial aspects—for instance, when "communal grazing rights" allow people to keep cattle and livestock and sell products, even if these grazing rights exist because of the lack of "land rights reform" (World Bank 2004b, 131). Furthermore, subsistence agriculture was also praised for relieving welfare budgets and helping keep unemployment in check in countries as diverse as Poland and Russia (Lerman and Schreinemachers 2005; Swinnen and Rozelle 2006).[5] In the World Bank readings characterizing the next phase, "subsistence" becomes a problem because it allows former collective farms to survive (World Bank 2004a, 95).

Phase 2. Late 1990s–Early 2000s: Fragmentation and Subsistence

Despite the massive scale of land reforms undertaken throughout Eurasia, by the end of the 1990s and increasingly throughout the 2000s, World Bank "stocktaking" documents and reports became critical of developments on the ground. Perhaps most importantly, reports criticized reforms as "nominal" in most countries of the Commonwealth of Independent States except for Moldova and the three Transcaucasian republics (Lipton 2009), because reforms had failed to dislodge the former collective farms. On the other hand, while claiming that reforms were "nominal," the reports also voiced concern over the extreme fragmentation of land produced by the land reform. Fragmentation and small size were seen as synonymous with "subsistence," with the majority of rural households producing for self-consumption rather than for markets in the countries that had failed to dislodge the former collective farms (Csaki, Lerman, and Feder 2002; Lerman 2006; Lerman et al. 2007). Subsistence became increasingly problematic in World Bank reports because of the withdrawal from markets it allegedly caused and because it was believed to keep former collective farms alive via the informal arrangements it involves (Swinnen and Rozelle 2006; Yefimov 2003). Despite the existence of these informal arrangements, the same stocktaking documents claimed that smallholders showed "strong psychological resistance" to joining cooperatives because of collectivization abuses and this reluctance vis-à-vis cooperation further fragmented smallholder farming (Gardner and Lerman 2006, 4; Csaki, Lerman, and Feder 2002, 163). In brief, subsistence is increasingly problematic because rural households involved in subsistence are far from the entrepreneurial or commercial ideal of World Bank experts, evident in the praise for the few "private farmers" found in these countries.[6]

To quote a mid-2000s report on Romania, "agriculture still acts as a buffer against the socio-economic effects of transition with farm miniaturization and a lethargic land market generally considered major obstacles for technological progress and efficiency improvements"; the "low supply of land [is] due to lack of alternatives for subsistence and land locked by elderly farmers" (World Bank 2006, 2). Similar conclusions also apply to Tajikistan and Moldova, somewhat surprisingly given that reports such as structural adjustment documentation generally praised these two countries for their privatization programs.[7]

The understanding of poverty changes from one of poverty due to lack of assets to one of "subsistence" due to absent markets (in Romania and Moldova) and the continued existence of informal arrangements between former state farms and rural populations (in Tajikistan and Ukraine). In these latter countries, smallholders and corporate farms are seen as basically "subsidizing" each other through informal arrangements that prevent investments and help perpetuate poverty, a situation that closely resembles that in Russia and Kazakhstan (Csaki, Lerman, and Feder 2002). Land reform documentation, while at times praising reforms in Tajikistan (see endnote 7) and even in Ukraine for finally individualizing land use rights and "the abolition of kolkhozes" (World Bank 2003b, 10), increasingly shifts back to a negative depiction of these countries (Lerman et al. 2007; Lerman and Sedik 2008). Regarding Tajikistan, the recognition sinks in that "private farmers" differ from rural or subsistence households and often do not even emerge independently of the former collective farm, hardly constituting a pro-poor development.[8] To cite again from a report on Tajikistan:

By mid-1999, the figure [of private farms] had increased to around 10,000, and has accelerated in the four months to November 1999 to 13,000. The process of obtaining dekhan [private property] rights is highly dependent on access to information, networks and resources. As a result, most of the new dekhan farmers are kolkhoz administrators and specialists, hukumat [government] officials, businessmen and relatives. The World Bank has consistently supported the "dekhanisation" [privatization] process. Most recently in the middle of 1999, the implementation commenced of the five-year Farm Privatization Support Project (FPSP). . . . It seems that the land converted and distributed may have been transferred largely to groups *which were already relatively wealthy rather than to the poorest or even poorer groups.* (World Bank 2000b, 61–62; emphasis added)

The introduction of individual ownership or land use rights did not bring about entrepreneurship to the extent envisioned by the World Bank experts who advocated it, not even in the countries that have advanced relatively vigorously in distributing land and disbanding collective farms, such as Moldova, Romania, and Tajikistan. What it brought about instead was widespread "subsistence," a rural population holding land titles but failing to commercialize production through official market channels and suspected instead of directly consuming production. The surprisingly high incidence of subsistence sets in only slowly, as research increasingly documents that more than half of the food produced in some of the largest post-communist countries comes from "subsistence farms" (Nagayets 2005). The reaction that characterizes Phase 2 is even more insistence on the necessity of land reform, in particular in cases such as Ukraine, where subsistence is believed to reflect not just the lack of assets, but as in Russia the agency of local yet "powerful vested interests," "kidnapping" reforms or stalling them at a suboptimal level. Thus, incomplete titling created a situation in which farmers and state structures could subsidize each other rather than undergo reforms (Yefimov 2003; Zorya 2003).

As in the first phase, when former collective farms were seen as "failing to adapt to the new economic conditions" (Csaki and Lerman 1997, xiii), the "pseudo-decollectivized" farms in Ukraine as well as in Russia and Kazakhstan are seen as "hangovers of State power, usually needing subsidy to survive" (Lipton 2009, 210). Arguing that the explanation for subsistence lies in the informal arrangements practiced between former collective farms and rural households, World Bank studies shift from an emphasis on "titling," or the simple distribution of property rights, to the actual "individualization of agriculture," meaning the increase of individual land use (Swinnen and Rozelle 2006, 183). If it also includes rights to buy and sell land, individualization would end such arrangements by allowing rural populations to opt out of them or out of farming altogether, because "functioning land markets" could facilitate the "consolidation" of land by allowing those unable to work the land to exit agriculture (Lerman and Cimpoieş 2006).

By the end of the 2010s, land reforms had failed to produce a *commercial* stratum among the rural poor, according to the World Bank's and other organizations' criterion for commercialization—namely, when farms sell more than half their production (Abele and Frohberg 2003a) on formal, officially sanctioned markets. As argued further below, the requirement to sell in formal markets was hardly explicitly formulated, yet the implicit expectation in most World Bank documents is so strong that they avoid regarding or even researching "informal commercialization" as commercialization proper.

The poor were not the addressees of reforms in Phase 2 anymore, but—due to the lack of means to work their land—they turned into a major obstacle to reforms that became more concerned with agricultural output and less with poverty reduction. Poverty reduction needed to advance not by increasing the assets at the poor's disposal but by reducing the overregulation in the formal economy so that the rural poor could sell their land and take up nonagricultural jobs (see the reports on Romania and Ukraine, World Bank 2003a, 2005, 2006). A rather well-established area of research showing that the poor "do worst when assetless" (Lipton 1988, 39) lost ground to the idea that the poor are better off if selling their newly received assets to take up nonagricultural employment. Reports and in particular the national development strategies of Romania and Ukraine (see next section) increasingly mentioned "consolidation," the necessity not to further "individualize" land usage but quite to the contrary, to reduce the numbers of smallholders by increasing the land of "viable" farms, usually meaning those of younger smallholders with above-average-sized farmland. Throughout the next phase, World Bank reports increasingly called for a different type of registration, not of land but of "viable units" at which to target state aid schemes—in other words, a system of subsidies covering certain production inputs such as seeds, fertilizers, and even machinery if purchased in ways that met official criteria.

Despite the fact that "subsistence" characterized post-communist countries irrespective of the extent to which they practiced land reform, it is during the late 1990s and early 2000s that the perception takes hold that transitioning countries can be divided between China-like and Russia-like ones, between those rapidly dismantling or restructuring collective farms and therefore successful and those that sought to maintain the farms. Early analyses highlighting China's rather unique path, which combined liberalization with state involvement in supporting smallholders (see this chapter's first section), were ignored in favor of insisting on the relevance of contrasting China and Russia for understanding the outcomes of land reform (Lipton 2009; Swinnen and Rozelle 2006).

What went unnoticed was the prudent takeoff, at that time, of more commercial smallholder farming. In the areas where I conducted fieldwork in Ukraine, this second phase of land reform coincided with a time when many respondents took up or returned to agriculture in search of higher incomes (see chapters 4 and 5). The world price for grain (wheat) quadrupled over less than a decade, reaching an all-time high in 2008. Fieldwork respondents describe how some even gave up employment in cities to return to their villages and work the land in search of profits. They called for and actively brought about the dismantlement of moribund former collective farms by "taking their land out of the [former collective] farm" [farmer, Banyliv, August 2016] (see chapter 5). These villagers usually had worked for the former collective farm as technical personnel, having better agricultural knowledge and access to farm equipment such as tractors and combines. They soon became embroiled in bitter competition over leasing the land of those villagers who had no resources to work their own land, but they also demonstrated to these other villagers the profitability of land. But these relations and developments were mostly informal, so unsurprisingly, states and their international advisors took little notice of them.

Phase 3. Beyond Land Distribution Programs: Commercialization and New Agrarian Reform

By the end of the second phase, it became clear that initial land reforms had failed to turn rural households into entrepreneurial farms. Instead of land sales between a growing number of entrepreneurial or private farmers, rural households practiced more or less formal lease arrangements, and, to the extent they sold their production, they did so locally and informally, making it difficult to document commercialization and creating the suspicion that such informal markets for land and production offer smallholders sub-optimal, predatory conditions, keeping them in a "vicious circle" of poverty (see chapter 5). World Bank reports and stocktaking documents, as well as the wider social scientific literature, were reporting already in the early 2000s that most rural households in "Russia-like" countries had left their land with the former collective farm or leased it back to the former kolkhozy for in-kind payments, usually in the form of grain to be used as animal fodder (Csaki, Lerman, and Feder 2002). Even where the former collective farms seemed to be gradually disappearing (as in Tajikistan, Moldova, and parts of Western Ukraine) or had been radically dismantled (as in Romania), it seemed that the actors populating these countries' rural spaces still practiced informal or in-kind arrangements that World Bank reports avoid calling markets. These arrangements kept rural populations in poverty by paying them very low wages or by preventing important investments; in short, these were not "markets," and the solution to rural poverty was "bringing agriculture to the 'markets,'" as outlined in the *World Development Report* (WDR) *2008* (World Bank 2007). To quote an agricultural competitiveness report on Moldova, broadly following the logic of the WDR 2008:

> Low incomes derived from agriculture stem primarily from weak links to markets and low competitiveness of the output produced. This situation is determined by constraints on both supply and demand sides that together form a vicious circle which is hard to break. On the supply side, farm size and farming patterns, problems related to produce safety and quality, lack of post-harvest storing, handling and packaging are the main culprits for limited marketing opportunities available to Moldovan producers. This in turn, is linked to demand side failures, i.e., the under-development of vertically coordinated supply chains in Moldova that should play a key role in driving demand and setting standards for agricultural produce in line with latest market requirements. (World Bank 2012, 2)

The underlying problem was a loss of control over smallholder agriculture, manifest in the failure to reach subjects and spur their commercialization through instruments such as land reform (see table 2.3).

TABLE 2.3. Land reform phases and underlying problem definitions and policy fixes of poverty. Source: Varga 2020.

	Phase 1	*Phase 2*	*Phase 3*
Underlying problem	Poverty as lack of assets	Subsistence due to informal arrangements	Subsistence
Policy fix	Land titling to produce entrepreneurial farms	Further individualization of farmland property	Farm registration, "consolidation," and "commercialization"
	Elimination of price controls, subsidies, export bans, and state-owned marketing		Integration in large value chains; introduction of subsidies for registered farms

The solution was partly to introduce monetary incentives to determine best-performing farms to register and operate on what the World Bank perceived as markets. These farms were to then integrate into value chains capable of exporting. Land titling was no longer expected to "work" in bringing about pro-poor results, but what the World Bank referred to as commercialization, increasing to at least 50 percent of their production what a select strata of best performing rural households—preferably officially registered as farms—sold on markets. Not any markets would do in the perspective of World Bank publications. They clearly identify the "vertically coordinated supply chains" rather than local periodic markets as the preferred marketing channel for smallholders. The measures of success changed from "individualization" to the numbers of "farms" registered and taking up state schemes in order to access vertically coordinated supply chains and to "consolidation" of their land. In other words, the measure of success ("consolidation") had become exactly the opposite of what it had been throughout Phases 1 and 2 ("individualization"): the situations created by land reform—a rural space inhabited by millions of rural households relying on agricultural land for subsistence—had become under Phase 3 precisely what needs to be fixed.

Throughout Phase 3, World Bank reports slowly gave up the Phase-1 goal of having a rural space dominated by small entrepreneurial farms. Ever since the late 2000s, the Bank has expected small farmers to integrate into the value chains dominated by large, "vertically coordinated" agribusinesses and has expected these businesses to play a leading role (see excerpt about Moldova above). With the exception of Ukraine, a country in which World Bank experts accuse large agribusinesses of stalling land reform (Deininger and Nizalov 2016; Nivievskyi 2018), for smaller countries such as Tajikistan and Moldova, the larger agribusinesses become the solution to poverty and agriculture lacking competitiveness. The general perception of former collective farms changes from "hangovers of State power, usually needing subsidy" (Lipton 2009, 210) to the claim of World Bank lead economists that former collective farms "were better able to deal with financing, infrastructure and technology constraints of the transition" (Deininger and Byerlee 2011, xxi). The continued existence of or role for smallholders as producers for local markets is devalued. To cite a report on Tajikistan:

> On the supply side, low farm productivity (resulting from poor access to investment and working capital finance and technological knowledge) limits the marketed surplus, and farmer capacity to market this surplus is constrained by inexperience with market activity and low economies of scale. The Rural Investment Climate Assessment (RICA, 2013) study reports that only one-third of crop producers currently sell their output, and of those more than half (52%) sell at the farm gate. An estimated 32% sell in local markets and 15% in national or export markets. (World Bank 2014, 3)

Accordingly, the Bank calls for a

> new Agrarian Reform Program . . . where the rationale for increasing agriculture commercialization is also recognized. Among its priorities, this strategy identifies the need to strengthen agricultural input and output markets and to increase agricultural productivity through improved access to seed, credit and extension services. In line with these strategic objectives, the Government of Tajikistan has requested Bank support for a project to increase commercialization of the sector, strengthen the links between producers and processors, and support producer associations. . . . The project will further the twin goals of the World Bank to reduce poverty and promote shared prosperity. (World Bank 2014, 4–5)

In Moldova, Romania, and Ukraine, countries where the World Bank assists governments in writing national and rural development strategies

(World Bank 2008), post-titling reforms take the form of farm registers: identifying "viable units," smallholder "farms" that offer growth prospects, which the country's government should assist with input subsidies, or, as in the case of EU-member Romania, "farms" at which to target the EU-subsidies system of the Common Agricultural Policy (Roger 2014; 2016). The crux of the approach is winning back some control over smallholder agriculture by monetizing the inputs of the households judged as "most viable." It is up to the state to identify these farms, incentivize them to register, and assist in their "modernization." In the phrasing of Ukraine's 2015 strategy and action plan for rural development, drafted with assistance from the World Bank and other international organizations, the authorities' "main objective" is to

> develop a set of legal, economic and organizational interventions to support small agricultural producers in order to promote the improvement of their productivity and profitability, modernisation, the diversification of agricultural activities, an increase of added value, the use of innovative market distribution channels, and the ensured access to finance. [Priority measures include the] creation of the economic, organizational and social conditions for small farm support (registration, taxation, insurance, credit, pension system) by enhancing the relevant legislative and regulatory framework [and the] design and implementation of a targeted investment support programme to assist small farm development and diversification. (Ministry of Agrarian Policy and Food of Ukraine 2015, 56)

In stark contrast to China's reforms, where maintaining the state's role as buyer of smallholder production also supported the emergence of local periodic markets, the relevance of local markets and the marketing channels existing in practice has been undervalued or dismissed throughout all three phases. During Phase 3, this rejection has taken its most explicit formulation in proposals such as "New Agrarian Reform," advocating for vertically coordinated supply chains as the most relevant marketing channel for smallholders. However, local marketing channels such as periodic markets and the interaction with traders buying produce at the farm gate should not be dismissed. As argued in the next chapters, these channels most often come with only little conditionality attached while—in the case of periodic markets—bringing local authorities taxes. They offer smallholders a stable income and even a strategy of incremental growth for which they hardly need credit or for which they can mobilize the monetary resources gained elsewhere, for instance, from migration.

Furthermore, throughout the third phase, there is growing explicit abandonment in World Bank reports of the idea that land reform alone can address rural poverty, calling instead for "land consolidation" reforms that increase the farm size of smallholders at the expense of those not "viable" enough. But the reports overlook that land reform was successful in providing rural populations with at least some means for subsistence during the time of the collapse of the Soviet Union, when it was the main direction for land reform advocated by the World Bank. If they address the successes of land reform at all, then reports depict these successes simply as increasing agricultural output and not as poverty reduction, claiming that countries in Central Asia or Transcaucasia have, because of "individualization" and the dismantlement of former collective farms, done a far better job in increasing output than the European post-Soviet countries of the "Russia-like" type (Lerman 2017).[9]

The next chapter will discuss how World Bank publications have mapped the Eurasian communist and post-communist countries and arranged them along a continuum from worst to best reformers while turning "subsistence" into a problem of land plot size that can and should be fixed through "consolidation."

CHAPTER 3
The Reform Continuum
From China to Russia

DESPITE LAND REFORM ADVANCING throughout post-communist Eurasia, "subsistence" as self-provisioning, low productivity, poverty, and market avoidance has remained a key feature of agriculture in many of the countries surveyed by the World Bank (Lerman 2017; Satana, Törhönen, and Adlington 2014; World Bank 2007). Important differences persist between country groups. On the one hand, a group of countries dismantled collective farms relatively quickly and, therefore, appeared as better performing in the World Bank's perspective. This group includes Albania, Romania, Moldova, and the three South Caucasus countries (Transcaucasia), as well as two Central Asian countries (Tajikistan and Kyrgyzstan). These countries have seen the dismantlement of the communist-era collective farms (the kolkhozy or *sovkhozy*), but despite land reform and the extension of land property or use rights, small-scale farming was very far from the World Bank's ideal of commercialization; consequently, World Bank publications refer to smallholders in these countries as practicing "subsistence agriculture."

On the other hand, the group of worst-performing "Russia-like" countries saw the survival of former collective farms coupled with moratoria prohibiting the sale of agricultural land. While Russia gradually eliminated the moratorium during the 2000s, Kazakhstan kept its moratorium and Ukraine eliminated it in only 2021. Despite the progressing cadastral land registration project in Ukraine, World Bank experts directly blame the moratorium for impoverishing and "violating the constitutional rights" of small-scale farmers (Deininger and Nizalov 2016). The most problematic aspect of subsistence in Russia-like countries is what World Bank experts refer to as the "dualization of agriculture—that is, the coexistence and even mutual interdependence between very large corporate farms (the former communist-era kolkhozy) and subsistence households, an interdependence considered to prevent both the households and the former collective farms from developing more efficient production. Dualization is the effect of incomplete land reform or of land reform being more "imaginary" than "real" (Yefimov 2003).

Using World Bank publications, table 3.1 lists Eurasian countries from worst- to best-performing countries, where *best* refers to countries achieving fast land reform, propertizing local populations, and dismantling or reforming collective farms. *Worst* refers to situations where land reform is incomplete and fails to transform collective farms. The survival of former collective farms receives a negative perception—turning a country into a worst performer—and is brought into direct relation with the sluggish recovery of agricultural production in Russia (Lerman 2017, 23) and Ukraine (Deininger, Nizalov, and Singh 2013). The table includes all post-communist countries mentioned in stocktaking documents reflecting on the state of agriculture in the aftermath of land reforms in Eurasia as well as China and Vietnam. Left out are the former Yugoslav republics and East Germany, which are usually not included in the World Bank publications reviewed.

Table 3.1, arranging post-communist countries according to land reform extent, summarizes the claims in World Bank publications and its knowledge network, including the World Bank's Development Research Group and the in-house publication *Word Bank Economic Review* (Swinnen and Rozelle 2006; Swinnen, Vandeplas, and Maertens 2010). Such an arrangement maps the world of reforming communist and post-communist countries as one in which China-like cases outperform Russia-like countries: East Asia (China and Vietnam) tops other regions, followed by East Central Europe and the Balkans, with most of the former Soviet countries coming in last. Yet arranging countries in this way hides several complications, discussed in the remainder of this chapter.

The first complication is that several Russia-like countries switched to more individualization in the 2000s; that is, they abandoned the land reform approach that gave households shares in collective farms rather than

TABLE 3.1. Post-communist countries and land reforms outcomes. Source: Author's elaboration based on Dudwick, Fock, and Sedik (2007); Lerman (2012, 2017); Lerman and Sedik (2009); Swinnen and Rozelle (2006); Möllers et al. (2016).

"Russia" Pattern		"China" Pattern		East Central Europe
Shares-based land reform		Propertizing land reform		
Worst performer	2nd-worst performers (low individualization, dualization)	Good performers (high individualization but coupled with subsistence)	Best performers (low subsistence)	Good performers but subsistence eliminated through smallholder exit from agriculture rather than commercialization
Belarus (private property rights only over household plots)	Russia Ukraine Kazakhstan Kyrgyzstan (1990s) Moldova (1990s) Tajikistan (early 1990s) Turkmenistan (early 1990s) Uzbekistan	Albania Azerbaijan Georgia Tajikistan (2000s) Turkmenistan (2000s) Kyrgyzstan (2000s) Bulgaria Moldova (2000s) Mongolia Romania	China Vietnam	Czechia Hungary Slovakia *At least 50% of land in individual use:* Estonia Latvia Lithuania Poland

property titles (or use rights) over the land of collective farms. Instead, they individualized land rights by transferring land into individual property or usage. Yet this hardly impacted the prevalent pattern of subsistence, and in the case of Ukraine, hardly helped to reverse "dualization." The other countries to have changed their land reform approach are Moldova, Kyrgyzstan, Tajikistan, and Turkmenistan. Ukraine stays nevertheless in the Russia-like category in table 3.1 because of the strong pattern of dualization present even after the change from a shares-based system to propertizing land reform; that is, despite individualization, most of the land is under the control of large corporate farms and subsistence farmers, with only few individual farms.

Second, it is important to note that data on whether subsistence and dualization also mean more poverty among rural households are rarely available. Most often, if there is such data from surveys, then these compare the incomes of subsistence households with those of larger farms, not with those of households lacking the means even to subsist. Most often the research focusing on the extent of land reform in post-communist countries provides data not on poverty but on productivity, based on the fact that in China and Vietnam smallholders experienced massive increases in productivity during the reforms' first years and even first decade, and these productivity increases went hand in hand with higher incomes and therefore a reduction in poverty. But throughout that decade, Chinese and Vietnamese smallholders could not increase the size of their land plots through market mechanisms because the allocation of land remained under the strict control of local authorities, as outlined in chapter 2; more than three decades after the start of reforms, 98 percent of China's farmers were smallholders, using two or fewer hectares of land per household (Rapsomanikis 2015).

And third, and most importantly, there is no numerical indicator measuring subsistence at the level of farms other than the size of the land plot, because productivity measures rely on official total output data. Thus, small farms—usually, those with land holdings below two hectares—are seen as practicing subsistence farming simply based on their land plot size. This leads to assuming that smallholders generally fail to engage with markets, an issue to which I return in this section and also in chapter 5. But whatever caused the increase in productivity and incomes in China, it was not the increase of landholding size through market transactions. By arranging countries as done above in table 3.1, the implication is that more land reform or more individualization of land use or property rights causes increases in incomes and decreases in poverty. However, the reality is that many countries in the China-like category achieved faster and deeper land reforms than China, but with far less success in limiting or decreasing subsistence.

Labor productivity (output per labor unit of farm worker) indeed differs considerably between, on one hand, China, Vietnam, East Central Europe, and one country of the China-like category (Albania) and, on the other hand, the vast majority of post-Soviet states irrespective of their land reform approach (table 3.2). In the latter group, only Estonia achieved a productivity increase after reforms, but a decade after land reform it maintained only 35 percent of the pre-reform workforce. Similarly, labor

TABLE 3.2. Productivity results of land reform in communist and post-communist countries. In the case of East Central Europe and the Balkans, ranges do not include Poland, which has seen less labor shedding but also needed less land reform because of its failed collectivization. Sources: Author's elaboration based on World Bank indicators database as well as the data presented by Swinnen and Rozelle (2006).

Labor productivity and labor use (in parentheses) as percentage of pre-reform levels				
	Russia-like		China-like	East Central Europe and Baltic states
	Shares-based land reform		Propertizing land reform	
Worst performer	2nd-worst performers (low individualization, dualization)	Good performers (no dualization)	Best performers (low subsistence)	Best performers but subsistence eliminated through small-holder exit from agriculture rather than commercialization
Belarus 72–86% (73%)	Russia, Ukraine, Kazakhstan 55–62% (92–102%)	Central Asia 39–98% South Caucasus 45–79% (100–200%) Balkans 63–104% (98–102%)	East Asia 107–146% (110–131%)	East Central Europe 132–220% (37–60%) Baltic states 65–163% (35–103%)

productivity advanced substantially in East Central Europe. But it did so not by increasing production but by shedding agricultural workers; a decade after the start of reforms, Hungary employed only 37 percent and Slovakia 60 percent of its initial workforce. In sum, the countries in East Central Europe and the Baltic states are the post-communist countries that have achieved the highest increases in labor productivity but with the largest labor force decreases. In contrast, China's use of labor stood at 110 percent and Vietnam's at 131 percent eight years following the reform.

The contrast between the best-performing countries and between China and the rest becomes more evident if yields are used to measure productivity (output per land unit). Five years into the reforms, China's average yields index stood at 145 percent of pre-reform levels. At the same time, no post-communist country except Romania reached the pre-reform level (with Albania coming close at 94 percent). Ten years after the reforms, all Baltic, Balkan, and Central European states had reached or surpassed pre-reform levels, except Bulgaria, Hungary, and Lithuania. China had reached 155 percent, while at the other extreme, the average yields index for Belarus, Ukraine, and Russia stood between 71 and 75 percent, with yields in Kazakhstan at 57 percent.[1]

Numerous World Bank publications, including landmark publications such as the *World Development Report* on agriculture, focus entirely on the story of recovery, downplaying how long it took most post-communist countries to reach even pre-reform production levels. They highlight in particular the contrast between the "best" performers in East Central Europe and the Baltics and the "worst-performing" countries such as Russia, Ukraine, or Kazakhstan, or between Balkan (Albania and Romania) and Transcaucasian countries and the Russia-like group. But East Central Europe's story of success is one very different from China's, with massive—close to two-thirds—decreases in agricultural employment, while the Balkan countries are still very far from the yields increases experienced in China. And the Russia-like group is more heterogeneous, with several countries increasing the pace of propertizing reforms without a decrease in subsistence.

Dismissing Informal Commercialization

More problematic for the relevance of advanced land reform for curbing subsistence is the World Bank data suggesting that the smallholders' propensity to commercialize production does not depend on land reform. Thus even in Ukraine, a Russia-like country with a strongly dualized agriculture, smallholders actually commercialize as much as or more of their production than China-like cases such as Moldova or the three Transcaucasian republics. Note that this data—presented in figure 3.1—goes back to the late 1990s, when Ukraine had done little to adopt propertizing land reform and most Moldovan smallholders still kept their land plots with the former collective farms.

The numbers in figure 3.1 come from the end of Phase 1 land reform, late 1990s–early 2000s. They include the percentages of agricultural land in individual use by the end of the 1990s in Armenia and Georgia and 2010

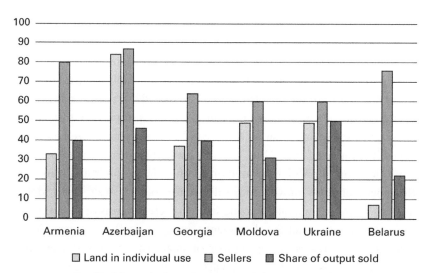

FIGURE 3.1. Smallholder agriculture (percentages), late 1990s–early 2000s. Sources: National statistics for the countries of the Commonwealth of Independent States except for Armenia and Georgia; all other figures are World Bank survey data in Lerman (2006).

data for the other countries, percentage of "sellers" (households selling at least part of their production), and share of total output sold by "sellers" by the late 1990s.

The World Bank survey results collected by Zvi Lerman in Transcaucasian countries as well as Belarus, Moldova, and Ukraine for the data in figure 3.1 show that irrespective of the type of land reform enacted (Russia-like or China-like), important shares of the household or smallholder sector do sell what they produce. Actually, it is Ukraine, a Russia-like country, that has seen a majority of its households selling production. Furthermore, the 2015 agricultural strategy for Ukraine documents the existence of an important share of smallholders that commercializes most production, claiming that "more than 20 percent of them [small farms] engage in commercial activities and offer their produce mainly through local markets" (Ministry of Agrarian Policy and Food of Ukraine 2015, 56). But after noting that commercialization in post-communist countries seems more widespread than assumed, Lerman's recommendation for the countries above is nevertheless that the primary tool to achieve more commercialization is to increase the size of farms. This in turn requires more market-making land reform, and not a better understanding of what allows households to commercialize production in their environment even when producing on very small land plots.

The striking aspect of how World Bank publications operate with the concept of subsistence is the tendency to equate "subsistence farming" with "farming on individual land plots" (World Bank 2004a, xviii). Confusing subsistence with individual land plots leads in practice to measure subsistence solely or primarily in terms of holding or farm size and numbers of subsistence farms. Thus, a World Bank document from 2016, drawing conclusions for Moldova based on commercialization from Poland and Romania seamlessly moves from subsistence to small-scale farms, defining *subsistence* and operationalizing it exclusively in terms of farm size, an approach present in all the documents surveyed for this chapter. Simple increases or decreases in the number of small-scale or subsistence farms are taken as measures of commercialization, even though these numbers can vary because of other developments, including migration and farm abandonment.[2]

Assuming by definition that there is no commercialization going on in the "subsistence sector," the implication is that subsistence farmers need to be clearly separated from commercially oriented farmers. Subsistence agriculture, to the extent it represents the smallholders' main source of livelihood, is the indicator for poverty, with the corollary being that commercialization is a sign of relative affluence. Yet it was World Bank data that showed that the number of rural households that rely mainly on agriculture for their livelihood through direct consumption has been declining and at best represents only a minority of the population in post-communist countries, highest perhaps in Moldova, not surpassing by 2015 some 20 percent of the rural population and actually steadily decreasing. *Subsistence* thus becomes a misnomer for characterizing rural households: the majority of the rural population in countries most often associated with subsistence (Russia, Ukraine, Romania, and Moldova) combine agriculture with incomes from off-farm work, including salaries, social benefits (pensions), and remittances from abroad (Romanian Ministry of Agriculture and Rural Development 2014; World Bank 2004a; Möllers et al. 2016). In my ethnographic sample, introduced and discussed in the following three chapters, the links between subsistence and poverty and between commercialization and affluence are tenuous. Subsistence is often a phase that commercializing smallholders go through, and they often need "subsisting" smallholders to buy up their production or to lease them their land. Furthermore, commercializing households—selling more than half of production—are either smallholders and entrepreneurial farmers, selling both formally and informally, or the ultra-poor that own only their household plots and are too old or too sick to sell their labor and instead are forced to sell their household plot production.

As figure 3.1 shows, most smallholders or subsistence farmers do sell parts of their production, mostly informally, even though they sell less than the 50 percent required to count them as "commercializing." While World Bank data shows that there is informal commercialization among smallholders, the World Bank knowledge network takes no interest in it and does not inquire when and how smallholders start to commercialize. In fact, what seems to trouble World Bank and national government experts is not the low level of commercialization but the lack of control over smallholders (see chapter 6), as this kind of commercialization is most often not registered or taxed. As pointed out in a personal communication by one of the authors who worked on a World Bank report on Eastern Europe, this type of commercialization was referred to as "informal commercialization" within the World Bank's knowledge network and was usually "dismissed" and not further looked into (personal communication with anonymous World Bank source, October 2019, July 2020). In other words, the World Bank saw only export and retail chains as allowing smallholders to market production and dismissed the notion that informal commercialization also means that smallholders deal with markets. As argued in the next chapters, it was vital for facilitating higher incomes and increasing production among my respondents. It is also closer to the scenario followed in China and Vietnam, where next to the state procurement system, the immediate environment consisting of local markets represented the smallholders' main channel for commercialization.

What Happened to the Idea of Addressing Poverty through Land Transfers?

To summarize part 1, the idea of reforming rural property relations through the distribution of property titles translated into a program believed to be of worldwide relevance for addressing rural poverty. The World Bank in particular has formulated and supported this reform program, and it still presents it as a key to solving development issues as varied as "rapid urban expansion, . . . climate change, disaster resilience, and social inclusion" (Deininger 2018); its Development Research Group has made tremendous efforts to emphasize the relevance of land reform, and in 2019 it held its twentieth conference on land and poverty, attracting "1,800 participants from government, civil society, the private sector, and academia representing 124 countries" (Deininger 2018). Yet as argued in this chapter and in contrast to the "landmark publications" discussed in chapter 1, the post-communist experience has been one of growing disillusionment with land reform. In the perception of World Bank reports' authors, it was not so much the reforms' effects on poverty reduction that were disillusioning but the failure to make a marked difference in producing more entrepreneurship. Consequently, the wave of reforms to follow has involved state action to deregulate labor markets in nonagricultural sectors to attract the rural poor and "registering" campaigns aimed at the larger farms to help them grow in size at the expense of those that should leave production altogether.

The land reforms' impact on livelihoods implies a direct link between land reform and subsistence. World Bank documents instead cast subsistence as the effect of informal arrangements, primarily due to the survival of collective farms. Perhaps even more elementary, the insistence on more land titling and propertizing, registration, and distribution of land simply did not provide households and farms with credit and investment. Instead, and as argued in the next part, land reform had the *demonetizing* effects of a retreat of former collective farms and rural households from the markets favored by the Word Bank, as both engage in informal, nonmonetary transactions underpinned by the land distributed during "titling" reforms. Smallholder agriculture again escaped the reformers' efforts to control it.

While acknowledging and criticizing this fact, World Bank reports long regarded informal transactions as resulting from insufficiently clear property rights, in particular during the first two phases of thinking about land reform: if only local populations would have a clear picture of where and how much land they own, they would evade such arrangements and work their land rather than lease it to the former collective farm. In other words, land reform contributed to a retreat of rural households from markets, a theme that all reports address and regard as the central problem to be addressed, even though it is not reforms per se that they blame but their partial enactment. This corresponds to the analysis of rural poverty in the 2008 *World Development Report,* in which the World Bank claims that smallholder agriculture needs to be "brought to the markets." Like the 2008 WDR, the policy documents studied here increasingly leave a focus on titling land reform behind and call for a range of measures that one could term—in line with the reports on Tajikistan—"new agrarian reform," breaking with the land reform's egalitarian approach and calling on the state to register and help integrate selected smallholders into larger—preferably international—value chains. After a brief period in which it seemed to favor an egalitarian smallholder agriculture, the World Bank's policies returned to approaches that recall the "urban bias" in development policy implicit in the "structural change" thesis, linking development to shrinking agricultural employment (Lipton 1977; Chenery and Syrquin 1975; for a critique, see Akram-Lodhi 2008).

Thus the idea that policies can address poverty by transferring assets to the poor and spurring entrepreneurship and growth as in China and Vietnam, an idea still widely circulated internationally, was relatively short-lived in the post-communist context and was eventually replaced by a stress on "consolidation," the need to overcome the fragmentation and small size of land plots. The idea of transferring assets to address poverty appeared to have lasted as long as World Bank reports could document that land reform and state retreat held promises of entrepreneurial creation among the rural population by transferring productive assets and increasing price incentives to produce. Yet as the reports on Ukraine have shown, the move to world prices raised the costs of basic food staples while land distribution facilitated subsistence as rural populations were forced to grow alternatives in response to price increases. This points to an intrinsic tension between poverty reduction and entrepreneurship to the extent that the latter mainly involved incentivizing production through price increases, and that pushed the countries included in this study toward an increase in subsistence production. Entrepreneurs did emerge, but they stayed in the informal economy. This crucial aspect of reforms is now often overlooked, and rather than an outcome of reforms, subsistence is assumed to be an effect of underdevelopment and of staying far from the reach of markets and policies.

Reading from their statistics that large rural and peri-urban populations were subsistence-oriented simply based on how much land they owned, World Bank and national government officials cast them as noneconomical and alien to markets. "Commercialization," the supposed antidote to "subsistence," then becomes a euphemism, measuring not how many small-scale farmers actually manage to increase marketed production but how many of them exit agriculture altogether. The land titling project, the deepening of "land reform" to produce markets for land, becomes in this context the main tool for driving commercialization, by facilitating the exit from agriculture of "noneconomical" actors, who are expected to sell their land plots to more productive farmers. But, as argued in the chapter and in line with a broader literature on governmentality and state and World Bank interventions, "subsistence" is a misreading, if it implies market avoidance and surviving mostly on self-grown food. It confuses subsistence with land plot size and casts social actors along a single axis while ignoring how commercialization looks from the perspective of the actors it attempts to shape.[3]

Part 2 will contrast the World Bank and national governmental perspective on subsistence and commercialization with the results of a fieldwork study carried out in a post-communist region with a very high incidence of smallholder farmers and contrasting land-reform patterns. In the region's southern (Romanian) part, reform followed the Chinese pattern in that it rapidly dismantled collective farms and transferred land to the rural population. Reform resembled the Russian pattern in the northern (Ukrainian) part, allowing collective farms to coexist with local smallholders. Farms were eventually dismantled, resulting in a proliferation of smallholder agriculture. Irrespective of the type of land reform pursued, smallholder agriculture was characterized by subsistence on both sides of the Romanian-Ukrainian border—that is, by the low incidence of farms producing for officially sanctioned markets. Part 2 takes a closer look at this outcome and rather than trace it back to insufficient land reform (Phase 2) or insufficient integration in global value chains (Phase 3), it traces the outcome back to the smallholders' need to secure their livelihoods by controlling as much as possible their exposure to markets. Smallholders do engage in markets, proving that the image of isolated and autarchic producers producing for self-consumption is misleading: the collapse of communism made room for a commercial agrifood chain that the World Bank calls "traditional," linking smallholders via traders with local consumers. While this process was assisted and encouraged by authorities in China, in post-communist countries this hardly was the case, even in countries that rapidly dismantled collective farms, such as Romania. Instead of supporting the local environment populated by smallholders and traders, the World Bank lent money to Germany's largest supermarket chain, Lidl, financing its expansion to Romania and other post-communist countries with 350 million euros in the 2010s (Provost and Kennard 2015). As the chapter on resistance (6) will show, governments further contribute to the isolation of the "traditional" agrifood chain by launching various campaigns to limit its spread and curb the informal activities it entails.

A "Monetizing" Perspective

CHAPTER 4
Smallholders
A Fieldwork Study of Resilience and Resistance

THE AGRICULTURAL LANDSCAPE that emerged from post-communist land reform seemed to resemble "traditional" or *fragmented* markets consisting of "numerous producers and retailers, generally small in size, with little explicit demand and supply coordination" (Lee, Gereffi, and Beauvais 2012). Following land reform, the most numerous producers turned out to be households in rural and semi-urban areas on city outskirts, worlds apart from the reformers' ideal of entrepreneurial farming or the productivity increases in China and Vietnam. Nevertheless, mirroring global trends of continued relevance of smallholders for food production (Cohn et al. 2017; Samberg et al. 2016), these households produced most of the food in the 1990s and much of the 2000s in post-communist and especially post-Soviet Eurasia. Statistics encompassed them under the heading of smallholders, understood by FAO as agricultural holdings "run by a family and using mostly their own labor" (Bosc et al. 2013, 23), producing on less than two hectares. A decade after the fall of communism and the start of land reform, statistical data documented the existence of 41 million agricultural micro-holdings in Europe's post-communist countries, representing 95 percent of all farms (von Braun and Lohlein 2003). While decreasing in number ever since, smallholders have kept high shares of agricultural output across transitioning Eurasia (see figure 4.1), especially in the crops that they specialize in and that have declining returns to scale (von Braun and Mirzabaev 2015, 19). But more generally, smallholders also

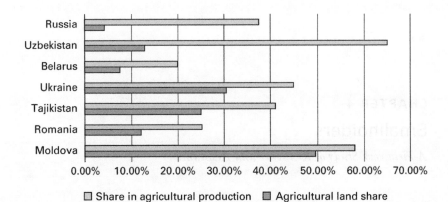

FIGURE 4.1. Smallholders and their contribution to agricultural production in selected post-communist countries (2013–14). For Moldova also including individual farms. Source: Burkitbayeva and Swinnen (2018).

played an important part in food security throughout post-Soviet countries, producing by the early 2000s in Russia and Ukraine more than three quarters of total vegetable and fruit production and between 51 to 73 percent of milk and 57 to 76 percent of meat production (Nagayets 2005, 363; Visser et al. 2015). In Ukraine, even with the rise of large agricultural corporations throughout the 2000s, smallholders still produced 40 percent of agricultural production and 54 percent of animal production by the time I started fieldwork in 2013, and in western regions, figures were well over 70 percent (Ukrstat 2018).

The continued relevance of smallholders for food production takes place against the background of numerous problems affecting them. While increasing in many countries throughout the first two decades of post-communism, smallholder numbers have started to decrease ever since the early 2010s in some of the region's largest countries, and Ukraine and Romania are no exceptions to this trend. Figure 4.2 exemplifies this, showing the reduction in "rural households" (Ukraine) and "subsistence farms" (Romania), referring to farms that consume more than 50 percent of their production. The figure also includes Poland, the country with the second highest number of subsistence farms in the EU, to show the difference with Romania: with almost twice Romania's population, the maximum number of subsistence farms in Poland was about one-third of the Romanian figure. Still, smallholder figures decrease throughout Europe,

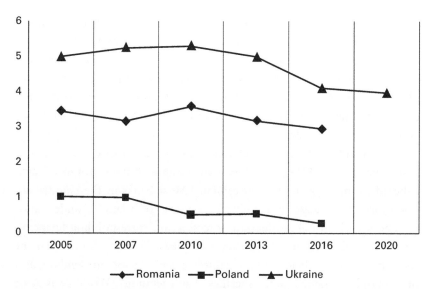

FIGURE 4.2. Smallholder farms in selected post-communist countries (*millions*). The Eurostat data for Romania and Poland refers to farms consuming more than 50 percent of production; the Ukrstat statistics for Ukraine count all rural households irrespective of holding size and commercialization. Only 1 percent of rural households have more than ten hectares of land. The Ukrstat data for rural households is at times contradictory, for some years ranging between 4.1 and 4.8 million households. Sources: Eurostat, https://ec.europa.eu/eurostat/ (2016 is the latest available figure); State Statistics Service of Ukraine, ukrstat.gov.ua.

with close to four million smallholders left in Ukraine and three million in Romania.

The most problematic aspect concerning the operating conditions of smallholder agriculture was elsewhere, and had been there since the early 1990s. Using a comparison with China's reforms introducing the household responsibility system, this book suggested in part 1 that it was, in particular, the collapse of official marketing channels after the fall of communism that negatively affected agricultural producers by pushing them into subsistence. The main difference between China's reforms and those pursued in post-communist countries was not land reform but the massive retreat of the state in the latter countries. In contrast, World Bank publications have focused on the lack of investment due in their perspective to the limited enactment of land reform in Russia-like countries, preventing the formation of land markets and the use of land as collateral for bank loans. Although lack of investment is a problem of worldwide relevance for smallholder agriculture (Bosc et al. 2013), post-communist countries were considered more severely affected, irrespective of whether their land reform programs were China- or Russia-like. This was due to the complexities of reforming or creating from scratch entire sectors, particularly private banking, and because the cadastral registration of private land proceeded only very slowly.

The World Bank and the Organisation for Economic Co-operation and Development (OECD) warned that the agricultural sector in Ukraine suffered from a chronic lack of capital: "Most banks in the country are unprepared to engage in agri-finance because of a lack of understanding about agricultural production processes and corresponding financing needs of the farms. There are no agronomy-based credit risk management tools; no lending policies and procedures specifically for agri-lending; and no loan officers trained on the specifics of agri-lending" (World Bank 2015; see also OECD 2012, 20). Even in Romania, for instance, one of the countries considered China-like in its approach to land reform, with more than 90 percent of land in private hands by 1993, only half the landowners had received land titles by 1996 (Swinnen and Gow 1999; Ciaian, Fałkowski, and d'Artis 2012, 37). In fact, due to the lack of investment, some studies voiced the concern that a drastic decrease in the number of farms was to be expected. As small farms lacked the capacity to access credit, they would lose market shares, get stuck in subsistence production, and eventually disappear by natural attrition.[1] A similar scenario was expected for Russia-like countries as soon as the subsidies to former collective farms were reduced, pushing them to shed their symbiotic relationship to smallholders (Lipton 2009).

This scenario has not taken place. Instead, what can be documented was the continued relevance of small farms for food production not only in China-like countries but even in countries where it was often argued that they received very little payment in exchange for their land, such as Ukraine and Russia. While the lack of credit mechanisms for small farms in particular is well documented, we know little about what supported smallholders in their activities, given that they lack established financing channels. In other words, we know little about how to explain what in a Western context has been called the "persistence" or "resilience" (Mac-Donald, Korb, and Hoppe 2013; Hall and Lamont 2013) of smallholders in securing or enhancing means of living and producing under difficult economic conditions.[2] Small farms were not just surviving but undergoing a process of differentiation, with some actually growing by informally taking over land and increasing production (Pallot and Nefedova 2007; Kuns 2017; Varga 2016). At the same time, inequalities within communities were increasing, as some of the most successful farmers were building their success on the unequal access to the resources of the moribund former collective farms (see chapter 5).

In studying the differentiation of smallholder agriculture in post-communist countries, few have looked at the immediate environment of smallholders, building on the assumption that in the absence of clear property rights, this environment hardly facilitates smallholder production. Yet, as argued in this book, it is this environment that helps smallholders informally commercialize production. To return to an idea first presented in the introductory chapter, land reform brought two unintended developments that take center stage in this book. On the one hand, there was an increase in subsistence, and on the other hand, there was a pattern of informal commercialization "from below" among smallholders, building on the production achieved in subsistence households and also on the smallholders' immediate environment, in particular on the extent to which local fresh product markets could develop. While this immediate environment and the informal commercialization associated with it are usually condemned in World Bank publications and governmental strategy papers (despite the important role it played in China), more attention to it could help better address subsistence.

Country Selection

Researching the link between subsistence and the smallholder immediate environment in post-communist countries requires selecting China-like and Russia-like cases, the two antipodes of land reform versions enacted. To summarize the differences between these countries presented in the previous chapters, table 4.1 lists several reforming countries of the once communist "East." Romania and Ukraine, the two countries selected for this study's ethnographic component, belong to different groups, experimenting with different land reform models, as discussed in the previous chapter. In Romania, individualizing or propertizing land reform merged with a fast dismantlement of collective farms. In Ukraine, a shares-based approach to land reform, largely regarded as nominal only, combined with an initial retention of collective farms. In contrast to China, both

TABLE 4.1. Land reform and state approach to procurement in Eurasia.

	State procurement	*State retreat*	
Nominal or no land reform	Belarus	Russia, Ukraine	
Collective farms dismantled/ privatized	Dismantled		*Privatized*
Land reform	China	Albania, Romania	Czechia, Hungary

Note: This table includes a selection of the countries listed in table 3.1.

countries massively reduced the state's role in procurement and both experienced only limited commercialization among smallholders.

Selecting Romania and Ukraine allows going beyond explanations of subsistence and lack of commercialization as effects of limited land reform or of the survival of "unreformed" former collective farms. This case selection and the associated differences between countries suggest the following explanations. A first possibility is that the commercializing effects of China's land reforms kick in only at a certain level of land reform, unreached even by the China-like countries in the Balkans (Albania and Romania) or the Transcaucasus. But this is not the case, since China did not go as far as most of these countries, avoiding land markets and keeping a high rate of state involvement in allocating and re-allocating land plots.

A second possibility is that it was the state retreat from procurement that pushed the smallest agricultural producers into subsistence, not the slow dismantlement of collective farms in post-Soviet countries such as Russia and Ukraine. This would also explain why countries that leave the Russia-like category by turning farm shares into land property titles (for instance, Moldova, Kyrgyzstan, and Tajikistan) never experienced the kind of productivity increases without labor force losses experienced by China. Instead, they ended up in the same category as Albania, Romania, and the Transcaucasus countries (see chapter 3).

The third possibility, running contrary to the first one, is that the *higher* levels of land reform enacted by China-like countries in the Balkans and Transcaucasia explain the poor results of these country groups relative to China. Land markets do not drive production up if there are hardly any commercial channels for that production. Instead, the outcomes might still be subsistence, as in Russia-like countries. The fieldwork enacted partly confirms this third possibility, but it also shows that land reform and associated subsistence contributed to the slow emergence of a vast informal economy that does in part play a beneficial role in supporting smallholders to commercialize production (chapters 5 and 6).

This research was conducted in areas of two post-communist countries with exceptionally high numbers of smallholders, Suceava County in Romania and Chernivets'ka Oblast' (Chernivtsi province or region) in Ukraine, yet with different institutional approaches in shaping the environment of smallholders. The two countries differ not only in terms of type of communist rule (and length, although parts of Suceava and Chernivets'ka shared a common past as the Austrian Bukowina and later Romanian Bucovina until World War II), but also in how post-communist governments conducted land reform. Authorities did not restitute collective farmland to former owners in Ukraine and instead divided it among former farm workers using a shares system. In contrast, Romanian governments pursued a policy of returning to pre-1947 owners up to ten hectares of their former properties and dividing the rest between collective farm workers. Ukraine experienced a gradual dissolution of collective property, while Romania saw an abrupt dismantlement of its collective farms (Swinnen 1999). The reason for selecting such differing countries to research was to construct a causal argument about smallholder resilience that goes beyond land reform and can cover an empirical reality wider than that of any of the two post-communist countries treated here. Nevertheless, the two countries are similar in one crucial aspect for this study: they both feature a high incidence of smallholder agriculture, as presented in table 4.2.

Land reforms in theory sought to reintroduce private property over agricultural land throughout post-communist countries. As outlined in part 1, this meant handing over property titles to the rural population formerly employed by collective farms or to pre-communist owners and their descendants. However, in post-Soviet practice, new owners received titles to land shares rather than clearly identifiable land plots and property titles. They predominantly leased their land shares back to the collective farms. They also returned the land to larger or former collective farms in other communist countries and even in Romania, where they had received property titles (Sabates-Wheeler 2002). Using inputs obtained in exchange for land from the former collective farms, owners continued production on land plots close to their households.

TABLE 4.2. Overview of agricultural indicators for Romania and Ukraine, with Italy and Germany for comparison, 2016. Source: Author's calculations based on Eurostat data at https://ec.europa.eu/eurostat/databrowser/view/ef_m_farmleg/default/table?lang=en; and Ukrstat data at http://ukrstat.gov.ua/operativ/operativ2017/sg/osg/osg_u/osg_0117_u.html.

	Romania (population: 20 million)	Ukraine (population: 44 million)	Italy (population: 59 million)	Germany (population: 83 million)
Total farms number (millions)	3.4 (highest in the EU)	approx. 4.8*	1.1	0.276
Average land plot size (hectares)	3.6	1.53**	11	61
Output (billion euros)	12	8.9 (output of rural households; 22 = total output)	51 (second to France in the EU)	49

* The number of total farms for Ukraine is an approximation by Ukrstat, which gives different values for the rural households' component, ranging from 4.1 to 4.8 million rural households in 2016.
** Average land plot size (Ukraine) refers only to households; does not include entrepreneurial farmers and corporate farms.

Furthermore, agricultural land sales were soon prohibited through moratoria, with a moratorium in place in Ukraine until 2021. With the eventual demise of the collective farm or its transformation into corporate farms, corporate actors and farmers became the new lessees. World Bank experts depict the local population as victims of such lease arrangements—the land-shares system and the moratorium—and corporate actors as the clear and undeserving winners (Deininger and Nizalov 2016; for an overview of how corporate actors emerged in Ukraine, see Sarna 2014). They argued that due to the polarization between corporate actors with access to vast swaths of land and a local population mostly working on household plots, the latter could hardly engage in anything but subsistence farming. The key to moving this population out of subsistence farming was the abolition of the land-shares system and replacing it with effective property rights (Deininger and Nizalov 2016).

However, the rural population's situation contradicts claims that small-holders are worse off when coexisting with former collective farms. Despite the restrictions concerning property rights, rural households in Ukraine produced most of the food throughout post-communism's first three decades (Nagayets 2005, 336; Visser et al. 2015). In the case of Ukraine, there are reports of "persistence" and also "intensifying" production among rural households (Kuns 2017; Varga 2016). In 2017 the four million rural households in Ukraine still produced some 43 percent of the agricultural output, down from 61 percent in 2000, and 54 percent of animal production; by 2020, rural households accounted for some 35 percent of total production and 47 percent of total animal production (Ukrstat 2021). The decrease from 2000 was due to the strengthening role played by corporate farms; rural households were producing in 2013–2017 between 25 percent (2013) and 19 percent (2017) more than in 2000, and between 8 percent (2013) and 4 percent (2017) more than in 2005 (Ukrstat 2018, 40).[3]

Given their subsistence and the allegedly negative implications of leasing arrangements, rural and peri-urban households should not have been in a situation to increase production. Yet they achieved yearly production increases even in areas with strong corporate presence—that is, in areas where the land-shares system should have forced them into subsistence. Figure 4.3 exemplifies these claims with data from the Ukrainian statistics office, Ukrstat. It shows the yearly production gains made by rural households in Ukraine and in selected regions: the fieldwork region (Chernivets'ka), two regions with a strong corporate presence in Central and Eastern Ukraine (Vinnyts'ka and Kharkivs'ka), and the region with the most robust smallholder presence, mountainous Zakarpats'ka. All these regions saw production increases until the deterioration brought by the war in the country's east in 2014 and the extreme drought in 2014–15 and 2019–20.

Similar expectations about the demise of "subsistence agriculture" also surrounded Romania's smallholders. One study stated (Vorley 2007, 107–8): "Plainly, the vast majority of micro-holdings of land are not commercially viable. . . . A lack of equipment and money for investment means that much of the agricultural potential of the country lies idle. Romania is one of the few places in the world where the poorest farmers have switched back to using horses for tillage and transport"(see also Mikulcak et al. 2015). Authorities regarded the vast majority of Romanian rural

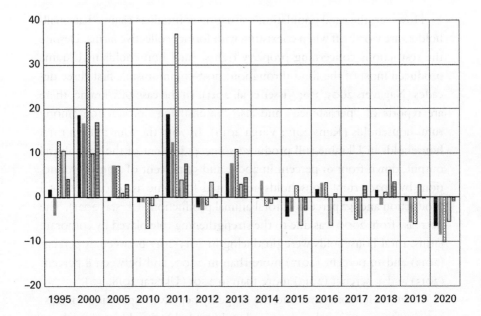

FIGURE 4.3. Rural household production fluctuation from the previous year in Ukraine and Ukrainian regions, 1995–2020. Source: State Statistics Service of Ukraine, https://ukrstat.gov.ua/druk/publicat/kat_u/publ7_u.htm (last accessed: 23.11.2021)

households as involved in subsistence agriculture, devoting most of their produce to their own consumption needs. Almost two decades after the start of land reform, the government relied on its 2010 agricultural census to claim that 3.8 million micro-holdings practiced subsistence farming, and only 1.2 million units qualified as registered "farms" even though these registered farms might have also practiced subsistence farming (Bailey and Suta 2014). A look at production indicators shows, however, a different picture, lending support to the thesis that the Romanian government's depiction of such a large share of households as subsistence agriculture had more to do with intentions to restrict access to financial assistance than with the reality on the ground (Roger 2014). If the subsistence thesis had been true, one would have expected lower or constant production figures for micro-holdings, but in practice, numbers stagnated only for cattle, while for sheep and vegetables (areas of smallholder production) they had fluctuated strongly since the 1990s (see figure 4.4).

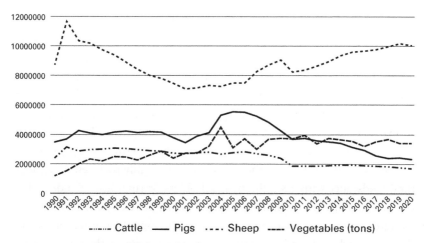

FIGURE 4.4. Production in Romanian smallholder farms: livestock (*units*) and vegetables (*tons*). Source: Data generated from the Romanian National Institute for Statistics website, http://statistici.insse.ro:8077/tempo-online/#/pages/tables/insse-table, last accessed November 18, 2021.

Given the difficulties usually associated with small-scale farming in Ukraine and Romania, the aforementioned production increases are puzzling. With hardly any credit lines for officially registered farmers (not to mention unregistered smallholders or rural households) and the limited availability of machinery, farming in Ukraine and Romania and post-communist countries more generally "entailed a level of risk that rural people were unwilling to accept" (Allina-Pisano 2008, 90, commenting on the situation in Russia and Ukraine). The following research, closing in on these two countries to conduct fieldwork in a trans-border region with a high incidence of smallholders, has helped answer how smallholders could at times increase and commercialize production.

Bukovina

The rationale for selecting the Bukovina region is that it suits a design using most different cases, similar outcomes. Despite the rapid dissolution of collective farms in Romania (where Bukovina's southern half is located) and their slow dismantlement in Ukraine (of which Bukovina's northern half is a part), the Bukovina region features some of the highest numbers of rural producers in each country. Thus despite the different approaches to land reform in the 1990s, agrifood chains on both sides of the border resemble the "traditional system," in which numerous producers supply a network of periodic and permanent markets in villages and cities. Currently it is predominantly smallholders (or rural households, as they are referred to in Ukraine) that own land on both sides of the border: in the Chernivets′ka Oblast′, the northern, Ukrainian half, smallholders own close to 70 percent of land, with an even higher share (some 90 percent) in Romania's Suceava County, roughly corresponding to Bukovina's south. In this sense, the two administrative units (the Chernivets′ka Oblast′ and Suceava County) represent the two countries' highly fragmented agricultural landscape, with 3.8 million smallholders or rural households in Romania and some 4.7 million in Ukraine at the start of fieldwork in 2013. Despite the distance from the two countries' capitals, the region is anything but secluded: an important European road passes through it (E85), representing the most important land route connecting Turkey and the Eastern Balkans with Ukraine, Belarus, Russia, and the Baltic countries. On the Ukrainian side of the border, the city of Chernivtsi is home to the thirty-three-hectare Kalynivskyi Bazaar. The region presents fairly large mountainous areas, with foothills and mountains being 34 percent of Chernivets′ka Oblast′ and 53 percent of Suceava. Main crops in which smallholders and farmers specialize are potatoes (up to 25 percent of cultivated areas in the Chernivets′ka Oblast′), cabbage, fruit (predominantly apples) and corn. Cereal grains such as wheat are produced mainly by the largest farmers and corporate entities (Holovne upravlinnya statystyky u Chernivets′kiy oblasti 2015).

Collectivization started in the northern (Soviet) part of Bukovina in the 1940s and entered its final stage between 1948 and 1953. Romanian communist authorities started collectivization in Suceava and elsewhere in Romania in 1949. The process was protracted and interrupted for several years in the 1950s, making Romania the last communist country to achieve "full" collectivization (Dobrincu 2009). Collectivization in Chernivets′ka occurred most quickly in Western Ukraine, reaching by 1949 some 90 percent of arable lands in only one year (Vitenko 2013), not surprising given that Chernivets′ka is the smallest of the western Ukrainian regions. The final stage of collectivization in western Ukraine (1948–1952) brought massive deportations of kulak, or relatively better-off households (Vitenko 2013). In contrast, collectivization in the Suceava area was protracted and met with resistance, reaching "only" 100 percent in the early 1950s, compared to 500 percent increases in other eastern Romanian regions (Iancu

2001). Revolts against authorities took place as late as 1962, when communist authorities announced the "success" of collectivization, meaning collectivization rates of 90 percent and above of arable land, including in Suceava County (Dobrincu 2009, 295).

In the Romanian fieldwork areas, collective farms were dismantled "instantaneously" in 1991–1992 (Sabates-Wheeler 2002; Hatos 2006). In the Ukrainian fieldwork sites de-collectivization was more protracted (in Novoselytsia, for instance, the collective farm closed only in 2007), and collective farms often continued to exist as private entities. The western Ukrainian agro-holdings Svarog and Mriya[4] have expanded throughout the region by leasing land from the rural population. Close to Brusnytsia, one of my fieldwork sites, Svarog established a strong presence by buying the former collective farm, including a large animal-rearing unit, and working the fields in the nine villages of the area. In both countries, large retail chains (supermarkets) have established a strong presence. The concentration ratio in the retail grocery market of Ukraine was 32 percent by 2012 (Ernst and Young 2014, 4); the same indicator in Romania was 30 percent in 2014 (European Commission 2014, 55). This indicator's values were lower than in most Western European countries but not that different from Greece (30 percent) or Italy or Poland (both with 40 percent). Between the 2000s and early 2010s, the increase in the concentration ratio in Romania was the highest in Europe, from close to zero in 2002 to 30 percent in 2012 (European Commission 2014, 56). The World Bank and the European Bank for Reconstruction and Development sponsored the expansion into Romania of one of the world's largest supermarket chains, Germany's Schwarz Group, which owns Lidl and Kaufland, with almost one billion euros in the 2010s. Both banks claimed that in this way, they would bring cheap products to "poor consumers"; Lidl opened "more than 185 stores" in Romania between 2011 and 2015, according to *The Guardian* (Provost and Kennard 2015).

Both Suceava and Chernivets'ka rank among the top administrative units in terms of fragmentation and smallholder numbers within their countries. The Romanian presidential rural development strategy singles out Suceava as being a problematic "pocket" of "subsistence farming" (Presidential Commission for Agricultural Development Policies 2013). The Ministry of Agriculture deals with some 50,000 individual farms in Suceava (ministry employee, Suceava, 2015), meaning that the county has one of Romania's most fragmented ownership patterns.[5] But despite its

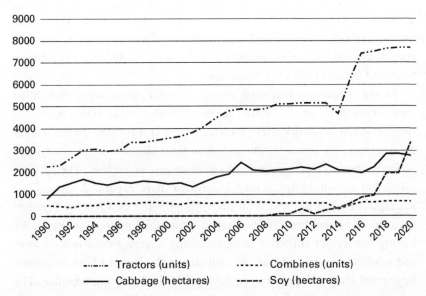

FIGURE 4.5. Selected crops (*hectares*) and machinery ownership (*units*) in Suceava, Romania. Sources: Author's calculations, using data from Romania's National Institute for Statistics website, statistici.insse.ro:8077/tempo-online/.

fragmented agriculture, the area achieved important increases in production and machinery (see figure 4.5). The development is surprising given that one would have hardly expected a region with such fragmented agriculture to raise funds for machinery investments and expand agricultural production, with private ownership of tractors going from 78 in 1990 to close to 8,000 in 2020. Numbers were far less dramatic for more expensive self-propelled combines, arguably a type of machinery less amenable to vegetables and other crops that smallholders specialize in.

Ukrainian statistical data allow disaggregation in order to see whether smallholder farms have grown or have further decreased in size given their alleged lack of commercial viability. As figure 4.6 shows, smallholders in the Chernivets'ka Oblast' (called "households" in national statistics) have managed to increase the land under exploitation over the past three decades. This seems to have happened not because of increases in total arable land but at the expense of those entities that official statistics refer to as commercial farms. Most likely, however, official surveys hide the extent to which households practice informal lease arrangements with entrepreneurial farmers and corporate farms and do not capture the expansion of the Mriya and Svarog agro-holdings throughout the region in the 2010s.

Nevertheless, output data further confirms the relevance of smallholders for food production. In the Chernivets'ka Oblast', the ratio between production levels in 2015 as compared to 1990 was 165 percent, and 134.2 percent as compared to 2000.[6] The rural households' share in total production went from roughly 50 percent in 1990 (when collective farms still existed) to 72.7 percent twenty-seven years later (Ukrstat 2021, 53).

Regions such as Chernivets'ka in Ukraine and Suceava in Romania, showing high numbers of smallholder density, represent a puzzle. The expectation was that the fall of communism and the adverse environment of the transition years would decimate the numbers of smallholders, leading to the "consolidation" of the sector—that is, to a reduction of smallholders. This should have been the case also because smallholders in Romania and Ukraine were largely and systematically excluded from bank credit to develop their activities. But countrywide, smallholder numbers peaked around 2010 and started to decrease only in the 2010s, markedly yet not fast enough for national governments. In my fieldwork areas, there were only slight decreases in farm numbers. Cultivation areas stagnated in Romania,

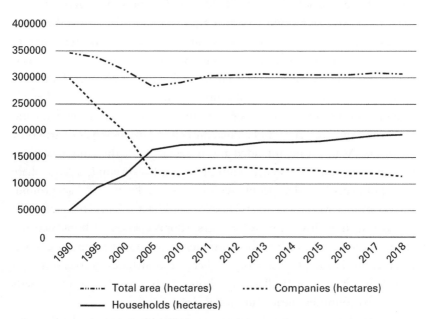

FIGURE 4.6. Total arable land and its use in the Chernivetska area (*hectares*). Source: Author's calculations, using data supplied by the Chernivtsi branch of the State Statistics Office of Ukraine, available at cv.ukrstat.gov.ua.

while cultivation areas held by smallholders increased in Ukraine. These developments raise the question of explaining the resilience of smallholder agriculture.

Data Collection

Interview data was collected through analytical induction, meaning that data was being collected to refine rather than test theoretical propositions (Curtis and Curtis 2011, 68). In particular, it was important to develop further the premise that land reform is not enough to explain smallholder resilience. Thus, selection relied on theoretical sampling and choosing a very wide variety of interview partners. These differed in size and type of farming operations (landless day laborers, smallholders, entrepreneurial farmers, corporate farm representatives, and intermediaries such as wholesalers, processors, retailers), locality, and length of entrepreneurial activity, as well as whether interviewees had been able to extend the areas under exploitation since taking up farming. Topics covered in the interviews included production inputs (physical capital, land, labor) and outputs, production and processing, market and market access. Questions also focused on whether and from where smallholders and farmers more generally had prior knowledge of farming. Table 4.3 provides an overview of the interviews carried out in Romania and Ukraine and used for chapters 5 and 6. The background of producers and traders was also important, because usually entrepreneurial farmers have emerged from what Natalia Mamonova (2015) refers to as "kolkhoz intelligentsia"—that is, people with higher education and managerial positions in former collective farms: general and processing shop directors and animal husbandry, machinery, or agronomy engineers. As this study intended also to research whether and how farmers can overcome subsistence without such a background, a large share of respondents included people without an "intelligentsia" background, such as former workers (industrial or former kolkhoz workers in sales and logistics such as drivers, merchandisers, shopkeepers, and bookkeepers), artisans, and others, such as former traders who had taken up agricultural production. Finally, the category "others" also includes various other respondents, from poor landless day laborers to businesspeople and experts in the two countries' agriculture ministries.

I carried out a total of seventy-five semi-structured, in-depth interviews (see the table in the appendix for a full list of respondents and their characteristics in terms of farm size and locality). I also followed

TABLE 4.3. Overview of interview respondents in Romania and Ukraine.

| | | Farm outlook | | Background | | | | |
	Activity	Grow	Stable/ decrease	Kolkhoz intelligentsia	Artisan/ rural worker	Industrial worker	Worker in sales/ logistics	Other
RO	Producers (20)	10	10	6	8	4	2	-
	Traders (4)	-	-	-	-	-	3	1
	Others (6)	-	-	-	1	1	-	4
UA	Producers (33)	12	21	10	10	5	3	5
	Traders (5)	-	-	2	-	1	1	-
	Others (7)	-	-	1	2	3	-	1

and interviewed people in four family businesses in each country repeatedly, over several years (2013–2019), observing how these family businesses produced and interacted with markets. The interviews with experts were used to identify and interview the largest farmers in each region; expert interviews also indicated which localities showed the highest numbers of smallholders and the biggest increases in output. A slowly developing contact base allowed me to approach and interview smallholders, who then intermediated contacts with the farmers they leased their land to. These in turn, further intermediated contacts with retailers, wholesalers, and day laborers. Interviews were carried out in Romanian and Russian or Ukrainian and recorded whenever possible; field notes were taken on the occasions that interviewees declined permission to record them. Further data came from direct observation of periodic markets and archival research. The research took place over yearly fieldwork rounds from summer 2013 to summer 2019.

I selected interview partners in five fieldwork areas; in order to trace differences in market channels, the areas featured both rural communities and peri-urban communities located on the outskirts of cities. In Romania, these areas were a mountainous rural area between Vatra Dornei and Moldovița, some 150 kilometers west of the regional center of Suceava (Dorna area), and a hilly, peri-urban area near Suceava (Ițcani area). In Ukrainian Bukovina, I interviewed people in an area to the west of Chernivtsi, roughly coinciding with the area of what had been one of the largest collective farms in the area, in Brusnytsia (referred to as the Brusnytsia area); in a peri-urban area near Chernivtsi, part of the Hlyboka raion (referred to as the Hlyboka area); and in a rural area to the east of Chernivtsi, in the Novoselytsia raion (Novoselytsia area). The rationale behind selecting these areas was to have varying numbers of commercial farmers (lowest in Hlyboka—only two, and highest in Brusnytsia, twenty) and different agrifood chains (meat, milk, and vegetables in the Romanian fieldwork areas and milk, potatoes, and soy in the Ukrainian areas).

Terminology: Rural and Peri-urban
Smallholders, Farmers, and Markets

The cutoff point for identifying a farm as a smallholder farm with the associated subsistence implication is a landholding size below two hectares. This is the standard criterion in most World Bank publications as well as government strategy papers. However, it would be more appropriate to refer to smallholders not only by reference to land-plot size but as a type of farming primarily using family labor and the household as the central unit of production. Farms owning more than two hectares also often operate around a central household, but the family's relevance as the central production unit decreases as landholding increases. Thus, the difference between smallholders and larger units—especially entrepreneurial farms—becomes less categorical. In this way, by approaching smallholders as households or smallholder households, it was easier to research when and how such farms grow, instead of excluding larger smallholders from the start. A further relevant continuum concerns the location of households; it makes a difference for commercialization whether smallholder households are located in rural or peri-urban areas. Peri-urban areas are in city outskirts or villages near cities, usually still covered by the city's public or private transportation network. Peri-urban areas offer producers the advantage of being closer to end consumers, but land is scarcer since urban dwellers often move into villages where they can buy or build houses. Nevertheless, more jobs are available to peri-urban dwellers, allowing them to more easily diversify their incomes and retreat into subsistence farming instead of being forced to sell on markets (chapter 5). Furthermore, the availability of "fallback resources," such as cheap housing and the household land plot allowing self-provisioning, facilitates the kind of jobs that peri-urban dwellers find in cities, offering them minimum wages but paying social contributions, a central concern for many respondents.

In the fieldwork areas as well as in the wider post-communist region, three types of smallholder households can be distinguished. First are the ultra-poor "subsistence" households that the World Bank and national governments presume to populate the post-reform landscape and allegedly survive by "subsisting" on agriculture (self-consuming production). As argued in chapter 3, such households are actually rare in post-communist countries. Even in an extreme case of a predominantly rural and agricultural-based post-Soviet country as Moldova, such subsistence households did not exceed 20 percent of all households in the 1990s, and they have decreased ever since. More prevalent in my fieldwork areas were assetless households with little to sell but their labor. These are the rural and peri-urban ultra-poor who were excluded from propertizing land reform and who own only their household plots. If too old to even sell their labor, they sell the little produce they can grow on household plots. For them, it is not subsistence that is the last-resort survival option, but commercialization.

A second category is the smallholder households that rarely sell what they produce and instead consume production themselves, without, however, relying on their production as their only or main source of livelihood. These are the households that predominate in post-reform landscapes, and it is usually for them and for those in the previous category that World Bank and national strategy documents use the term *subsistence*. But, as discussed in chapter 3, *subsistence* is actually a misnomer as it implies "subsisting," or barely surviving on agriculture. These households do have sources of monetized income, from migration remittances and wage labor more generally to social welfare transfers; they have received land but lease it out, receiving in exchange fodder for the animals they raise. They use these together with agricultural products on their household plots for self-consumption and occasional sales of meat and dairy products. *Self-provisioning* would be a more accurate term for denoting the actual use of food production in these households, but the term has not entered the terminology of World Bank publications. I reserve the term *mixed-income households* for this category, to draw attention to agriculture being only one source of livelihood. However, it is consequential for the immediate environment of these smallholders: it offers other, commercializing smallholders and larger farmers access to land and a market for products such as fodder. The mixed-income households represent an important area of continuity with communist and pre-communist eras, combining several sources of income rather than specializing in farming (Hann 1993, 303).

A third category is the smallholder households regularly commercializing production. These households combine monetized incomes from the sale of agricultural products with off-farm income sources, such as wage labor, remittances from migration, and welfare transfers such as pensions. As a rule, the household counts on the income from the sale of agricultural production, and such sales together with other income sources support the household's livelihood needs and can be invested in further developing production. Such commercializing smallholders lease land from other members of their community, usually the mixed-households introduced before. Typically, there is a gendered division of tasks, with the male "head" of the household in charge of land husbandry directly or with the help of seasonal workers, while the female household member and other, especially elderly household members take care of the household area and in particular animal husbandry and production on land plots in household vicinity, cooking for the seasonal day laborers, and so on. In these households, self-provisioning is not only consumption oriented, feeding household members, but also production oriented: household members seek to take on production and marketing steps so as to lower the market price of their products (van der Ploeg 2008; see next chapter).

All three categories of smallholders have in common that in much of the post-communist region they are unregistered as farmers or agricultural producers. To the extent they own land, they are usually found in statistical categories as rural or peasant "households" in Ukraine and Romania or as "individual" landowners in Romania, although the latter category also covers owners with far larger land plots. Important to note, national statistics can hardly detect the actual level of commercialization among such households, except for those based on surveys, as presented in chapter 3, and that document far higher levels of commercialization (production sold both formally and informally) than usually assumed when smallholder agriculture is regarded as basically synonymous with subsistence as self-consumption.

The next category is entrepreneurial farmers; like the smallholders, they lead most activities through and from the family household. They are, however, registered as legal entities and usually own or lease more, sometimes far more, than two hectares. Their main source of income is agriculture, commercializing most production, with only occasional income from other sources. Here too there is a gendered division of tasks. The male "head" of the household takes over the legal aspects of running the farm, sales, and land husbandry (employing seasonal or permanent laborers), while the female household member and others take care of the household, the nearby land plots, and animals. While many of the entrepreneurial farmers studied during fieldwork originated among the technical personnel of the collective farm, others had started as smallholders. The task of fieldwork research for this study was then to find out how these smallholders had turned from smallholder agriculture to entrepreneurial farming. I discuss in chapter 5 how much of the answer to this question builds on peasant farming, characterizing the farming operations of both commercializing smallholders and those entrepreneurial farmers that avoid official credit and investment schemes as well as the registration of their entire range of operations and land holdings.

The last category is the corporate farms or enterprises, employing a permanent as well as a seasonal workforce; they are run by managers and corporate structures, not by households. In the fieldwork areas in post-communist Romania, the corporate presence was weak in agricultural production and strong in the processing sector, buying up the production of smallholders and entrepreneurial farmers but without competing with them if the latter stayed out of processing. To the extent they survived the collapse of the Soviet Union, corporate farms in Ukraine throughout the 1990s and the 2000s were predominantly the direct successors of the collective farms established under communism. They continued many of the local arrangements practiced by collective farms, covering the costs of educational, cultural, and recreational institutions in local communities and supporting production through informal arrangements with the rural households. Repeated mergers throughout the 2000s turned many former collective farms into larger corporate units, so-called *agro-holdings* (Plank 2013). Predominantly export-oriented, these corporate actors count among the largest globally by landholding size and participate in or have their own vertically coordinated supply chains, controlling them from production to export or retail. As in Russia, in Ukraine too there is a declining interest in maintaining community-level institutions or arrangements with rural households (Kurakin, Nikulin, and Visser 2019).

Table 4.4 summarizes these distinctions between the types of agricultural producers encountered during fieldwork. It suggests that commercialization actually characterizes smallholders as well as entrepreneurial

TABLE 4.4. Agricultural producers in Bucovina fieldwork areas.

	Commercialization (Income coming from agriculture)		
	Low		High
	Family farm as basic production unit		
	Unregistered producers		Registered
Landholding size	Only household plots	Lease out land	Lease land
Below half a hectare	Ultra-poor households		
Around 2 hectares: smallholders		Mixed-income households	Commercializing households
Below 10,000 hectares			Entrepreneurial farmers
10,000 hectares and more			Corporate farms

farmers, but the income it brings varies with landholding type. It is a last-resort act of despair for the ultra-poor families that own only their household plots, but for the smallholders included in the land reform program, it is an important—and regular—source of livelihood.

"Periodic markets" and the system of markets that has resurfaced after the fall of communism deserve a special mention, because for many smallholders and entrepreneurial farmers, this system of local markets provides the main channel for commercializing production. It is also a crucial component of the smallholders' immediate environment. While markets existed also under communism, they were primarily permanent markets restricted to urban areas, and only producers from close, peri-urban areas could sell in them. There was no specialization of roles between producers and traders and therefore, producers from more remote areas hardly had any possibility of accessing these markets. It needs to be remembered that it was illegal to sell to intermediaries and difficult to transport and sell produce during one's spare time, as producers would as a rule still work for the collective farm and could engage in household production on subsidiary plots only when off work (Feldbrugge 1984; Kideckel 1982; Varga 2017).

After communism, however, various types of markets resurfaced, re-creating what William Skinner (1985) called in the Chinese context a "hierarchy of markets": periodic markets in villages form the base of the hierarchy, with permanent wholesale and retail markets in urban areas at the top. Wholesale markets are the central element, with smallholders and entrepreneurial farmers either directly present in such markets or selling to traders that supply wholesale markets. Other traders supply from these markets urban retail and rural periodic markets; the fact that these latter markets are periodic facilitates a large participation of traders that can attend each day a different market. Sale in such markets, whether permanent wholesale or periodic, involves informal aspects in all areas in which I conducted fieldwork. While traders usually carry documentation detailing the quantities they transport and present it during controls, the produce is sold without any accompanying receipts or documents. Authorities in both Romania and Ukraine have made different efforts to regulate such markets, as detailed in chapter 6.

To summarize, this study's ethnographic component relied on fieldwork conducted in regions of two post-communist countries showing exceptionally high numbers of smallholders, yet nevertheless showing different institutional approaches shaping the environment of smallholders, in particular collectivization, which was generally far more protracted in Romania than in the Soviet Union, and de-collectivization, which was far more rapid in Romania than in Ukraine. By selecting such contrasting environments, this study constructs a most-different-cases research design. The countries differ in institutional environments but both feature the same outcome of a highly fragmented ownership structure and high incidence of smallholder farming. This design allows questioning accounts about the high numbers of alleged subsistence farmers, tracing subsistence back to insufficient or failed land reform. Irrespective of how land reform was carried out, land titling reforms produced highly fragmented ownership and very high numbers of smallholders. Yet, as argued in the next chapter, it also facilitated ways out of poverty.

CHAPTER 5

Resilience

Survival and Growth of Smallholder Agriculture

IT IS OFTEN ARGUED THAT smallholders must, in order to survive and grow, approximate the logic of entrepreneurial farming, taking up credit, adding land, and investing, realizing economies of scale through cooperatives and joining supply chains dominated by large agribusiness (Ashley and Maxwell 2001, 403; McCullough, Pingali, and Stamoulis 2010, 57; World Bank 2007). Ideally, this is to be achieved by increases in farm size, leading to higher incomes and investment in better machinery to respond more timely and more efficiently to soil and market opportunities (World Bank 2007). But such increases in farm size and investment are difficult as smallholders typically lack access to credit. Instead they "make investments through family labor," risking "impoverishment spirals" if family members cannot work anymore (Bosc et al. 2013, 24). This chapter shows how smallholders evade impoverishment: in much of post-communist Europe and Central Asia, as well as China and Vietnam, few smallholders had access to credit markets; nevertheless, agriculture operated more as a safety net (in post-communist Eurasia) and cure to poverty (in East Asia) than as a mechanism of impoverishment. As for Ukraine and Romania, while the numbers of smallholders are decreasing (see chapter 6), the areas that they cultivate are increasing, suggesting that while some smallholders indeed have to leave agriculture because of the impoverishment spiral, others are capable of surviving and growing.

Another perspective has argued that smallholders evade impoverishment not by realizing economies of scale by acquiring more land and better machines (see World Bank, 2007), but by ensuring "self-provisioning" and "autonomy" (van der Ploeg 2010), controlling upstream and downstream links in value chains. Self-provisioning—less in the sense of self-consumption and more in the sense of internalizing production steps—works to prevent the "impoverishment spiral" from negatively affecting livelihoods because increasing control over value chain links also means an increase in cash income and in the availability of cash for investments, as well as for family-related expenditures. In other words, smallholders have a strong interest to resist the loss of control over or monetization of inputs. Thus, understanding smallholder survival and growth needs reconceptualizing the logic of smallholder actions as self-provisioning, seen by Jan Douwe van der Ploeg as "reducing dependence on external resources," and reducing "monetary costs while overall levels of production are maintained or even slightly improved" (2010, 6; see also Dorondel 2016, 198). The tendency among farmers is not one of growth toward and through economies of scale but through self-provisioning understood as internalizing and demonetizing costs, growing not at the expense of other producers but by controlling upstream and downstream links in the value chain and setting up niches protecting the price of their products from competition.

Autonomy does not succeed in isolation and autarchy; it is possible even in a fragmented smallholder agriculture because smallholders interact with an immediate environment consisting of small traders, mom-and-pop retailers, and secondhand machinery suppliers, as well as larger entrepreneurial farmers or even corporate farms. This chapter discusses how this environment emerged after communism to facilitate the internalizing logic and the savings associated with it. The smallholders' immediate environment translates into a viable alternative to interacting with an environment composed of corporate suppliers, wholesalers, and retail chains. The next section presents this argument in detail, while the third section illustrates the argument with the empirical material introduced in chapter 4, the fieldwork carried out in the two neighboring post-communist administrative units, Suceava County in Romania and Chernivets'ka Oblast' in Ukraine.

The Smallholders' Immediate Environment: Post-communist Re-emergence

Smallholders usually specialize in crops that are relatively safe from large agribusiness competition (Mamonova 2015; Kuns 2017; Varga 2017). But self-provisioning facilitates smallholder resilience not only because it limits competition with agribusinesses but also because it embeds smallholders in environments populated by numerous other actors who supply them with signals about the profitability of certain crops and lands, as well as with cash incomes. Key to this insight is the argument that markets function as "tangible cliques of producers watching each other" (White 1981, 518), turning our attention to the central role of interactions between producers and flows of information between them for the emergence of markets and survival of economic actors. Furthermore, economic actors and other actors do not just exchange information over volumes traded. They do not just "watch" each other, but they also attempt to counter and overcome the unequal "distribution of strengths" between them through specialization (Bourdieu 2005, 195–96, 203). Field theory achieves a synthesis of these arguments. It posits vertical integration (together with diversification) as the logic that allows economic units to alter unequal market structures without being exposed to direct competition and destructive price wars (Fligstein and Mara-Drita 1996, 659). Whereas field theory broadly deals with organizations (firms), this study applies its insights to smallholders and argues that economic units survive and even grow by establishing control over the nearest links in value chains. However, rather than through mergers or acquisitions, they grow by emulating the activities of the closest suppliers and customers. By gaining control over valuable inputs and outputs, smallholders can use monetized incomes for making investments, allowing volumes to grow while minimizing monetary costs.

Following field theory and building on the idea that smallholders emulate suppliers and customers in order to internalize certain production and marketing steps, markets can be approached as "reproducible role structure[s]" (Fligstein 2001, 94). Markets exist and stabilize to the extent that there is a diversification of actors that translates into a "status hierarchy" (Fligstein 2001, 30; White 2002, 152). Particularly in high uncertainty contexts, such as the post-communist context, the diversification of market roles created opportunities for "low-status entrants," as large firms tended to engage only with peers (Podolny 1993; Soulsby and Clark 2007, 1426). The implications for this study is to check which other actors matter and how they matter for the actions of smallholders and to uncover a variety of actors populating the smallholders' environment. Smallholders might in fact depend for their survival on the presence of these other actors and on their capacity to interact with these other actors, including by emulating the larger and more successful farmers. Smallholders—as this study found them—are embedded in environments referred to by the Food and Agriculture Organization (FAO) as "traditional markets," differing from the "modern procurement systems" of "structured markets" in which the various traditional traders have been replaced by retail chains and their logistics. Research published by the FAO sees such traditional markets as predominantly detrimental to small farms, as "traders might depress prices through collusion" and might "charge irregular fees"; worst of all, traditional markets are informal, "with [smallholders] bearing many of the costs associated with poor market performance" (McCullough, Pingali, and Stamoulis 2010, 61; Bosc et al. 2013).

But "traditional markets" can also be approached as value chains (Lee, Gereffi, and Beauvais 2012) in which the survival and growth of small farms depend on the smallholders' coexistence with complex scenes of suppliers and customers. Traders are the most important element in this perspective, as they are the first to approach small farms and buy production at the farm-gate, thus constituting for smallholders an initial source of cash income. It is this income that can be saved, to the extent that producers hold additional incomes (from secondary jobs or migration remittances), and later on invested. In the empirical cases studied, this investment took two directions. One option for smallholders was to move downstream and take up trading themselves. They used the investment to buy the necessary transportation means, such as secondhand four-ton trucks, usually of the Mercedes Sprinter or the Ford Transit variety. This meant replacing only the farm-gate traders and taking the produce to wholesale markets to sell it to small retailers. The other option was to ensure some control over inputs, and while many inputs seemed intangible to farmers, machinery inputs were especially relevant and prone to be controlled by smallholders. Briefly put, due to the abundance of tractors on secondhand markets, buying up such machines became the main alternative to renting or leasing them.

Value chain analysis helps summarize this argument. A value chain in the food sector comprises the following links: Seed design (1) > Growing (2) > Post-harvest processing (3) > Exporting (4) > Retailing (5) (Kaplinsky and Morris 2000; Varga 2015). Adapting this framework to agricultural producers as depicted throughout this chapter, the value chain comprises the following links: Energy and raw resources including water, electricity, and gas (1) > Seeds (2) > Machinery (3) > Growing produce (4) > Harvesting (5) > Post-harvest processing / Storage (6) > Exporting / Local trading (7) > Retailing (8). Producers from smallholders to entrepreneurial farmers seek to control links 2 to 7 of the value chain through family labor, with "internalizing machinery" meaning internalizing maintenance and repair. To return to the puzzle of smallholder farmers' survival and even growth in post-communist countries, this chapter argues that the possibility of expansion and growth within value chains is crucial for the continued existence of these producers.

A field theory approach further helps to explain smallholders' resilience and their demonetizing or internalizing logic by seeing "traditional markets" as markets *as such* rather than an artifact impeding the development of smallholders and bound to be dismantled by the arrival of more "modern" market actors. Such markets stabilize because there is a reproducible structure of roles that allows smallholders to gain knowledge and cash incomes. Similarly, such markets can be understood as institutions, surviving as they endow participants with cash incomes as well as with "templates for action" (Fligstein 2001, 121), guiding actors in establishing or accessing cash flows and making investments.

In the writings on the "modern procurement system," its "traditional" or "informal" counterpart is seen as usually dissociated from change, apparently constant at least until the modern procurement system challenges it directly. The traditional system has a past before the advent of the modern procurement system, and this past is conceived in similarly immutable terms, as "peasant agriculture" (Reardon et al. 2009). The rise of modern supply chains and the "supermarket revolution" that started in the 1990s is often assumed to be the most "radical change" affecting the traditional system (Reardon et al. 2003). Other studies have questioned the view that the modern system, with the supermarket as its central embodiment, necessarily dislodges traditional fresh product markets; trader networks can find many ways to compete with retail chains and depending on product and demand, even achieve inclusion in international networks (Jonge 1993), unless state intervention "peripheralizes" them (Applbaum 2005, 277).

But the "traditional" agrifood system that took shape in the 1990s could not simply be a reenactment of pre-communist times, because it emerged under different conditions. Collectivization had swept over villages, centralizing resources and know-how around collective farms, and a centralized collection and processing system guaranteed these farms the purchase of production. Trade was illegal, even though communist authorities tolerated the existence of "spot" or periodical markets or bazaars and allowed the direct sale of private plot produce (Hann 2005). Communist authorities regarded "private trading," or buying and selling produce, as "speculation," a serious criminal offense, punished by imprisonment from two to ten years (Feldbrugge 1984, 533). As most communist countries governments heavily relied on the production achieved on household plots, smallholders could only sell their household plot products to state processing units or directly as producers on state-owned markets (Kideckel 1993, 58; see also Feldbrugge 1984, 530). This system imploded in the 1990s; centralized collection and processing disappeared in the massive deindustrialization of the 1990s. Key elements of the traditional system, such as "buying in the spot market from traditional wholesalers of processed and fresh food products" (Reardon et al. 2009) had to re-emerge after 45 years of communist rule for Eastern Europe or even longer for most post-Soviet states. Such wholesalers indeed re-emerged, but they are hardly traditional, as the wider environment of which they are part operates between different "modernizing" projects. These include the dismantlement of the communist central product collection (procurement) system and of collective farms, in addition to the land reform of the 1990s, with its failure to bring about entrepreneurial farming as envisaged by reformers (Allina-Pisano 2008).

These reforms influenced the emerging agrifood system through a massive state retreat from buying agricultural production and through an abundance of relatively cheap inputs, from land to labor (Verdery 2003); from the former collective farm, there were production inputs to be used in animal and crop husbandry (Pallot and Nefedova 2007), as well as used machinery (Swain 2013). The inputs from former collective farms facilitated the involvement of smallholders in food production, giving the traditional system a strong footing in the area, and, as this chapter argues, also facilitating the rise of traders specializing in food trade. As outlined below, this differentiation of roles between producers and traders in turn makes smallholder resilience possible: it allows smallholders to market production and thus receive an income that adds to the savings realized through family labor.

The Demonetizing Logic and Its Underpinnings

The Kolkhoz Intelligentsia

Smallholder resilience requires the demonetizing logic of self-provisioning and its supportive environment: a model of production in which the household is the central production unit, using family labor on the farm and raising funds for investment through off-farm wage work; the myriads of traders allowing smallholders and farmers to reinvest profits in their farms even where they receive no bank credits; and the existence of secondhand machinery markets allowing labor-saving investments and internalizing—and thus demonetizing—specific production steps. But what proved important for interviewed smallholders that started commercializing their production was less the availability of "investment" than a signal from other producers (in ways reminiscent of White's theory of markets as cliques), from entrepreneurial farmers to large agricultural holdings, that farming in the region was profitable.

As in wider Eastern Europe (Szelényi 2002; Swain 2013), the former "kolkhoz intelligentsia" (Mamonova 2015) gave a strong impetus to the establishment and spread of private farming in the Suceava and Chernivets'ka regions. Also at the time of my fieldwork, the farms owned or run by members of the former kolkhoz intelligentsia were the largest farms on each side of the border. Among my respondents, these were entrepreneurial farmers owning or leasing thousands of hectares (for exact data, see the appendix). Under communism, they had worked as the kolkhoz director, veterinarians, and animal husbandry and farm machinery engineers. Other owners of large agribusinesses in my sample started by making money in different business areas—such as imports and shipping—and only later on invested in agriculture. Many of the interviewed small farmers had a past in the kolkhoz workforce. Some of them had served as machine operators or drivers and thus had access to specialized knowledge and machines, which allowed them to build connections and a potential base of customers. In the words of a respondent, implying that while in charge of the kolkhoz machinery it was the standard for him to charge fellow villagers for helping them out informally with knowledge or machines,

> I wasn't taking any *chubuk* [local expression for bribes or milder forms
> of informal payments, derived from the Turkish word for pipe]. But
> I was helping out those I could [by driving machines to their subsid-

iary plots and helping them with various production tasks]. You understand, I was responsible for 120 machines. (Farmer, Hlyboka area, August 2017)

Since particularly in Ukraine and to a lesser extent in Romania, the ownership of at least some land after the fall of communism depended on having had been a kolkhoz employee (or the child of one), it is not surprising that that there is continuity between present-day agriculture and the communist-era collective farm. Irrespective of whether one was a member of the kolkhoz intelligentsia or had a blue-collar job in the kolkhoz, the kolkhoz offered not only technical knowledge about running farms but, in Ukraine, also employment after the fall of communism. Future producers holding such jobs could support their initial involvement in agriculture and dedicate at least one part of their income to farm investments. Alternatively, they would wait in such jobs for signs that agriculture was becoming profitable.[1] In Romania, where collective farms disappeared early in the 1990s, some interviewees were shifting between farming and trading or between farming and seasonal work on construction yards and in agriculture in Italy, Spain, or Greece.

What is important about these members of the former kolkhoz intelligentsia is that they played a pivotal role in triggering the entry into business of smallholders. In some cases, the establishment of small farms was the effect of the positive example set by the larger entrepreneurs. In the Vyzhnytsia raion west of Chernivtsi, such positive examples came in one village from the former kolkhoz veterinarian (who became one of the largest farmers in the Chernivets'ka Oblast', leasing close to 900 hectares) and from the Mriya agro-holding (a large corporation consisting of several former collective farms). In the words of one of the farmers, Mriya "proved to us the productivity of land," attracting him out of his combination of self-provisioning agriculture, lathe operating, and carpentering and into working as an entrepreneurial farmer on an area of over seventy hectares in his village (farmer, Lukivtsi, August 2015). In the case of the kolkhoz veterinarian, his village became the one with the highest number of farmers in the region, which other farmers link to the fact that many more could follow his example. Thus farmers learned waiting not so much in alternative jobs as in their own community, where the first and most successful farmer later on became mayor and shared his knowledge with other villagers (farmer, Banyliv, August 2015).

The Mixed Household and the Post-reform Poor

A common observation throughout my fieldwork sites concerned how the work performed by household members served as the most critical resource for expanding agricultural production. Most households operated as mixed-incomes households, combining agriculture on small plots with other incomes, such as from work for larger farms, self-employment (most typically as artisans), off-farm work, and social benefits. Households often decided which income source to prioritize—abandoning, for instance, commercialization in favor of self-provisioning and waged work—depending on their needs. These ranged from paying for everyday needs (electricity, food items such as oil and sugar) and seasonal expenses (firewood) to securing social contributions long enough to receive a pension after retirement, to informal payments needed to enroll children in school, pass exams, and receive jobs paying social contributions. Major concerns were securing access to health services and social security schemes (particularly retirement) and supporting children in receiving education and jobs.

The key to this balancing act between incomes and monetized needs was whether smallholders could demonetize a sizable amount of farming costs by involving unpaid family members in production and machinery maintenance. With both spouses working, households could not only demonetize labor costs but also gain access to money available in their community that would serve as the initial funds used in production. The wedding was a central event, allowing young couples to raise money through their family and local community circles. The money was then used to buy or lease land and machinery. For many couples, the capacity of both members to work on the farm without a salary since moving in together was a key element in making sense during interviews of how their farm survived and expanded: "What got us out of trouble was that she [the respondent's wife] could start working together with me since she was eighteen—that is, ever since we got married. She didn't go to school [after her 18th birthday]; she directly started to raise sheep" (farmer, Suceava, August 2018). This reliance on family work had intensified over time for many households; as more and more of their neighbors and fellow community members left their community to work abroad, there was more land to work but also fewer people to employ in seasonal jobs: "Why should they stay here for 10 euros a day while they can earn 50 euros a day in Belgium?" (farmer, Suceava, July 2015).

A gendered division of tasks in the household meant that male household members worked on the larger land plots received from the former collective farm or leased from other households, while female members took care of household tasks, animal husbandry, and the vegetable and fruit plots near the house. Household members adapted this gendered division to facilitate new arrangements that ensured a stable income or the growth of their farming operation. Most importantly, female household members spent long periods abroad as migrant care or cleaning workers to raise funds that would be invested in agricultural production. A respondent explained how a local farmer could pay authorities the large sum of money required for leasing a well-situated land parcel after a tender for 25,000 euros in 2015: "His wife simply left, went abroad, to Germany, to pay back the state its money. They still don't have their home ready and have three children, but she had to go" (farmer, Suceava, August 2018). During these periods, men performed both farm and household tasks, often assisted by their parents, although in some households, it was the elderly that migrated abroad and sent money back home. Especially among the smallholder households involved in commercialization, men migrated less often or only seasonally to avoid interrupting farm operations. The money earned abroad paid debts, repaired housing after a fire, or expanded the household and bought land and machinery.

Relative poverty was, among my respondents, often an outcome of the "impoverishment spiral," mentioned at the beginning of this chapter, of households falling apart due to conflicts or the sickness or death of one of the spouses. It was also the outcome of having less land than others, as not everyone had a past in the former collective farm and therefore did not benefit from land distribution. Or, in the Ukrainian communities visited during fieldwork, because the distribution of higher-quality collectivized land was often informally conditioned on being able to carry out unpaid work in the former kolkhoz. This proved impossible for single-member households. Rather than retreat into subsistence, some of these respondents had to commercialize products grown on their household plots. They were *forced to sell* their produce, unable to subsist on it since they needed monetized income to cover other expenses.

Maria, for instance, a respondent living in the peri-urban area on the outskirts of Chernivtsi, owned only her household plot because being a widow without family kolkhoz past, she did not receive any land. When the textile factory Graviton in Chernivtsi closed, she lost her contributions paying job. With her eyesight worsening over the years, she could no longer secure waged work over longer periods and survived by selling household plot production. Many women like Maria often group together in Chernivtsi's central squares and sell homegrown products in what authorities and media call "spontaneous markets," populated by older women too poor and with quantities too small to sell on official markets. But Maria could not afford even the bus to the city, so she sold her produce on the road to Chernivtsi. In the interview excerpt below she describes her biggest worries; like most respondents, she is concerned with having officially worked enough years (*stazh*, or minimum number of years in a job paying social contributions) to be entitled to a better pension and with paying for firewood to get through the winter. Although she sells most production, she could not get by without financial help from her son, who works abroad:

> I lost my courage. . . . When I was working at Graviton, there was a rule, to work for ensuring a better life for our children, we paid that [wage] money [into the pension fund], but we lost all *stazh* when the factory went bankrupt. Now, no one hires me anymore. They're telling me to come again in half a year, they're looking for young people, they're not taking me. The Turks [Turkish firm] in the village are hiring again, but [informally] without *stazh*, our people work there as day laborers. I worked for them for seven years, but they're looking for young people, with better eyesight. . . . For me, the big problem is [fire]wood; that is the biggest expense. But at least the soil is good and fruitful, thank God for that. I'm not going to the market; I'm staying on the road. That's why people sell on the streets. . . . If you sell such small amounts to traders, they offer you a price that won't even cover your transport. But the big problem is the wood. I need big money for it, two full truck[load]s for passing the winter, 16,000 [Ukrainian hryvnia, roughly 500 euros]. I can't save all this money even in a year. If my family [son working abroad] did not help me out, I'd have to collect wood in the riverbed. (Maria, Chernivtsi, August 2018)

Access to social security—such as the state-backed pension scheme that Maria had lost access to—was a considerable concern for all interviewed smallholders and explained why smallholders—who as unregistered producers receive no social benefits—took up or abandoned the direct commercialization of their products. To take another example, Antonia, unlike

Maria, had a choice between commercializing agricultural products or taking up a contributions-paying job that offered her a wage near the living minimum. By the time of the interview, she had worked for sixteen years for a textile factory, which paid her some 5,000–6,000 hryvnia (156–187 euro) a month if she reached a daily quota of 450 suits sown; if not, the factory would pay her 3,500 hryvnia per month (109 euro), just short of the 2018 minimum wage of 3,723 hryvnia. What mattered for Antonia was that the job paid social contributions, so she took it even though she had enjoyed "going to the bazaar" (the way she referred to commercializing products):

> I first went to the factory when I was young. I wasn't very much aware of what I was doing. I simply wanted to have my own money but didn't really like it. What I liked was going to the bazaar and selling, but I couldn't get a foothold [especially after the local market was flooded by cheaper imports]. And I also thought that if I continue going to the bazaar, I won't have the *stazh*, and what will I do then when I am old, so I went back to the factory. (Antonia, Ostrytsia, August 2018)

Antonia further emphasized that she could take up factory work because she could rely on her husband's income. Their household had not received any land from the former collective farm and only inherited a household plot from a relative elsewhere in their village; Antonia's land possessions totalled—with the family's household plot—less than half a hectare. But the family benefitted from both spouses working together to increase their monetized incomes, with Antonia's husband struggling in informal groups ("brigades") of construction workers or as an occasional taxi driver taking villagers to the nearby city:

> My husband goes around looking for earnings, to Odessa, looking for construction yards. Earlier he was at a company in Vinnytsia, transporting glass, furniture to schools, shops, as drivers do. And when that company went bankrupt, he started growing cucumbers in the greenhouse, and when that closed, he started taxi driving and he's been doing that ever since, if he has no orders to go somewhere for construction work. And if he has orders, he goes there, but he's gotten old and so far he's doing taxi driving [to pay] for oil, electricity [literally, "for light"], for gas. One dollar [for a ride] there, one dollar back. (Antonia, Ostrytsia, August 2018)

Both Antonia and Maria emphasized that most industrial workers were women from their peri-urban communities; urban dwellers could not live on the low salaries paid by the textile factories. Antonia explained:

> It is women from the surrounding villages [around Chernivtsi] that work at the factory. There are buses taking them to the factory; she [the factory manager] pays for them; the drivers collect their *stazh*. . . . Those city women don't want to work too much for such a low wage, and piece-rate work is very tough. But a village woman can grow potatoes, she has something to live from. For those [women from the city] the salary is too low, but this one over here in the village can grow a pig, she has something to live from. With what she earns over there, she can come back to the village and build something. She has something to live from . . . a pig, potatoes, a cow, an onion . . . that's why most of them [working at the factory] are from the village. (Antonia, Ostrytsia, August 2018)

The concern with securing contributions-paying (*stazh*) occupations characterizes not only mixed households in general but also the smallholders in my sample who had increased the land under their control. Vanya, a former kolkhoz machine operator who in twenty years had extended operations from less than two hectares to seventy, combined farming activities with a contributions-paying job—in his case, as a fireman in his community's volunteer fire brigade. He described his solution to combining the two: "I found someone to hold my shift [at the fire brigade] for the time I need to do [agricultural] work. This way, I keep collecting the *stazh* [years needed for retirement]. I already have forty" (farmer, Hlyboka area, August 2017). In the passage below, Vanya expresses his regret of not being able to spend time with his son as a child because of the yearly seasonal spikes in farm labor. He saw what he perceived as neglecting his child as nevertheless justified, as the money he earned helped him cover the financial expenses of having his son in the military firemen school in Kharkiv, 1,000 kilometers east of his village. What makes a fireman's job so desirable is that it pays a lifetime of social contributions. In the end, nevertheless, Vanya did not have the money to secure his son a job as a fireman in the city.

I couldn't take care of Vasya when he was a child. During summer, there was so much to do, [that] our house was full [of seasonal workers]. They slept everywhere, on the floor, in the kitchen. Vasya couldn't study; he had no place to go. But he was good with technical stuff, machines. I sent him, nevertheless, to school—the military firemen school in Kharkiv, a good school. That year in the whole of Chernivtsi, they [the Kharkiv military school] only took four people. Vasya was one of them. I asked how much this would cost me. My friend there told me he would tell me later. He never brought it up. Because, you understand, for this kind of stuff you have to pay a great deal. And I am only talking here about a place in [military service] school, not about actually landing a job as a fireman, which, if you pay a high *chubuk* [slang for "tip," meaning a bribe], you can even get without military service. [Because in the end his son did not get a fireman job] I got him a job as a care worker. He's taking care of his 92-year-old grandmother. This way, he collects the years needed for his *stazh*. (Farmer, Hlyboka area, August 2017)

Better-off households (such as Vanya's) owning some land made farming for markets conditional on access to social services. If such a balancing act was not possible (as in Antonia's case), households abandoned farming for markets in favor of employment in jobs paying social contributions coupled with growing food for their own consumption. The worse-off households—like Maria's—were unable to secure such jobs and covered expenses by taking up any informal occupation, including the direct commercialization of the little produce from their household plots. Poverty pushed them into commercialization, not into subsistence. But despite the difficulties of having to balance monetized expenditures and the small incomes from growing agricultural products and from off-farm work, mixed households nevertheless kept a strong presence in food production. They were the first building block in the re-emergence of the "traditional system" in my fieldwork area, consisting on the producer side of a diverse scene ranging from numerous mixed households to just a few entrepreneurial farmers and coexisting with consolidating corporate producers to which the households leased their land. Understanding how smallholders can develop so as to commercialize production requires a further type of actor, informal traders, a critical element in the smallholders' immediate environment because they make monetized incomes available to smallholders without contractual conditioning. In the next section, I discuss the traders' role in facilitating production-oriented self-provisioning and internalizing costs, helping both smallholders and larger farmers to counter the monetization of their livelihoods by selling on local markets.

Traders as Investment Facilitators

Field theory uses the concept of vertical integration to capture the growth of economic actors through mergers with suppliers or customers. Vertical integration is, however, ill-suited for capturing the situation of interviewed smallholders; mergers with suppliers or customers were not feasible even when or if reaching the stage of entrepreneurial farming. Instead, the monetization perspective captures how agricultural producers sought to occupy upward and downward links in the value chain as the key to their survival and growth. Rather than merge with other actors, smallholders sought to fulfil some of the tasks controlled by suppliers (regarding machinery) and customers (intermediaries or traders). Traders such as wholesalers and retailers, therefore, played an important part in making the smallholder equivalent of vertical integration possible, because they offered smallholders the first opportunity to enter markets as sellers and also an essential source of cash. With traders buying production at the farm-gate, smallholder farmers with no transportation or storage capacities could engage with product markets and receive cash money for their production. For instance, most smallholders started by selling production to traders, who came and took products directly from the smallholders' households. At this stage, smallholders would still hold another occupation (usually waged), but the incomes from that occupation and profits from selling production would be used for buying a car, allowing them to deliver produce directly to wholesale markets. Here production could be sold further to traders (present in far larger numbers and offering higher prices than at the farm-gate), or smallholders could sell production themselves to end consumers, an option usually far less preferred because of time limitations.

To take examples from surveyed families on both sides of the border, the M. family produced vegetables such as cabbage on some five hectares on the Romanian side of the border, while the I. family produced cabbage and potatoes on eighteen hectares near Chernivtsi. Typically, production was sold directly to end customers in periodical markets, one or two days a week, but when seasonal crops abounded, one family member needed to stay daily at a wholesale market, selling production to traders. The two families and other producers did not complain about "collusive" traders because the wholesale market offered many traders to choose from. Both families perceived the presence of one of their members at the wholesale market as beneficial: they received far higher prices for their production than at the farm-gate, since there were more wholesalers to choose from. What they complained about was the time loss, because instead of working on the farm, they needed to spend long hours selling production in the nearby cities: "I do not wish to be here. For me, this time is dead. I could be home taking care of the harvest or something else. But I have no better way to sell my produce" (farmer M., Bursuceni, August 2015). However, for these two families, as for most of the region's smallholders and entrepreneurial farmers, participating in the "modern procurement system" hardly constituted an alternative. When they approached large retail chains, they were told that produce such as cabbage and potatoes was available earlier and in larger quantities in more southern locations. Even if they teamed up with other producers in a marketing cooperative to increase marketable output, they could still not beat the advantage of regions that sold their produce earlier. The consequence was reliance on informal traders or, as in the my observations during fieldwork rounds in 2015–16, taking up trade on markets for themselves.

Large numbers of small traders populating periodic markets are nearly extinct in Western Europe, disappearing along with the respective markets following the rise and expansion of supermarkets;[2] they have been replaced by a few large logistics and distribution chains connecting farmers organized in producer organizations and retail chains such as supermarkets (Chen and Stamoulis 2008). In Ukraine and Romania, intermediaries such as transporters or shippers are populating local periodic markets as well as ports and export sites. Usually coming in the guise of drivers of small trucks such as the four-ton Mercedes Sprinter or Ford Transit, some traders have taken the step of buying or building their own storage facilities, usually close to or on the very premises of local periodic or permanent markets (personal observation, Chernivtsi and Suceava, August 2013 and 2015). Most, however, continue to operate informally, owning only one or two vans and storing produce on their household premises.

Although traders are portrayed in an undifferentiated manner (World Bank 2007, 119) and as potentially predatory (McCullough, Pingali, and Stamoulis 2010), they tend to specialize in certain roles, corresponding to the type of market they sell at: periodic or permanent, wholesale or retail, rural or urban. Some act as wholesalers, buying produce from farmers and transporting it to periodic as well as permanent wholesale markets. Others act as retailers, to be distinguished from the integrated logistics networks of retail chains. They also often involve household members in their operations (Díaz, Lacayo, and Salcedo 2007, 73–74) and prefer buying from markets rather than at farm-gates and from producers rather than from wholesalers in order to advance in the value chain and get a better price. As soon as they become capable of taking their produce to markets, producers can meet such trader-retailers and keep them as customers, at a larger profit also for themselves. These trader-retailers could beat supermarket prices for seasonal products bought from local producers, an important factor behind the survival of informal trade despite the presence of large retail chains: *seasonal* products sold *locally* to end consumers are cheaper than produce sold in retail chains. The retail chains' arguments against buying up the M. family's produce were quantity and availability, but not price.

Traders in my fieldwork areas appeared hardly capable of imposing their price on farmers, except for the soy value chain, an export commodity in Ukraine's Novoselytsia fieldwork region. There the trader scene was no longer as fragmented. At the downstream end of the value chain, soy traders differed from the van drivers buying up farm production at the farm-gate: they were a handful of warehouse owners close to export ports in Odessa and Mykolaiv. For instance, there were only three large private warehouses in Odessa and two state-owned ones at the time of fieldwork. Farmers and traders did complain about these owners being collusive, but they also noted that they drove prices down for the entire upstream value chain, including for smaller traders. This suggests that the "traditional" system benefits producers if it is fragmented and allows producers to choose from several traders.[3] Interviewed farmers, especially smallholders, decried the low prices offered by traders at the farm-gate. However, they also found solutions, such as the practice of teaming up in what would qualify as an informal marketing cooperative in order to increase the quantities sold to traders and get a better price. Showing me the tens of traders' telephone numbers in his phone, a respondent told me that

> Even when we have small quantities, we team up. We get together several producers and increase the quantity of produce to be sold. We call various traders until someone agrees to our price and comes over with his truck. (Farmer, Banyliv, August 2015)

Informal traders were the preferred partners not only of smallholders teaming up but also of entrepreneurial farmers. For instance, a farmer working close to two thousand hectares of land close to the EU border between Romania and Ukraine said, "Everyone complains about the so-called *samsari* [a pejorative term for intermediaries]. [But] over the years, they changed a lot. They built warehouses and work with large amounts of turnover cash," and he preferred selling to them, as "they buy twenty to forty tons," paying on the spot in cash and taking the produce— potatoes—at once from farm-gates. He continued:

> Over the years [traders] have grown from small truck drivers to owners of storage facilities, forty-ton vehicles, and large capital stocks. I prefer selling to them. They pay in cash on the spot and take large quantities. Supermarkets wanted me to transport to them some five tons [at the farmer's expense to cities 400–500 kilometers away]. If the produce would sell, they would pay me the money in a few months. (Farmer in Bălcăuți, August 2015)

Another farmer, heading one of the few legally registered marketing cooperatives in the area, also resented interacting with retail chains:

> Retail chains impose their conditions. They force upon you a certain price, but they also pay you only when they want—for instance, sixty days after you delivered your produce to them. How can they keep your money for sixty days? How can you grow? (Farmer, Iaslovăț, July 2015)

A farmer who owned a twenty-hectare apple orchard continued selling to traders even though he was one of the few regional farmers to gain contracts with international retailers. He praised the presence of traders because they helped him establish the right price for his production: "If too many of them line up at the gates, my price is too low. If there are only few of them, then I need to lower my price" (farmer, Fălticeni, March 2015). In this way, he also knew what to charge retail chains. In order to make the best use of the two systems (the "modern" and the "traditional" ones), he had changed the juridical status of his operations: roughly half the orchard was listed as the property of his private company, while the other half was listed as his individual farm (not a company). On paper, all sales to retail chains were made from the first half, but in practice he could allocate quantities informally between the two juridical halves of his operations according to the signals coming from the retail chain and the intermediaries.

Smallholders and entrepreneurial farmers in Ukraine criticized how authorities and private managers run periodic and wholesale markets, allowing traders to occupy the best places in the market, by keeping cars parked in those places day and night. This practice harmed not only producers but also other traders, one of them declaring when interviewed:

> It is really very tough, because [market authorities] don't really lease the places available, but you occupy them. Many intermediaries simply keep a car parked there, day and night, and pay the 4 euros per 24 hours just to keep others out. (Trader, Chernivtsi, August 2015)

Consequently, smallholders and larger farmers were forced to sell not on the markets' premises but directly on the streets leading to the markets (personal observation, Chernivitsi Zelenyi rynok, August 2015). Nevertheless, most smallholders and farmers selling on the streets leading to markets sold production to traders and received prices 30 percent higher than what they would have obtained if they had sold the production at their farm's gates, because many traders were present and competing. Traders, who as a rule, buy large quantities of products, represented an important, if not the main source of cash for producers and also helped them save time by limiting the time they spent at markets.

Areas of Investment

The cash incomes realized from selling to traders together with incomes from the waged off-farm work of family members were the main sources of investment for the interviewed smallholders. These funds were used in two ways, both of which further increased self-provisioning. First, these funds were used to facilitate control over machinery. With new equipment too expensive and leasing schemes inaccessible to unregistered smallholders, the smallholders relied heavily on machinery bought at secondhand markets. Without exception, machinery, especially tractors, came from the secondhand machinery markets emerging in countries, including Romania, that had witnessed a more rapid dismantlement of collective property than Ukraine, or from Western and post-Yugoslav countries in the case of Romanian farmers. Thus smallholders as well as entrepreneurial farmers could buy tractors at prices ten to twenty times below those for new equipment (taking, for instance, the price of EUR 85,000 in Ukraine for a new Western-produced tractor). A respondent told me how he bought his first combine and brought it to Ukraine:

I talked to some people, who were working for a car-dismantling business [in Germany], and they were sending spare parts home, sometimes legally, sometimes by smuggling them. I asked them to find me a combine in good condition for 8,000 dollars. I then paid the transport to the [Polish-Ukrainian] border. It cost me in total 12,000 dollars. I had it for eight years. (Farmer, Brusnytsia, August 2015)

For most respondents, this equipment, however, worked only to the extent that producers could internalize maintenance and repair work; many interview partners took care of maintenance and repair on their own, at times creating spare parts themselves with lathes. Lathes are machine tools performing various operations from cutting to drilling and deformation, and those in use among the interviewees had been bought online, were from the 1970s, and came from dismantled Soviet factories at prices of some EUR 1,000 each.

Second, funds from the sale of production and off-farm work were used to facilitate control over land. In both Ukraine and Romania, respondents barely bought new land. If they decided to increase the land that they worked, they usually leased it from smallholders more interested in self-consumption than in commercialization (see the discussion on terminology in chapter 4) or from local authorities in case of communal land. The predominance of leasing was due in Ukraine to the agricultural land sales moratorium, and in Romania because ever since EU accession, villagers and agricultural landholders had had an interest in owning land as they received EU subventions (a possibility not excluding further leasing the land). In one fieldwork area, the lease system favored competition among respondents for other villagers' land, and producers needed increasing incomes to secure control over land. For instance, in one Ukrainian village (visited in 2013 and 2015), the five entrepreneurial farmers operating in the village were paying a lease twice as high as what an agro-holding in a nearby village paid landowners. In 2015, the price came close to one ton of produce per hectare. Important to note, the lease was predominantly paid in-kind, even when the lease-paying farmer actually needed to buy the respective product—usually grain—in order to distribute it to landowners; preference went to grain as smallholders could feed it to livestock, which facilitated cash incomes if the landowning smallholder commercialized livestock or meat (see also Kuns 2016; Agarwal, Dobay, and Sabates-Wheeler 2021).

The lease tenure system shows that there hardly was a neat division between entrepreneurial farmers and smallholders. Farmers and smallholders interacted in tenure arrangements as lessees and lessors, a relationship that also existed between those smallholders trying to increase output and interested in leasing land and those involved in agriculture primarily for reasons of self-consumption. In fact, the economic survival of the lessees might depend on not everyone seeking the same involvement in agricultural production and therefore freeing up land; in other words, their economic survival depends on the specialization of roles in the producers' wider communities.

Conclusions

This chapter argued that it is difficult to identify how the agrifood system that emerged in the 1990s in de-collectivizing, deindustrializing post-communist Europe was "traditional." The new system did not resemble the highly centralized communist food value chains, nor could it simply be a version of what existed before communism. The context was too different, shaped by the moribund collective farms and the unfolding land reform. Rather than pursue economies of scale and face competition, the agricultural producers emerging in this system sought to escape competition by integrating production steps upstream and downstream in the value chain. This can explain how they could survive and expand operations when they barely had access to credit. Larger farms mattered for smallholders as examples showing how and when land is profitable. They provided "a cost-discovery function: by engaging in new economic activities, they help map out the underlying cost structure of the economy, providing valuable information to other entrepreneurs about what can be produced profitably" (Rodrik 2008, 102). Smallholders and larger farmers are not to be seen as separated from each other, with the former operating in "traditional" or informal markets of the "periodic" type, while the latter operates in "modern" markets. In fact, smallholders and larger farmers interact in informal markets by competing (if selling the same products) and cooperating when exchanging information or supplying each other with land and products and when smallholders receive inputs for livestock rearing in exchange for leasing land.

The mixed household's reliance on family labor engaging in animal and land husbandry as an important means of livelihood resembles "peasant" farming (Shanin 1966, 6–7; see also Edelman 2013, 6). At first sight, the symbiotic relationship that households established with the former collective farms in most post-Soviet (Russia-like) countries goes against explicitly referring to such households as peasantry, at least in Ukraine, because unlike autonomy-seeking "peasants," rural households relied heavily on inputs from the collective farm. However, these production inputs are often demonetized. That is, their exchange takes place in-kind, usually in the form of households leasing land to former collective farms in exchange for grain (in turn usually fed to livestock). This arrangement offers households greater autonomy and control over supplies than having to procure them on markets. Specifically, the in-kind payments going to households for leased land parcels were of fundamental importance for smallholders in the fieldwork areas. They allowed smallholders to keep livestock without having to work the land for forage. This could explain why in the Chernivets'ka Oblast', rural households strengthened their dominant role in animal husbandry from 52.7 percent in 1995 to 76.8 percent in 2015 (State Statistics Service of Ukraine 2016, 208). Even though using parts of production for self-consumption, respondents keeping livestock also sought to market their products. Land reform failed to produce entrepreneurial farmers in the expected numbers but did strengthen the mixed-income households' involvement in food production.

The local population's interest in marketing production represented an important factor for the development of traders in the areas under study: the first traders—and later on, larger farmers—were the people trading the meat they bought from fellow villagers and then transported to cities to sell it further. Traders emerged to market what fellow villagers produced; some were not ordinary villagers but had held jobs in the collective farm, which had prepared them for commerce. Perhaps most importantly, their peasant background explains why traders also participate in traditional agrifood chains: villagers themselves, they have the knowledge to recognize and market good produce.[4] Over the years, some of them developed and invested in increasingly large transportation means and even warehousing, thus being able to buy up the production also of larger farmers. However, one element stayed largely unchanged: namely, their preference for immediate cash transactions, offering producers a so far unmatched possibility of receiving an immediate monetized income from production.

The development of trade in the "traditional" agrifood chain suggests the advantages this chain offer participants compared to the "modern" procurement system. From the perspective of interviewed farmers, the challenge of joining modern supply chains was not so much that of meeting quality and safety requirements but the very conditionality involved in the contractual relationship favored by retail chains: payments are postponed and conditional on sales, and requirements regarding quantities and delivery are in terms that farmers perceive as unfair. The contractual relationship involves power issues, with producers (including larger farmers) the weaker contractual side when dealing with large retail chains or banks. In contrast, the traditional market can offer less concentration; instead of a few retail chains, it is an immediate environment consisting of traders of various sizes that buy up products. And instead of contractual arrangements that involve late payments and require certain quantities and often distant delivery locations, traders pay in cash, on the spot, and buy up the entire production, transporting it at their own cost. The immediate environment of the traditional market type facilitates resilience by allowing smallholders to save and invest in production. It therefore translates into a viable alternative to interacting with an environment composed of corporate suppliers, wholesalers, and retail chains.

As the next chapter will show, following Phase 3 land reform logic, governments in the two countries discussed here took little interest in the smallholders' immediate environment. Instead, they have sought to transform it to resemble the modern procurement system, by driving the commercialization of the sector through measures that increase the smallholders' dependence on monetized inputs.

CHAPTER 6
Resistance
Smallholders against Commercialization

WORLD BANK PUBLICATIONS ON land reform blame the low commercialization levels among post-communist smallholders on surviving collective farms, slow cadastral land registration, and the banning of agricultural land sales through moratoria. Ukraine receives much attention for epitomizing these problems, moving only slowly along the path of World Bank–supported reforms and from 2001 on, introducing a moratorium on the sale of agricultural land (Deininger and Nizalov 2016). Romania, a country that replaced collective ownership through the far-reaching distribution of land titles as early as possible, has also failed to accomplish land reform promises of widespread emergence of entrepreneurial farming. Quite surprisingly given the differences in de-collectivization, Romania and Ukraine resemble each other, both seemingly reaching "dualist" agricultural landscapes, lacking entrepreneurial farmers but populated by millions of smallholders and only a few mega-farms, large corporations vertically integrating multiple value chain links. In fact, as discussed in chapter 3, this development characterizes most of the post-communist space, with the main exception being the Central and Eastern European countries achieving production increases by drastically decreasing the number of people in agricultural occupations. Elsewhere in post-communist Europe and Central Asia, the outcome was a highly fragmented landscape of struggling agricultural producers, irrespective of the form that land reform took, with minimal—if any—productivity increases. This was a far cry from the productivity increases coupled with growing agricultural employment achieved in China and Vietnam.

World Bank experts and government strategists see the particularly high incidence of smallholders in these countries as one, if not the main problem of post-communist agriculture. The key reform proposed by World Bank and government experts to deal with the high incidence of subsistence farming after land reform was commercialization. This meant increasing the amounts smallholders sell on markets to turn market sales into the main income source for smallholders, or in the phrasing of the 2008 *World Development Report*, to "bring agriculture to the markets" (World Bank 2007). The call to bring smallholders to markets materialized in several concrete recommendations for achieving commercialization. First, it was believed that *more* land reform, particularly the introduction of tradable private property rights, would drive the commercialization of agriculture by allowing those capable of producing and commercializing to acquire more land. The small size of land plots read as an obstacle to reform because to increase production, smallholders must be able to acquire more land (Lerman 2004). Second, commercialization implied not only the registration of producers coupled with the development of credit and insurance mechanisms to assist smallholders in developing production but also setting up producer organizations or cooperatives to allow them to access international retail chains.

Together with calls for commercialization went also the perception that smallholders "resist" or "oppose" the reform of their sector, mainly for "psychological" reasons, fearing the risk of giving up their "dependency" on "subsistence agriculture" (Lerman 2004, 2017; World Bank 2004a; Ministry of Agrarian Policy and Food of Ukraine 2015; Romanian Ministry of Agriculture and Rural Development 2014). The "resistance" imputed to smallholders is hardly public, collective action calling the attention of power holders and media. Instead, it consists of smallholders ignoring the course of economic action proposed by authorities and international advisors, operating far from the mechanisms supposed to support entrepreneurial farmers, such as credit and insurance. Authorities and advisors explain this resistance by claiming that states lack the capacity to commercialize the smallholder sector and overcome the resistance of smallholders (Ministry of Agrarian Policy and Food of Ukraine 2015)— that is, drive out those that fail to commercialize by incentivizing them to sell their land (see the policy recommendations in Lerman 2004, 2017).

This "commercialization" perspective casts smallholders as if existing in a noneconomic realm or one that hardly manifests any economic rationality, untouched by state reform. This depiction is misleading, as it leaves little room for acknowledging that what authorities and international experts perceive as "resistance" to "commercialization" in fact represents an adaptation to previous reforms that have influenced the monetized realm faced by smallholder households and have turned these into mixed-income households, pursuing various income sources rather than specializing in entrepreneurial farming. Interviewed smallholders indeed had—as the World Bank studies argue—vested interests not to commercialize, but hardly because of the unreformed collective farm. This type of farm, while present in Ukraine throughout the first two post-communist decades, is absent in Romania, yet smallholders in both countries were reluctant to engage in the formal commercialization favored by the World Bank. They avoided official commercialization even where the break with the past was radical (as in Romania), because of the increasing monetary needs that formal commercialization implies. The empirical material that follows exemplifies this argument by discussing policies seeking to increase official commercialization in Ukraine and Romania and the smallholder response to them: curbing informal land use practices in Ukraine, increasing the regulation of "traditional markets" in Romania, and incentivizing cooperatives among smallholders in both countries. These examples show that authorities did not pursue commercialization just out of a concern to help smallholders but sought to depict practices in the smallholders' immediate environments as deeply unfair toward registered economic actors and therefore—particularly in the Romanian context—directly sought to curb them.

State Strategies of "Commercialization"

Romania is the European Union country with the highest share of "subsistence" farms, rural households consuming more than 50 percent of production. Even in absolute numbers, the close to three million small-scale farms by the mid-2010s in Romania far outnumbered those in the EU countries coming in next: Poland, Hungary, and Italy, all three totalling less than a million (Eurostat 2016). This reality is the starting point in all strategy papers issued by Romanian officials. It forms the background for a depiction of Romanian agriculture that casts such a high number of small-scale "farms" as deeply problematic, as a "brake on the development of high productivity agriculture" (Presidential Commission for Agricultural Development Policies [PCADP] 2013, 27). Despite the number of such small-scale farms decreasing by 800,000 in half a decade (2010–2016), Romanian officials insisted on calling this "development . . . too slow" (PCADP 2013, 25). They even called for the state to buy up land from small-scale farmers in order to diminish their numbers, which would mean a reversal of the land titling reform. They also called for increased registration and taxation of small-scale farms, as they suspected such farms to be part of a vast "grey market, over which state controls have no effect" (PCADP 2013, 153). Such taxation should build on mechanisms created by EU accession, with more than one million farmers registering with authorities to qualify for EU subventions. Nevertheless, even though Romanian authorities have tried to use registration to increase taxation, they "lost the public debate" around their 2008 taxation offensive and eventually gave up their plans, a fact decried in the strategy document (PCADP 2013, 152).

While the long-term strategy document presented "subsistence" as a rational response to economic hardship and as something that was facilitated by the extension of private land property rights (PCADP 2013, 26), this take on subsistence was absent from Romania's National Rural Development Plans (2007–2013 and 2014–2020), drafted with World Bank assistance. The plans also cast smallholders as subsistence farmers and as the main obstacle to the country's agricultural development, leaving out any attempt to understand subsistence as a rational response to the farms' economic environment or as an outcome of land titling, the introduction of private land rights in the 1990s. Instead, the documents claimed that 89 percent of Romania's farmers were "lacking entrepreneurial spirit" (Romanian Ministry of Agriculture and Rural Development [RMARD] 2014, 608). They called for "assisting" them in either developing "viable" business plans or for persuading them to leave agriculture altogether (RMARD 2014, 97). The plans depict subsistence farming as a danger to public health and the "competitiveness of the entire sector," since "animal disease outbreaks occur typically in these small holdings" (RMARD 2008, 23). They stress psychological factors of small-scale farmers and devalue the skills they might have:

> Most of these people are either not educated or have limited skills or knowledge. For them, farm and household activities become

inseparable. They typically opt for mixed production patterns: granivores (poultry and pig) in combination with field crops. Given this production mix, and their very loose connection to the market, they remain immune to adverse price fluctuations. (RMARD 2008, 23)

What these documents thus reproached small-scale farmers for was not just their lack of involvement with markets but also their low vulnerability to market mechanisms, preventing such mechanisms from turning their holdings into more "competitive" units. They "keep aggregate agricultural performance low by offsetting the achievements of otherwise high performing large farms, and preventing the consolidation of semi-subsistence farms into viable and more competitive farm units" (RMARD 2008, 23). The solution envisaged for these problems was a "more active land market"; the plans stated that the costs of registering land and land transactions deter farmers from selling and buying land (RMARD 2008, 26).

Ukrainian strategies for the agricultural sector were less virulent in their approach to "rural households," the term used by government and World Bank officials to denote small-scale farming in Ukraine. Nevertheless, they share several commonalities with Romanian documents. First, in Ukraine as in Romania, the drastic reduction of rural households over the last decade went unnoticed, even though the number of rural households had declined from 5 million plots in 2005 to 4.2 million in 2013 (Keyzer et al. 2017, 146). The Ukrainian strategy paper for 2015–2020 estimated the number of households engaged in farming at some 4 million, including more than 14 million people (Ministry of Agrarian Policy and Food of Ukraine [MAPFU] 2015). Second, the "household sector" was, as in the Romanian documents, depicted as the locus of informality and above all, poverty. But in Ukraine, as in Romania, it was not really subsistence agriculture alone that supported local households; in Ukraine, only 10 percent of rural household incomes came from agriculture in 2013, down from 30 percent in 2002. This "subsistence reading" of households ignores that mixed-income households were the most numerous actor of the post-reform landscape, for which agriculture was but one source of livelihood.

Third, Ukrainian documents, like Romanian ones, assumed that psychological "characteristics" prevented small farmers from becoming commercially oriented, such as "prevailing conservative attitudes" and "psychological hurdles to self-organization/cooperation," as well as the "inability to adapt: the very small, less educated and older farmers may not have the capacity to adapt to the upgraded agricultural standards" (MAPFU 2015, 18). Major policy instruments proposed included extending "registration, taxation, insurance, credit, pension systems" also to rural households MAPFU 2015, 56). This is an important difference from previous strategies. Although also psychologizing rural dwellers as characterized by an "absence of work motivation," they did not target policy measures directly at these (MAPFU 2007, 2). The 2015 strategy document, drafted with World Bank assistance, posits registration as the foremost measure supporting the extension of other policies to the household sector, ensuring that "small farmers become better trained, more efficient, and market-oriented." The main threat identified by the document is again "resistance to change or acceptance of business orientation amongst small farmers" (MAPFU 2015, 56–57).

Government strategy papers in Romania and Ukraine were straddling two contradictory objectives. On the one hand, they stated the intention of "assisting" small-scale farmers in setting up "official" commercial operations. On the other hand, there was a preoccupation with the "unfair" practices that small-scale farmers allegedly engaged in. As argued in the next section, Ukrainian strategy documents locate these unfair practices at the level of land use, referring to informal and untaxed tenure arrangements as "shadow production" and "shadow lease" (MAPFU 2007). Consequently, government strategies called for "fairer" taxation of rural households, a call reflecting a distrust of small-scale farming that hardly met smallholder sympathy. In Romania, quite surprisingly, given the assumption that smallholders are not commercial, strategy papers located unfair practices at the level of the sale of agricultural production: "a vast grey market" of undocumented sale of products (PCADP 2013). Because of their involvement in such informal practices, smallholders were expected to resist government plans. In these plans, improving agriculture overlaps with overcoming smallholder resistance, presumed to have developed interests and mind-sets that run contrary to government intentions. Unsurprisingly then, a major measure in "commercializing" agriculture in the two countries is distinguishing those that have a chance of turning "commercial" from those producers that are too small, unskilled, or unwilling to become so (Roger 2014; Varga 2018).[1]

Shadow Lease

Authorities and the international organizations advising them assume that the informal practices of smallholders originate in a pre-reform, communist past. However, it is important to note that at a closer look, what authorities and World Bank incriminate represents a reaction to earlier rounds of reform and earlier monetization of needs. A case in point is the "shadow lease," a phenomenon that the Ukrainian development plan for the late 2010s intended to combat and that was present in Romania at the time of fieldwork. "Shadow lease" is an informal arrangement under which smaller owners temporarily transfer unused land they had received during land reforms to larger producers for agricultural use without notifying authorities. This practice is problematic for the state because the land was put to productive use for which no tax was paid.

In the fieldwork areas under study, the general lease of land was widespread. Entrepreneurial farmers and commercializing smallholders on both sides of the border did not buy up the land they worked (although on the Romanian side they are allowed to do so), relying instead on lease arrangements with smallholders, as outlined in the previous chapter. Where land was scarce, such arrangements usually took the form of the entrepreneurial farmers paying some one-and-a-half tons of grain per hectare to smallholders each year. Larger farms preferred this arrangement to buy up land because payment would not take place in money, and thus access to land would not depend on a resource "produced" outside the farm—namely, money. Larger farmers and corporate actors registered these lease arrangements with authorities; they employed lawyers that registered hundreds of lease contracts in each community.

Smaller farmers and commercializing households did not register these lease arrangements. They praised the importance of "shadow lease" for facilitating the operation of their farms: "The secret is that some people left me their land, and I can work as much as twenty hectares just like that. I don't have to pay back anything [for the land]" (farmer, Chernivtsi, August 2016). They judged the relevance of signing lease contracts from their perspective—ignoring the state's interest in collecting tax—and underlined that they did not need contracts: "There is no need for any contracts. The people know that I give them seven hundred kilos [of grain] for fifty acres. I even give [them] a ton. If they're not happy, they give it [the land] to someone else." The respondent, an entrepreneurial farmer producing on more than two hundred hectares he leased in three villages, justified such informal dealings by claiming that what the state loses in land tax, it gets back in the fines that farmers pay for bookkeeping mistakes: "I paid 1,000 dollars last year for a two-comma mistake of my bookkeeper" (farmer, Chernivtsi, August 2018). On the Romanian side of the border, where land taxes are significantly higher, it is still the smallholder that pays the land tax to the state. A larger farmer emphasized that she would not buy the land even if it were up for sale, as the lease arrangement is far more beneficial. If you bought the land, she said,

> you would need to pay the land tax. Look, I have a neighbor that bought some land. He has two deceased sons, and still has two daughters [implying that the daughters would not be interested in working the land]. What's he supposed to do with the land? Let the land lie fallow? But he still needs to pay the [land] tax. See, [owning land] is like a double-edged sword. (Farmer Lia, Suceava, August 2017)

These interview excerpts are indicative of the reasoning behind my respondents' decisions, making sense of their situation in terms of the monetary burden it imposes. Whether one buys up more land or whether one develops production for markets is likely to be evaluated from this perspective of reducing not only costs but, in particular, their monetization. Land tenure arrangements came at no monetary cost for the farmer, who paid no land tax and paid the lease in kind. In some cases, farmers participated in arrangements that did not even pay smallholders a lease in exchange for their land, or in the case of interviewees in the Romanian fieldwork area, it even came at a monetary cost for the smallholder who still paid the land tax.

The standard depiction of such arrangements in World Bank publications is that they are "predatory" and "detrimental" to smallholders, who should sell the land rather than enter or be forced to enter such arrangements. While it is obvious why the entrepreneurial farmers and corporate farms might take an interest in such an arrangement, since they receive free or cheap access to land, the smallholders' reasons for participating are far from clear; World Bank experts assume that they are forced into such arrangements or that they hardly have a choice (Deininger and Nizalov 2016). The smallholders' reasons become more evident if one avoids equating smallholders with subsistence farming and recognizes that the reality of the vast majority of them is far more complex. In the case of shadow leases, it is not the subsistence smallholders that participate in such arrangements; according to the definition, if achieving only enough production to subsist on, leasing out their land would cause them to starve. The smallholders that participate in such arrangements owe their livelihoods to other incomes. Such smallholders include the local village teacher, who "leases" land for free to the large farmers simply so that "someone keeps the land in order" (teacher, Chernivtsi, August 2016). As a rule, such farmers most often come from the same community as the smallholders, as they seek to enlarge the land available to them in their community and close to the farm or household from which they run their operations. Without this tenure arrangement, smallholders unwilling to work or sell their land fear that other land users might slowly take over their land never to return it, irrespective of whether the land shows up in the land cadaster or not. A Romanian trader observed that if no one works the land, potential land rights usurpers

> will slowly move the *hat* [unworked land separating land plots] to di-minish your plot until it's gone. Then you can go and sue them and wait until justice is done. In the meantime, they can keep working your land. (Trader Iulia, Suceava, August 2017)

These cases might seem extreme, and respondents in communities with several entrepreneurial farmers practiced the arrangement portrayed in the previous chapter, receiving grain in exchange for land. While they charged farmers for using their land in products to be used for feeding livestock, they kept such arrangements informal—that is, in the parlance of respondents, "without papers"—so they could switch between farmers from one year to the next and thus extract a higher lease. On the other hand, as pointed out in chapter 5, numerous communities are experiencing a steep decline in numbers of smallholders willing or able to work their land in Romania and Ukraine more generally. Despite the government strategy papers' alarmist tone about the incidence of small farming, the reality is that in each country, smallholder numbers have decreased by more than half a million in the last decade (Keyzer et al. 2017; Presidential Commission for Agricultural Development Policies 2013; Eurostat 2016). Furthermore, rural areas in both countries have seen increasing outmigration and general demographic decrease. In Romania's northeast region, of which Suceava is a part, the population declined from 3.7 million to 3.2 million inhabitants in ten years. This means that land often remains fallow, and there are plenty of opportunities for entrepreneurial farmers to engage in "shadow lease" arrangements of the type documented above. What government strategy papers read as "resistance" is, in fact, a local adaptation to the fragmentation produced by the land titling program.

A "Vast Grey Market" of Undocumented Sale of Products

Strategy documents in Romania approached the existence of a large number of "traditional agricultural markets" (periodic markets), the traditional places for smallholders to sell their produce, as a "vast grey market" and a major sign of underdevelopment (Presidential Commission for Agricultural Development Policies 2013, 153). This relates to broader approaches that see such markets as predatory and potentially dangerous for smallholders (McCullough, Pingali, and Stamoulis 2010, World Bank 2007), which argue that smallholders should form producer associations and tap into the regional or international value chains dominated by retail supermarkets. Rather than seeking ways to support such traditional markets, the World Bank and the European Bank for Reconstruction and Development were financing in the 2010s the expansion of the supermarket chains Lidl and Kaufland to Romania without any requirements that they cooperate with local producers or traders (Provost and Kennard 2015). Romanian authorities too eagerly embraced the preference for international chains in their development plans, particularly since it entailed building on export possibilities that seemed underused. In practice, this preference brought a massive offensive by tax authorities to curb undocumented and untaxed sales in "grey" or "traditional" markets and, as argued in the next subsection, only a little progress in incentivizing smallholders to set up and join producer organizations.

The national authorities' most relevant registration offensive sought to extend EU and other agricultural subsidies to smallholders. At least 75 percent of subsidy recipients in Romanian agriculture should represent "farms" owning between one and five hectares of land. However, most smallholders in Romania failed to qualify for subventions (Fox 2011; Roger 2014). The EU Common Agricultural Policy framework and Romanian authorities introduced hierarchies of subvention recipients that excluded those actors deemed to be "subsistence farms" because only "semi-subsistence" farms qualified for subventions. This meant that as much as 91 percent, or three million "farms" or "peasant households" did not fulfil eligibility requirements (Bíró Boróka 2015; Şerban and Juravle 2012).

Rather than register successes in having smallholders join cooperatives or access EU subventions, authorities concentrated on fighting tax evasion. After timid attempts in the 2000s, tax collection "campaigns" took off in 2015, aiming to uncover and fine those involved in undocumented sales of agricultural products. They went hand in hand with a registration offensive, aiming to differentiate "producers" (smallholders) from "intermediaries" (traders); authorities have considered that the former are entitled to sell in fresh product markets, while the latter's presence in markets should be prevented. From 2015 on, the paperwork required for counting as a "producer" specified that producers monitor and declare all quantities sold, irrespective of landholding size and amount of products. Tax collection campaigns took place every year from 2015 until 2019, with tax inspectors from Romania's National Agency for Fiscal Administration raiding markets throughout the country.

The reaction in the fieldwork areas under study was that sellers—both producers and intermediaries—simply chose to sit it out, paying the fines involved or avoiding markets for the duration of the campaigns and waiting for the controls to pass. While the ethnographic study for this article involved regular visits to seven markets in the Suceava County from 2013 to 2019, I could see the extent to which the new regulations—in force since 2015—took hold. The required practice of producers handing out receipts to buyers was simply unheard of three years after authorities had made it binding for producers to carry "commercialization cards" (*carnete de comercializare*) uniquely issued to them based on acquiring from town halls individual "producer certificates." What clearly contradicted the initial intentions of this reform was that even traders ("intermediaries") could easily obtain such certificates and corresponding cards, since, given their peasant background, they often owned and worked the land. Most problematic for the authorities' approach was that few smallholders were happy with selling in markets, as discussed in the previous chapter; for them, selling in such markets was "dead time" and landing deals with traders was considered a success. Smallholders thus saved time and avoided the risk of altering their products.

In the neighboring Chernivets'ka Oblast', where Ukrainian authorities were also planning similar registration offensives, the abusive practices that some traders pursued were eventually dealt with differently, not through registration but by expanding market facilities. The large wholesale market in Chernivtsi was, until 2016, practically out of the reach of smallholders.

Since such markets worked by driving one's truck into a paid-for slot and then selling from the truck, some traders occupied more slots by simply keeping extra trucks parked day and night in these slots. Smallholders, who rarely owned more than one car or van, were forced to sell on the neighboring streets, and authorities often fined them or chased them away. This changed from 2016 on. Instead of registering sellers, authorities expanded the wholesale market, making more spots available and making sure that sellers—traders or producers such as smallholders—actually sold from their slots instead of only keeping them occupied.

Resisting Cooperatives

Governmental strategists and World Bank advisors blame the smallholders' reluctance to enter or establish cooperatives on a communism-induced legacy of distrust toward organizations that reminded them of collectivization's excesses. It is "a strong psychological resistance to cooperation, bred by years of abuse of the whole concept" (Gardner and Lerman 2006; Lerman and Sedik 2014; Hagedorn 2014). This language is present also in national strategy documents, claiming, in Ukraine, that the creation of cooperatives was at "risk" because of the "lack of confidence between members, no respect for the internal rules [of cooperatives], insufficient capacity of members to evolve" (Ministry of Agrarian Policy and Food of Ukraine 2015, 53). In Romania, strategy documents connect the very low figures of newly established "producer groups" in the late 2000s primarily to smallholders' "reluctance" due to "a negative perception of the character of common marketing arrangements in the shadow of communism experiences" (Romanian Ministry of Agriculture and Rural Development 2008, 97). Even the word *cooperative* allegedly reminded the post-communist smallholder population of the repressive communist cooperative (collective farm), making them reluctant to join anything using the same terminology.

As ethnographic research has shown, the local populations' memories of collective farms are far more mixed, if one explores these not only through public opinion polls mirroring wider societal discourses but through fieldwork gaining the trust of respondents and allowing them to share their thoughts more openly: While resenting the brutal communist collectivization drive, former collective farm workers valued the welfare and informal production arrangements that collective farms facilitated (Creed 1998; Hann 1993). Research has also questioned claims of smallholder "psychological resistance" to cooperatives or cooperation more generally. It has shown how even in places with fast de-collectivization and dismantling of former collective farms, such as Romania, new owners returned 43 percent of land to cooperative forms of farming in the early 1990s, with close to half of these being informal associations among relatives and neighbors, without statutes or legal basis but as of 1993 recognized by law (Sabates-Wheeler 2002; Brooks and Meurs 1994; Agarwal, Dobay, and Sabates-Wheeler 2021; Hatos 2006).

Not all negative experiences with cooperatives in my fieldwork area hark back to communism. On the northern (Ukrainian) side of the border, farmer Ivan derided a local cooperative established in his village with Western know-how and money, recalling how the money went to buy the most expensive equipment that was also very costly to maintain in good condition. As the Western combines broke down, there was no money or knowledge for repairing them. The combines stood idle and abandoned, unlike the old Soviet-era or Belarus-made equipment that smallholders usually owned or shared and often could repair themselves. However, there was plenty of informal cooperation among smallholders and the larger, entrepreneurial farmers in Ivan's community, passing on advice about market opportunities or grouping together to increase quantities for sale and thus get better deals from traders.

This grouping together thus functioned as an unregistered marketing cooperative, suggesting that much of the opposition to cooperatives had more to do with the formal requirements of setting up cooperatives than with the idea of cooperation per se. Respondents perceived the establishment of formal cooperatives as hardly addressing the power imbalances inherent in dealing as smallholders with large retail chains and with the legal-juridical conditions that states impose. Joining cooperatives requires formal registration and involves double taxation, because local laws treat cooperatives as intermediary traders to which producers sell.[2] The interviewed members of the few formally registered marketing cooperatives in Suceava County point out the fiscal regime, in particular the value-added tax (VAT) that also applies to sales within cooperatives, making it more profitable to sell directly to firms (cooperative member, dairy producer, Suceava, 2016).

In fact, cooperatives in the area are highly diverse, stretching from production cooperatives resembling communist-era collective farms (usually presented negatively by the World Bank) to cooperatives supplying various services from investment in or maintenance of infrastructure to marketing. These might, however, be registered under different juridical forms (not only as "cooperatives") or not at all, making it difficult to count them (Agarwal, Dobay, and Sabates-Wheeler 2021). More attention should go, if one wants to make inferences about the cooperative character of small-holders in the area, to cooperation aimed at local problem-solving such as managing water and irrigation and other local resources and services. This might be as relevant to smallholders as the marketing cooperatives favored by World Bank experts. On the southern (Romanian) side of the border, one member of the M. family (see chapter 5), recalled how he and other community members established a village cooperative involved in water management and irrigation. They registered it formally as an as-sociation and not as a cooperative, showing that counting only formal cooperatives but not associations can be a misleading indicator for the extent of cooperative organization. Nevertheless, the farmer understood the association as a form of cooperation. For him and other villagers, the terminological problem was hardly an obstacle, with locals able to come up with alternatives to *cooperative*, such as most often *uniune* (union), usually not even used as a substantive but as a verb in the imperative: *Să ne unim!* (Let us join together!). And on the Ukrainian side of the border, in a meeting with several villagers on the outskirts of Chernivtsi, a respondent detailed a local practice of mutual collective aid when com-munity members come together over weeks to help one fellow villager to build a house for free. She refers to this practice as *clacă* (Romanian) or *klaka* (Ukrainian), an old practice of mutual help in rural communities in Central and Eastern Europe:

> We take turns helping each other, when someone needs to build a house. One time we work for them, then the other way around. This is how young people build their houses. They measure it by counting the days [of work]. You worked this many days for me, I work so many days for you.
>
> INTERVIEWER: How do you call this practice?
>
> *Clacă*! Don't you call it the same in Romania? There are people that cannot return the favor, as they are away, and they offer money, de-pending on how many days of work they owe. . . . We all built our houses in this way. (Villager, Chernivtsi, August 2018)

While in other communities, respondents said they had not encountered such practices over the last decade, the survival of communal mutual aid nevertheless suggests that any conclusions about cooperation among smallholders or farmers should take into account the variation in cooperative behavior extending beyond formal organizations to comprise informal cooperative behavior more generally, including whether and how smallholders participate in community services and share resources informally within their local communities.

Resisting "Economic Reasoning"

The state's insistence on cooperatives shows a recurring feature of "plans to improve," claiming to know better how to go about the situation of the subjects involved than the subjects themselves.[3] This feature was similarly present in a state-backed initiative of influencing animal-rearing in the late 2010s, attempting to incentivize Romanian smallholders to abandon dairy cattle and opt instead for beef cattle. This meant relying less on raising cattle to earn money from selling milk and dairy products and instead to earn far more from selling the cattle for beef; this implied acquiring new breeds of cattle. Smallholders—or "peasant households," as authorities refer to them—hold close to half of Romania's cattle. According to the data of the last EU-wide agricultural census, some 1.3 million cattle (40 percent of the total) were held in about 900,000 "peasant households"; only 20 percent of the milk produced reached processing units, while around two-thirds was consumed in the corresponding households or most likely sold by smallholders directly and informally with or without further processing (Romanian National Statistics Institute 2011). Authorities read such data to indicate lost profits and called for raising more profitable beef cattle. This was a recommendation made in several strategies issued by the authorities, including the National Rural Development Plan for 2007–2013 drawn up with World Bank assistance (Romanian Ministry of Agriculture and Rural Development 2008), as well as the National Framework for Sustainable Development of 2014 drawn up by a presidential commission (Presidential Commission for Agricultural Development Policies 2013).

Yet in Suceava County, Romania's administrative unit with the highest number of cattle (Bogdan 2017), local authorities regard the drive for beef cattle as largely failed: in 2018 the cattle held for milk production in households still outnumbered those held by larger, "registered" farms by a factor of ten. In decline over the last decades, cattle numbers had not improved, and the county's six abattoirs (meat-processing units) struggled to find the necessary beef for production (Paiu 2018). Experts who I interviewed blamed the smallholders' "mentality," saying smallholders were too risk-averse and too resistant to change to abandon the milk cattle breeds or too unskilled in managing the paperwork necessary for receiving the higher EU subvention for beef cattle. In 2016 Romanian authorities even paid exceptionally high, one-time subventions of EUR 1,248 per animal as compared to only EUR 844 per animal for milk cattle; nevertheless, the promise of such payments did little to incentivize smallholders to adopt beef breeds. In the words of the agricultural agency's payments expert in Suceava: "We can't convince peasants to move on to beef breeds. They don't understand what's a breed. For them, a cow's simply a cow" (agricultural agency expert, Suceava, August 2016). Authorities acknowledged the high initial investment necessary for acquiring beef cattle, of at least EUR 2,000 per animal. Nevertheless, they emphasized beef production as a safe investment because of high prices for meat, especially if producing for export.

Yet the few farmers rearing beef cattle complained about the intense price fluctuations for meat due to often recurring scandals concerning its quality (Patrichi 2013). Furthermore, what experts more generally perceive as resistance to their plans and unwillingness to reason economically looks, from the perspective of smallholders, more like going on with a model of production that ensures them a *steady* flow of income. Smallholders interviewed by the author between 2015 and 2017 preferred the small but certain sums of money from selling the little milk production achieved to the possibly high but uncertain sums paid by abattoirs, which would also need to be high enough to offset the considerable investment required for buying beef cattle.

What is more, animal breeding was the responsibility of women in most households, who controlled the steady and unregistered income generated from the sale of dairy products. This income was often the only income of women in smallholder households and was earmarked for household expenditures about which, in the communities studied during fieldwork, it is typically women that decide. These expenditures include the education or the wedding of their children. Because of the formal registration it entails, the move to beef cattle would transfer this income from female household members to the male owners of the land and was perceived reluctantly by women (as a rule, land and housing were registered as the property of the male household "head").

Finally, smallholders also preferred going on with a model that requires little investment and allows feeding animals without pasturing them much. In contrast, beef cattle require not only high initial investment but also a feeding model based on pasturing (greatly affecting meat quality), and therefore access to far more land. In particular, those smallholders living in mountainous areas, characterized by even more pronounced land ownership fragmentation, held the prospects of grazing more than six cows as unrealistic, given that they did not have enough land (smallholder, Vatra Moldoviței, August 2015). Thus plans to incentivize more beef cattle breeding require a different land property structure and also more labor: whereas milk cows rarely demand extra labor force, beef-cattle rearing requires a more intensive labor force and possibly also extending the household labor force by taking up employees. When recommending that smallholders owning one or two cows transform their operations so as to reach a farm size of at least fifteen to twenty cows, the authorities' "plan to improve" consisted of a recommendation disconnected from the realities of a very fragmented ownership situation—that is, disconnected from the reality produced by land reform.

Resistance as Ignoring Official Plans

Given that official plans to improve their situation devalue or even vilify their practices and cast them as unknowing or unwilling-to-reform subjects, a common response of smallholders to state strategies vis-à-vis their operations was to simply ignore them. Such plans were not just about improving the situation of those very few it deemed as worth it but also about claiming to restore fairness by levelling the field so that all actors would face the same regulatory burden. This leads to the contradiction of claiming to support smallholders and at the same time seeking to discipline them. The expert plans to "improve" smallholder agriculture delimit which subjects stand a chance of being "improved" and target support policies toward these "improvable" subjects. The others are considered at best incapable and at worst unwilling to change and characterized by unsound economic reasoning, preventing investment and the spread of more profitable crops and breeds.

The ethnographic material for this chapter indicated that the smallholders' economic reasoning made sense of their situation not in categories of credit availability and investment returns but in terms of the monetary burden it imposed. Whether to buy up more land or develop more production for markets by having more beef cattle was likely to be evaluated from this monetary burden perspective. A household's capacity to maintain its livelihood was likely to depend on the extent to which it could minimize monetary expenses and diversify sources of income. As publicly provided services require monetized payments, the monetary burden for households was acutely felt throughout my fieldwork areas on both sides of the border (see the respondents detailing how they had secured access to jobs paying social contributions in the section "The Mixed Household and the Post-reform Poor" in the previous chapter).

More fundamentally, the governmental and World Bank strategies decrying and seeking to improve the low level or lack of commercialization of smallholder production in Romania approach smallholders as if trapped in a pre-reform realm of "traditional" or "peasant" production methods and relationships, or in the case of Ukraine, a realm that owes more to the logic of the communist collective farm than to market economy. In the latter case, strategy documents downplay the importance of land reform, decrying its lack of completion due to the introduction of the 2001 moratorium. Yet as in the neighboring post-Soviet countries (Russia, Moldova) that pursued similar programs of turning collective farm workers into land-title holders, it is difficult to understate the impact of land titling: it reversed the relationship between previous owners (farms) and tenants (workers), with the new "owners" now being the former collective farm workers and the former collective farm as the new "tenant." The owners now outnumbered the tenants, and the dependency relationship was reversed: owners owed part of their income—and most of what could be realized in the post-reform village—to the capacity of tenant farms to pay the rent. That tenancy was demonetized—with "rents" as a rule still being paid in kind today—decreased the cash needs of both owners and tenants, allowing them to at least partly retreat from the disciplining sphere of the monetized realm. This retreat—and not the presumed survival of a communist-era realm—is perhaps the biggest problem for the World Bank's discourse on land reform, showing the contradictions of land titling, intended to irreversibly dismantle the collective farm but at the same time allowing local populations more control over the monetization of livelihoods.

In Romania, official strategy documents strengthened the message about the pre-reform past by contrasting Romania's smallholder agriculture with agriculture in Austria, Italy, and France. The latter left Romania's agriculture far behind in commercialization, diversification, and development indicators. The bottom line of such comparisons was to suggest the many opportunities that the country missed because of failing to reform its vast smallholder agriculture. However, it is important to remember that as in Ukraine, the world of smallholders is to a large extent shaped less by resistance to change and unwillingness to reform than by previous and profound reforms such as de-collectivization and land titling and is paralleled by registration offensives increasing the conditionality that smallholders face if seeking to qualify for state support programs. It comes then less as a surprise that busy as they are with maintaining their livelihoods, the most common form of "resistance" among smallholders is to simply ignore the official plans to "improve" their situation.

CONCLUSIONS
The Limits of Pro-poor Land Reform

NEARLY THREE DECADES HAVE passed since countries in Eurasia started reforming their collectivized agricultural landscapes through propertizing reforms seeking to fight poverty by spurring entrepreneurship among smallholders. A glaring divergence emerged between the egalitarian focus of the initial 1990s land reform proposals and the support for commercialization on the ground since the 2000s, involving the "consolidation" of agricultural holdings and seeking to persuade "subsistence" farmers to leave agriculture altogether, including by selling their land. The specificity of the market project pursued by governments and international advisors throughout post-communist Eurasia deserves a special mention: it turned out that both the World Bank and national governments supported a very specific version of markets dominated by retail chains, while ignoring the markets that the actors of post-reform landscapes were actually engaged in.

One should see in land reforms more than what Jamie Peck (2010) called the hybridization or "mongrelization" of neoliberalism (see chapter 1), the mixing of neoliberal with other reform components, explaining in part the enduring nature of neoliberalism. Instead, the specificity of the market project behind land reform means that reform proposals changed throughout the years as long as reforms missed their rarely openly admitted initial goal: addressing poverty through increases in *formal* entrepreneurship. What changed over the years was that as formal entrepreneurship failed to materialize, there was a deepening stress on institutional aspects: the rules and regulations surrounding smallholders' activities and environments from land reform as titling to cadastral registration and the registration of "viable" units involved in the commercialization project. The land reform project turned into a project of control over populations allegedly beyond the reach of initial reforms.

This perspective about the Bank's pro-poor land reform eventually ending up, despite its initial egalitarian intentions, as a project of control helps explain the tensions in the World Bank's approach—for instance, between claiming to enact pro-poor schemes supposed to facilitate commercial smallholder farming while at the same time depicting smallholders as alien to business orientation (as outlined in chapter 6). The latter component followed from the misreading of post-communist smallholders as "subsistent" and of subsistence as an outcome of anything *but* land reform. This misreading had, by post-communism's second decade (the 2000s), much in common with post-communist elite depictions of local populations as problematic and damaging to reforms. There was little disagreement between the World Bank and national elites regarding smallholders, even in those countries that the World Bank perceived as most adverse to reforms, where governments delayed the dissolution of collective farms. National elites across the post-communist region read smallholders and their environments as "subsisting" on agriculture and as obstacles to development.

This was clear from the strategy papers enacted in Romania and Ukraine, as well as elsewhere in those post-communist countries where reforms least fitted the Russia-China land reform continuum outlined in World Bank publications (see chapter 3)—for instance, in Lithuania, Czechia, Poland, and Slovakia (Mincyte 2011; Pasieka 2012; Smith and Jehlička 2013; Smith and Rochovská 2007). In these countries, an anti-smallholder discourse was taking root even without a World Bank presence, albeit reflecting in Lithuania the influence of other Western advisors (Mincyte 2011). Furthermore, this discourse operated at a more general societal level, including not only political elites but also media and academia. It involved a self-applied dose of orientalism (Buchowski 2006), characterizing various social practices and the populations involved in them as incompatible with and problematic for Western-oriented market reforms. In brief, there was a strong tendency, articulated in elite discourses throughout post-communist Eurasia, to see local populations, from industrial and agricultural workers to rural dwellers and farmers, as both individually responsible and psychologically unfit for market economy (Ost 2005; Pasieka 2012; Varga 2011). Despite these elite actors' claim to break with communism, they, in fact, replicated the nineteenth- and early-twentieth-century anti-peasantry discourse of many socialist thinkers, starting with Karl Marx's "sack of potatoes"—and "idiocy of rural life"—metaphors for describing peasants and their lifeworlds.[1]

The Bank's advocacy for propertizing reforms briefly interrupted the prominence of such perceptions; as Andrew Coulson (2014) noted, the concern with peasant or smallholder lifeworlds was by the 1990s far more a component of World Bank–affiliated economists' discourse, such as Hans Binswanger, than of the discourse of local elites and reform planners. The Bank produced in the 1990s arguments and empirical material supporting the importance of land reform for development and poverty reduction irrespective of local smallholders' mental or psychological predispositions. It mirrored both the hopes of neoliberals such as Peter Bauer and Milton Friedman about the entrepreneurial propensities of the global poor and the agrarian "neo-populist" strand following in the footsteps of Alexander Chayanov and Amartya Sen in documenting the efficiency and rationality of production among smallholders. There was little counterevidence present in the 1990s, and the little empirical material pointed in the direction that the Bank at that time favored, in particular because of the crushing nature of Chinese and Vietnamese evidence amassing behind the Bank's studies in the 1990s. China appeared as the case where land reform had miraculously addressed poverty. Despite the increases in inequality, China's development seemed to confirm the successful prospects of market-making and commercialization among smallholders, and this reception would travel in the form of land reform advice to post-communist countries.

However, in the 2000s, the World Bank's reporting on the post-communist area would align, as discussed in chapter 2, with those elite accounts that problematized the high numbers of smallholders, and by the 2010s, it advocated policies aimed at curbing their numbers. While the market-populist arguments would survive in more global-oriented publications such as the *World Development Report* dedicated to agriculture (World Bank 2007), the alignment with local elite discourses would take place at the level of publications more directly addressing the post-communist world, country reports in particular. These reports saw smallholder agriculture as too feminized, too old, and too exposed to communism to foster the entrepreneurial promise of land reform. The Bank not only abandoned the market-populist stance it had had in the early 1990s, but it also reinterpreted the level of market creation from one involving smallholders within countries and communities as producers to one centered on the export capacity of national producers. The Bank thus achieved a phenomenal U-turn in its country reporting, away from vilifying surviving former collective farms in the 1990s to seeing them as the key to international competitiveness in the late 2000s and the 2010s. This helps identify a further tension within the Bank's land reform plans. On the one hand, the Bank's land reform perspective at least initially assumed that the *fragmentation* of private property over land would spur entrepreneurship and commercialization, as it would foster the market participation of smallholders seen in the case of China's and Vietnam's land reforms. On the other hand, from the 2000s on, the perspective changed to claiming that only property *accumulation* (or "consolidation") would allow amassing the capital needed for investments and, ultimately, export capabilities.

By the late 2000s, preference would go to accumulation over fragmentation, the latter seen as a sign of underdevelopment and as a synonym of poverty—rightly so, given that the Bank's poverty alleviation meant an exclusive focus on private property at the expense of other reform components. As such, the Bank's land reform in post-communist Eurasia replicated the nineteenth-century land reform in southeastern Europe and the land reforms after World War I in Central and Eastern Europe (Dorondel and Serban 2014; Mitrany 1951; Thompson 1993; Van Meurs 1999). These also focused exclusively on land redistribution, driving up subsistence and neglecting that peasant participation in markets as producers required far more than just land transfer.[2] Early-twentieth-century governments in Eastern Europe too sought to solve the problem of fragmentation through consolidation, encouraging the creation of larger peasant farms—or "kulak" households, to follow Mitrany's use of the Russian pejorative term—of fifteen to twenty hectares.[3]

Rather than consolidation, what post-communist smallholders required—if one is to follow the comparison with China further than World Bank reports did (chapter 2)—were investment sources and support for marketing to encourage and protect the smallholders' immediate environment as a source of investment and as the main destination of smallholder products. In the Bank's reform, the mistake was an understanding of markets as being about and emerging only from private property. This reduction of markets to property was not an error of local reform planners; as outlined in chapter 1, it was a key component of the World Bank's reform design, owing much to the impact of neoliberalism and the neoliberal criticism of the Bank's 1970s community-oriented programs. Despite the focus on smallholders, the Bank's construction of Chinese reforms was, in fact, a simplification that downplayed the statist elements in China's reform program. The fulcrum of the Bank's perspective on China still is the "land reform" component, epitomized by the household responsibility system and seen not from the systemic perspective underpinning it but from the perspective of "poor people respond[ing] to market incentives" (Ravallion and Van De Walle 2008). Even in later writings acknowledging the complexities of China's rural reforms, the Bank's perspective on China avoided admitting institutional complementarities between state and market components of reforms. It aligned the evidence from post-communist Eurasia to further rule out *any* such complementarities.

As such, China, Vietnam, and post-communist Eurasia became for the World Bank and its wider epistemic community cases from which there was hardly anything new to learn. This group of countries seemed to simply confirm "the basics" that "the ingredients for a dynamic market economy are already well-known" (Sachs and Woo 2001). The World Bank overlooked the feature of Chinese reforms that made them most interesting for non-Western settings: the fact that the Chinese had addressed poverty and spurred entrepreneurship *without* formalizing property rights and establishing formal markets for the exchange of such rights. One can, at this point, revisit the arguments of Johanna Bockman and Gil Eyal (2002) about the Eastern European "origins" of neoliberalism, showing how neoliberal intellectuals incorporated in their criticism of statism ideas about socialism developed in transnational dialogue with economists in communist countries (Bockman 2011). Eastern European and Asian "transitioning" countries enabled more than proof of communist failures. After the abandonment of communism as an economic system, they also offered the *empirical* support for the workings of neoliberal reforms even under the most unwelcoming conditions, the landscapes of collectivized agriculture. This empirical support would complement the few non-Western examples that neoliberals at that time could mobilize in defense of their cases, such as Chile; transitioning countries presented the advantage of having none of the statist elements characterizing East Asian non-communist economies, including Japan, South Korea, and Taiwan (Amsden 1989, 1994; Johnson 1999).

But there was also more to learn. Even though the World Bank used China as the central reform benchmark and source of inspiration for de-collectivizing countries, elsewhere in Eurasia land reform led to subsistence. And while this study took issue with subsistence as a concept over-simplifying the post-reform situation, the concept nevertheless reflects a pattern of productivity far below the outcome of reform in China. Proper-tizing land reform produced subsistence in the sense of self-provisioning, or growing food for self-consumption rather than for sale on markets. Self-provisioning was a massive help to impoverished local populations facing the market-making reforms of the 1990s. At the same time, land reform also offered local populations the means to slowly overcome sub-sistence by fostering an immediate environment, helping smallholders commercialize production, albeit at levels far below those of China and without preventing an exodus from agriculture. Despite the reduction in smallholder numbers throughout the 2010s, subsistence embarrassed lo-cal governments and international advisors, who depicted subsistence as evidence of insufficient reforms and not following the Chinese blueprint closely enough. They acknowledged the connection between subsistence and land reform when arguing that land reform had pro-poor objectives and effects but ignored the impact of land reform on subsistence when designing strategies for "commercializing" subsistence farms and read subsistence as an impediment to development. While the survival of the former collective farms usually carried the blame for subsistence, sub-sistence in the sense of fragmented agriculture and low productivity is, in fact, present in post-communist Eurasia irrespective of the degree of propertizing land reform and survival of collective farms. Even China-like post-communist cases that quickly dismantled collective farms were very far from smallholder productivity in China or Vietnam. The usual expla-nation for subsistence in such countries is that they were slow to facilitate the cadastral registration of land and create land markets. Furthermore, the World Bank and national governments assumed that subsistence and small-scale agriculture overlapped, and they approached subsistence less as an economic reaction to existing conditions and more as a psychological inclination, or "mentality."

However, these interpretations of subsistence overlook that based on the World Bank's reading of Chinese reforms (seeing productiv-ity increases as an outcome of transferring land from collective farms to smallholders), even the little land reform experienced in post-communist countries should have spurred productivity increases approximating developments in East Asia. In post-communist countries, too, land reform eventually took the form of dismantling collective farms and transferring land to local populations, without, however, also spurring the productivity increases that China achieved. Field research suggested a different reading: namely, that land transfers alone cannot prevent subsistence, even though land distribution did help local populations get by during the prolonged economic recession of the 1990s. To recall, fieldwork took place in the northeast of Romania (Suceava County) and Ukraine's southwestern Chernivets'ka Oblast'—two nowadays separate administrative units that once constituted the historical Bukovina region. They represent areas that in both countries stand out in how World Bank and national governments in these countries understand "subsistence": namely, agriculture predominated by extremely small holdings, allegedly subsisting on self-grown produce instead of selling it. Research followed a design using most different cases and similar outcomes. Despite the rapid dissolution of collective farms in Romania and their slow dismantlement in Ukraine, the Bukovina region featured some of the highest numbers of rural producers in each country. Despite the different approaches to land reform, areas on both sides of the border featured high numbers of small agricultural producers. And despite their large populations of subsistence farmers, both areas, north and south of the border, experienced increases in the land used as well as in the production realized by small-scale farmers.

The high incidence of subsistence in the fieldwork areas suggests that subsistence appears as an outcome of reforms concerned *only* with property rights; despite the differences, reforms in both countries featured the common trait of an exclusive focus on transferring land away from collective farms. Fieldwork further suggested that the fragmentation specific to smallholder agriculture does not impede participation in local markets, as the Chinese case also clearly illustrates. Quite to contrary, it facilitates such participation, allowing smallholders to grow incrementally by internalizing production steps (chapter 5). Such a fragmented scene of smallholders could have benefitted from a *gradual* reduction of the state's role in procurement (buying up smallholders' production), as in China. Instead, the post-communist countries across Eurasia abruptly ended state procurement, leaving smallholders alone, without credit lines, machinery, or know-how but with the enormous task of increasing production under the conditions of a largely unprecedented recession in the 1990s coupled with the introduction of a new economic system based on market relations.

A central fieldwork insight was that the rural and peri-urban poor in my sample had little to do with subsistence farming; they could not survive by consuming their own production because they too faced monetized payments, and survival was not possible without any monetized income. Poverty in the fieldwork areas had far more to do with land reform's on-the-ground results that were very different from the initial egalitarian intentions. Research on land reform had long argued that the few entrepreneurial farmers to emerge in post-communist Eurasia developed out of the collective farm by making use of the superior knowledge and access to networks and capital they had gained as former engineers or farm directors (Verdery 2003; see also Allina-Pisano 2008; Swain 2013). In the fieldwork areas under study, this rise of the former kolkhoz intelligentsia as entrepreneurial farmers was not the only source of inequality. What amplified inequalities was that the post-communist planners of land reform had not considered that collective farms had been different in land-holding size and quality and that not everyone had been a collective-farm employee or member in the past. Collective farms had differed tremendously in size and quality of their land holdings and in machinery ownership. Land reform could not compensate for these differences in endowments and thus introduced an important source of inequality *between* communities. And by turning the local population's past in the collective farm—or in Romania, their pre-communist past ownership of land—into the main criterion for distributing land, reform planners failed to consider compensation mechanisms for those without such a past, amplifying inequalities *within* communities (see also Dorondel 2016, 66). It was those households with too little or no land except for their household plots that were the poorest members of their communities, forced to commercialize household production and sell their labor to meet their family's monetary needs.

Fieldwork findings imply that despite the manifest interest of international organizations in the protection and empowerment of vulnerable groups overrepresented in rural populations, such as women and the elderly, the effects of some of the reforms enacted are difficult to reconcile with the notion of empowerment, if understood as increasing the rights of and resources at the disposal of vulnerable groups in rural producer households. To take the example of women, while the study found little to prove that land reform does by itself negatively affect the rights and resources of women, some of the policies enacted to deal with the land fragmentation produced by land reform suggest that there were important consequences for women. "Commercializing" measures, aimed at incentivizing farmers to register and sell more of their production, were found to shift monetary resources within the households away from women, because some of the money gained from informal production passes through the hands of women. Furthermore, much of the informal retail trade with agricultural goods was also run by women in the Ukrainian fieldwork area, constituting an important additional source of income.

The small amount of income and food generated by the little land that rural households generally possess allowed the women in the fieldwork area to take up employment in low-paid "light industry" jobs (textiles or food), jobs usually avoided by or unavailable to men. Reforms aiming at overcoming land fragmentation by reducing the availability of land in the countryside would greatly influence the capacity of women to take up such jobs or have such incomes because the various sources of a household's incomes are interrelated. Offensives to incentivize smallholders out of subsistence and agriculture risk diminishing the smallholders' capacity to access the few—and poorly paid—jobs available to them in their communities or nearby cities. If smallholder households give up agriculture and self-provisioning, they require incomes above what local employers pay, and even more would be forced to leave their communities. The broader consequences of institutional reforms on the incomes of "subsisting" populations and vulnerable groups is thus an important area of future research, exploring how such reforms touch upon the arrangements prevalent between producer households and broader communities. Equally important is research on how endowments in such communities—from land and the social practices around it to the social environments of diverse producers and traders—facilitate the operation of formal, export-oriented sectors of the economy, such as the textile industry employing women in this study's fieldwork areas.

A further fieldwork insight was that smallholders and entrepreneurial farmers hardly operated in separate formal and informal halves of the economy, and the success of entrepreneurial farmers depended on interacting with smallholders. Entrepreneurial farmers relied on smallholders to gain access to land and sell them their production; other entrepreneurial farmers had grown by collecting and selling the meat production achieved in smallholder households. Thus, some entrepreneurial farmers were thriving precisely because smallholders engaged in livestock rearing for their own consumption or limited commercialization and had not left agriculture or their local communities. That is, they were thriving because "subsistence"—or self-provisioning—had kept at least parts of the local population involved in agriculture. Entrepreneurial farmers further benefitted from tenure arrangements with smallholders. Where land was scarce, such arrangements usually took the form of the entrepreneurial farmers paying some one and a half tons of grain per hectare to smallholders each year. They preferred this arrangement to buy up land because payment would not take place in money, and thus access to land would not be monetized, a finding that also applies to the areas where land was abundant because of abandonment.

World Bank experts have long argued that such tenure arrangements are detrimental to smallholders and that "land markets," the smallholders' "freedom" to sell their land, would bring them higher incomes. But the argument overlooks that soaring land prices might hurt the few entrepreneurial farmers to have emerged while incentivizing corporate farms to opt out of the "symbiotic" arrangements with local smallholders. There is a tendency in analyses of World Bank experts and government strategists to see subsistence farmers and their peri-urban and rural communities in isolation from the wider economy. But the trick for policy makers will be their capacity to recognize endowments as such, rather than as obstacles to development, even if such endowments are rooted in the informal economy. While proponents of titling reforms present the informal economy as a response to an overregulating state, sociological and anthropological work has found the informal economy to be a reaction to market-making projects, which also involve substantial regulation (Portes and Schauffler 1993; Hart 2006; Maloney 2003; Centeno and Portes 2006). In both Eastern European countries on which this book's ethnographic part has focused (Romania and Ukraine), the informal economy developed together with official markets. Rather than battle informality, governments and international advisors should recognize how it contributes to the resilience of local populations.

Fieldwork findings suggested a different logic of smallholder farming than usually implied in the analyses of national governments and international organizations. Despite the noneconomic reasoning usually imputed to smallholders in the region, success in economic activities depended on minimizing monetary expenses. Most smallholders did monetize at least parts of their production and therefore engaged with markets, yet they usually conditioned increases in marketed production on minimizing monetized inputs. Smallholders and entrepreneurial farmers even more acutely felt this reality. In post-communist Eurasia, they still were—just as outlined by Mitrany (1951) in his contrast of western and eastern farmers in the early twentieth century—predominantly family farmers, and monetary needs came from both the farm and the family household. They came from the former, because even a self-sufficient farmer producing most inputs on the farm would still have to pay for energy, from gas to electricity; they came from the latter, because household needs included such expenses as schooling for children, medical care, and accessing social security. The household thus further enforced the smallholders' economic reasoning and monetary needs, although it is often depicted as problematic for farmers since it incentivizes them to spend their incomes on household needs rather than farm investments. But the household was virtually inseparable from the farm; it was its main production site and labor source in the case of smallholders and even most entrepreneurial farmers in my sample. Irrespective of the degree of commercialization, the monetization of household and farm needs thus forced smallholders to seek monetized incomes to meet those needs.

Subsistence as poverty and isolation due to self-consumption thus appears to be a misnomer obscuring the extent to which local populations in the post-reform landscape actually have to engage with the wider economy and earn a monetized income. Rather than assume commercialization as an exception, fieldwork supported the expectation that commercialization and smallholder presence on local markets are, in fact, widespread, if one opens the concept to include both formal and informal markets and to speak of commercialization also in the case of those households that sell less than half of their produce. Rather than approaching subsistence and commercialization in categorical terms divided by the cutoff point of selling half of the production, this study argues for researching how smallholders increase quantities sold irrespective of the subsistence cutoff point. Informal traders represented a crucial presence in the smallholders' immediate environment, and fieldwork identified several ways how they supported commercialization among smallholders. First, smallholders met traders in wholesale markets once the combined financial resources gained from reinvesting profit and waged work allowed them to transport produce from farm to market. Because traders also compete among themselves, smallholders found more buyers for their produce on wholesale markets. And as these buyers bought large quantities, they allowed smallholders to save time, because few smallholders could afford the time needed for selling produce directly to end consumers. Second, traders also specialized in certain roles, such as wholesaler or retailer. Retailers preferred buying the produce from markets rather than farm-gates and from producers rather than wholesalers. In periodic and wholesale markets, producers (including smallholders) met such trader-retailers and kept them as customers at a larger profit also for themselves. Thus traders and small retailers offered smallholders cash inflows that represented an important source of investment in cheap, secondhand machinery. The smallholder's own labor or family labor was then further "invested" to internalize the maintenance and repair of machinery. Finally, production increases resulting from machinery use then enlarged the land under exploitation, usually by leasing from other members of their community.

This take on small-scale agriculture contradicts the reading of subsistence in World Bank and national government strategy papers, but not the data. The data confirms that a substantial number of those referred to as "subsistence farmers" engage with markets, as the World Bank readily admits, even though it dismisses such involvement as informal and does not look into it further. Ukraine exemplifies this point. Because of the land-sale moratorium, Ukraine was for the World Bank a prime example of the link between insufficient titling land reform and high incidence of subsistence. But as early as 2001, a World Bank, OECD, and Ukrainian government strategy paper readily admitted that around 33 percent of households were "grow[ing] for sale" even in a context of acute economic hardship at the beginning of the 2000s (World Bank, 2004, 92). Household production has increased ever since. By the mid-2010s, some 20 percent of Ukrainian small-scale farmers were, in fact, selling *most* of what they produced and represented small-scale "commercially oriented" unregistered farmers (Ministry of Agrarian Policy and Food of Ukraine, 2015). Research should have focused on studying these 20 percent, since they had achieved commercialization in the absence of the land markets that by that time the World Bank portrayed as crucial for entrepreneurship.

One of the few but influential volumes on subsistence, constituting a major source in defining *subsistence* in World Bank and FAO studies, starts by claiming that subsistence is somewhat of a myth (Abele and Frohberg,

2003a). In its conceivably purest form, in which people "subsist" based on the food they produce, without any other sources of income, it is at best a marginal phenomenon (Heidhues and Brüntrup, 2003). Despite that warning, international organizations and national governments continue to read smallholders as practicing "subsistence" farming and devise programs to "pull them out" of it and bring them to "markets." In their practical formulations, these programs translate in major registration and monetization offensives for the sake of "commercialization," the antipode of "subsistence." But the type of commercialization that addresses subsistence is about more than easing the small-scale actors' access to formal markets. It is about increasing the monetization of households and forcing the adoption of crops and breeds that meet increased monetary needs. Thus, markets are not just supposed to help small-scale farmers access investments and credit and grow by transferring land. They should also discipline a sector often perceived as alien to "business orientation" and owing its existence not to markets but to surviving past structures such as the former collective (now corporate) farm, as well as to its "subsistence mentality." One needs, however, to question the utility of subsistence for capturing the realities of post-reform populations. Subsistence is not a mentality, to the extent one sees in it a fragmented landscape of diverse agricultural producers ranging from self-provisioning households to commercializing smallholders. Instead, this fragmented landscape is part of a resilient environment of actors, from day laborers to informal traders and entrepreneurial farmers, too poor to access the formal economy or too exposed to unequal power relations in formal contractual arrangements and therefore seeking to engage with markets on their terms.

List of Respondents in Romania and Ukraine 2013–2019

TABLE A.1. List of respondents in Romania and Ukraine 2013–2019.

Activity	Locality (county in Romania, raion in Ukraine)	Farm size (hectares)	Product or activity	Years in activity / background / observations
		Romania		
Wholesaler / retailer, Burdujeni	Suceava	-	Wholesaler / retailer	10–15 / kolkhoz merchandiser
Smallholder, Sucevița	Suceava	1	Bees; honey products	20 / former factory engineer
Wholesaler / retailer	Suceava	<1		1 / former meat-processing plant merchandiser
Farmer, Horodnic	Suceava	<5	Sheep-rearing; grew from 5 to 300 sheep (2013)	12 / n.a.
Farmer, Burdujeni	Suceava	60	Livestock: cattle (main activity; some 30 animals, 2013-15), supplements income with poultry-rearing	2nd generation or more (peasant family) / blue-collar worker in Italy, former wholesaler
Farmer, Moldovița	Suceava	5	Some 5 cattle (2013), down from a maximum of 12 (son owns 8)	2nd generation or older / former village mayor, head of producer organization
Farmer, Moldovița	Suceava	10	19 cattle (2013–15)	2nd generation or older (peasant family) / started farm in 2011 after selling father's forest
Smallholder and wholesaler, Vârfu Câmpului	Botoșani	2.5	Wholesaler / retailer of fresh produce (vegetables in 2013, strawberries in 2015)	Business management graduate
Farmer / processor, Sadova	Suceava	30	35 cattle (2013); retailer (owns diary store)	Former communist-era employee (collector) of dairy-processing plant

Role/Location	County	Ha	Production	Notes
Farmer, Fălticeni	Suceava	15	Fruit (apples) production	10 / former communist-era agricultural research farm employee (pomiculture engineer)
Farmer / processor, Fălticeni	Suceava	50	Fruit (apples) and juice production	15 / former communist-era agricultural research farm employee (pomiculture engineer); grew from 3ha initially to 50ha in 2015
Farmer, Fălticeni	Suceava	20	Fruit (apples) production	22 / former communist-era agricultural research farm employee (pomiculture engineer)
Farmer, Buneşti	Suceava	9	Fruit (apples)	12 / former bookkeeper
Farmer / processor, Iaslovăţ	Suceava	8	Vegetables; pickle packaging and export	2nd generation (peasant family) / former restaurant employee, small-shop owner
Ministry of Agriculture employee, Suceava	Suceava	-	-	Assists farmers in setting up producer organizations
Farmer, Bălcăuţi/ Balkivtsi	Suceava	1800	Grain, potatoes	2nd generation (peasant family) / started in 1993 from 0.5 hectares
Ministry of Agriculture employee, Suceava	Suceava	-	-	Assists farmers in accessing EU grants
Farmer, Dumbrăveni	Suceava	65	Livestock (50 cattle, 130 sheep; 2012–15: 10,000 poultry)	25 / former kolkhoz veterinarian; also runs metal fabrication shop
Farmer, Câmpulung Moldovenesc	Suceava	175	Livestock (40 cattle, 500 sheep); retailer (owns dairy store)	25 / former kolkhoz animal husbandry engineer; dairy collector for communist-era dairy-processing plant

(*continued*)

Activity	Locality (county in Romania, raion in Ukraine)	Farm size (hectares)	Product or activity	Years in activity / background / observations
Smallholder and worker, Dorna Arini	Suceava	2.3	Livestock (13 goats); also lives from picking berries and mushrooms	10 / also part-time employee in a barbershop
Farmer / wholesaler, Fundu Moldovei	Suceava	26	8 cattle; buys and resells milk from other farmers	2nd generation or more (peasant/ shepherd family); former dairy collector for post-communist dairy-processing plant
Head of producer organization, Vatra Dornei	Suceava	-	-	2nd generation or more (peasant family)
Farmer, Burdujeni	Suceava	23	86 cattle in 2015	2nd generation or more (peasant family); former blue-collar worker in auto-repair shop
Farmer, Bursuceni	Suceava	7	Vegetables	22 / 2nd generation or more (peasant family)
Employee of the State Statistics Office	Suceava	-	-	-
Farmer, Campulung Moldovenesc	Suceava	105	Livestock (40 cattle, 70 sheep in 2015)	2nd generation or more (peasant family) in area with no collectivization
Farmer / retailer Grănicești	Suceava	120	60 cattle in 2015; sells in wet markets	22 / former kolkhoz director
Head of Beef Cattle Producer Organization, Suceava	Suceava	-	-	-

Farmers, husband and wife	Suceava	10	Livestock rearing (200 sheep)	2nd generation or more (peasant family); always worked as shepherds

Ukraine

Retailer, Myhove	Vyzhnytsia	1	Fruit and vegetable sales	Former communist-era forestry engineer
Processor / wholesaler, Myhove	Vyzhnytsia	2	Wood-processing	Former communist-era forestry engineer
Farmer, Stanivtsi	Hlyboka	5	Livestock (5 cattle, 5 pigs, 100 poultry)	n.a.
Nonagricultural worker, Ropcha	Storozhynets	<1	Construction worker	Former blue-collar worker at spirits-producing plant
Farmer, Ropcha	Storozhynets	1	80 sheep	25 / former policeman
Farmer, Dranytsia	Novoselytsia	60	Wheat, corn, and soy	15 / university graduate (law)
Farmer and processor, Dranytsia	Novoselytsia	800	Sunflower oil-extraction; livestock (1,000 sheep)	20 / former wholesaler
Farmer/ meat processor and wholesaler, Dranytsia	Novoselytsia	30	Corn, soy, livestock (pigs)	20 / former meat-processing plant worker
Local politician, Chernivtsi	Chernivtsi	-	-	No agricultural background; long-term head of administrative subdivision
Vice-governor, Chernivtsi region	Chernivtsi	-	-	-
Farmer and retailer, Nedoboivtsi	Khotyn	27	Fruit	Businessman with no local kolkhoz background, local politician
Farmer	Khotyn	2,500	Orchards, grain, soy (took over local bankrupt kolkhoz)	Businessman with no local kolkhoz background, former local politician

(*continued*)

Activity	Locality (county in Romania, raion in Ukraine)	Farm size (hectares)	Product or activity	Years in activity / background / observations
Company manager, Boyan	Novoselytsia	205	Soy (180 hectares)	Company initially grew in wholesale and retail, and in construction; agriculture is a side investment
Farmer, Boyan	Novoselytsia	100	Fruit (apples)	10 / initially large-scale wholesaler, with a 14-truck fleet (specializing in imports)
Farmer, Boyan	Novoselytsia	87	Soy, wheat	Former kolkhoz chief agronomist
Farmer, Banyliv	Vyzhnytsia	900	Soy, wheat, corn, other cereals (in the past also owned 300 cattle)	Former kolkhoz veterinarian
Farmer, Banyliv	Vyzhnytsia	22	Potatoes, grain	Son of kolkhoz workers
Nonagricultural worker, Mamaivtsi	Kitsman'	0.5	Potatoes	Guards the premises of the former kolkhoz director's farm
Company director, Orshivtsi	Kitsman'	3,200	Cereals (predominantly soy and wheat), 1,000 cattle	Former kolkhoz director; sold the kolkhoz in 2008 to Svarog, a "megafarm" (90,000 hectares in Western Ukraine)
Farmer, Banyliv	Vyzhnytsia	0.5	Potatoes	Construction worker in Kyiv, makes an additional USD 1,000/year from agriculture
Trader, Banyliv	Vyzhnytsia	<1	Wholesale: cereals, vegetables	1 / former construction worker in Spain

Farmer, Lukivtsi	Vyzhnytsia	70	Cereals (soy)	10 years / former kolkhoz lathe operator, later earned income from selling processed wood
Nonagricultural worker, Sloboda-Komarivtsi	Vyzhnytsia	3	Leases all land to the Mriya "mega-farm"	Medical assistant in nearby town
Farmer, Brusnytsia	Kitsman'	15	Grain and soy (300 pigs in 2003–2010)	Former head of the kolkhoz meat-processing shop
Businessman, Berehomet	Vyzhnytsia	1.5	Soy	Former kolkhoz director, currently owns several businesses, including a hotel
Head of the Agricultural Unit of the State Statistics Office, Chernivtsi	Chernivtsi	-	-	-
Farmer, Chereshenka	Vyzhnytsia	1,000	300 cattle	17 / former kolkhoz director (in another region)
Family of retail sellers, Kolinkivtsi and Chernivtsi	Hertsa	<1	Sell production from own orchard	Former kolkhoz workers, now selling in the Chernivtsi bazaar
Legal expert	Chernivtsi	-	Prepares land lease contracts between smallholders and large agribusiness	
Farmer, Valia Kuzmina	Hlyboka	27	Sells hay to local population (as livestock fodder)	Former kolkhoz machine shop employee
Farmer, Molodiia	Hlyboka	200	Soy, grain, maize	Former local meat trader, no kolkhoz past
Farmer, Kostychany	Novoselytsia	150	Soy, grain, livestock	Local mayor, former border security officer

(continued)

Activity	Locality (county in Romania, raion in Ukraine)	Farm size (hectares)	Product or activity	Years in activity / background / observations
Farmer, Voloka	Hlyboka	60	Soy	Former kolkhoz worker
Mayor, Valia Kuzmina	Hlyboka	-	-	Former police officer
Smallholder, Ostrytsia	Hertsa	< 2	(leases land to agribusiness)	Former kolkhoz engineer
Day worker, Valia Kuzmina	Hlyboka	<1	Grows vegetables, keeps livestock	No kolkhoz past
Day worker, Valia Kuzmina	Hlyboka	<1	Grows vegetables, keeps livestock	No kolkhoz past
Artisan (mason), Valia Kuzmina	Hlyboka	0.5-2	Grows vegetables, keeps livestock	No kolkhoz past
Smallholder, Valia Kuzmina	Hlyboka	<2	Grows food for self-consumption	Former kolkhoz worker
Farmer, Valia Kuzmina	Hlyboka	27	Keeps household, garden, livestock (farmer husband)	No kolkhoz past (marries before joining formal labor market)
Smallholder and seller on informal markets, Ostrytsia	Hertsa	0.5–1	Sells vegetables and fruits	10 / retired industrial worker, now sells farm products informally
Teacher and smallholder, Ostrytsia	Hertsa	2	Teacher, grows animals and vegetables for self-consumption	
Industrial worker, Ostrytsia	Hertsa	0	Construction worker, lives in village, works informally in Chernivtsi and Germany	
Industrial worker and smallholder, Ostrytsia	Hertsa	0.5	Grows animals, vegetables, and fruit for self-consumption	16 / Gave up commercial farming and took up industrial employment for roughly EUR 150/ month

Notes

Note on Transliteration

Throughout this book, I use the Library of Congress system for transliterating Cyrillic Ukrainian source material.

Introduction

1. As outlined in this book, although widely cited in the international organizations' literature on subsistence, many of their warnings regarding the use (and abuse) of the subsistence concept were overlooked and replaced precisely by readings of subsistence as driven by a noneconomic "mentality" or "psychology" (see chapter 6).

Chapter 1

1. Narratives represent "sequence[s] of causally linked events and their underlying sources, unfolding through time" (Akerlof and Snower 2016, 58). In times of increasing uncertainty, they represent important "coordination mechanisms that facilitate and channel decisions over multiple periods and thus have a long-lasting impact" (Boyer 2018). They "sustain attractive but frequently unfounded stories that drive markets," influence political agendas (Boyer 2018, 41), or, as in the case of this study, attempt to influence poverty reduction policies worldwide (see also chapter 2).

2. Identifying the World Bank's positions on land reform involved the selection of a core group of World Bank experts working on land reform (see page 19) and

consulting the bank's oral interviews database as well as analyzing their and other World Bank publications from 1972 to 2003 (the years that cover most World Bank publications on the topic), including papers, reports, and book-length volumes, published by this team in World Bank outlets and economics journals. The oral interviews were used for reconstructing the intellectual climate within and around the Agricultural Department by the time Anne Krueger, a notable neoliberal, became the World Bank's vice-president for research in 1982. The selected interviews cover staff members in the Agriculture and Rural Development Department (Hans Binswanger, Uma Lele, John von Pischke, Stephen Eccles, Willi Wapenhans, and Leif Christoffersen) as well as Montague Yudelman, Mahbub ul-Haq, Hollis Chenery, Anne Krueger, and Ernest Stern. These led the bank's Agricultural Department (Yudelman, director of the Agriculture and Rural Development Department, 1973–1984), the bank's research activities (Chenery, vice-president from 1972 to 1982, and Krueger, vice-president from 1982 to 1987), policy (ul-Haq, 1972–1982), and operations (Stern, 1980–1987, senior vice-president of operations, "the most powerful staff position at the bank" [Wolf 2019]).

3. These landmark publications reflect earlier work (Binswanger, Deininger, and Feder 1993, 1995; Binswanger and Deininger 1993; Binswanger and Rosenzweig 1986; Feder 1985).

4. There were several publications preparing this argument (e.g., Feder 1987, 1988; Deininger and Binswanger 1999).

5. An exception is a paper by Arnold Harberger (1970) that expressed understanding for the landless in Latin America and saw land reform as a solution to poverty.

6. It was organized by the Fraser Institute and its then director Michael A. Walker, which a decade later would launch the Economic Freedom Index and in 2015 would launch with the Cato Institute the Human Freedom Index (Slobodian 2019). The 1986 conference would see an early version of Douglass North's seminal "Institutions and Economic Growth: An Historical Introduction," a paper published in 1989 that would form the basis of his 1990 volume on institutions, new institutionalism's most important work. The full conference proceedings are available as an edited volume (Walker 1988), and page numbers in this section refer to this volume.

7. Krueger was associated with a brand of neoliberalism called New Political Economy, responsible for producing the theoretical approach behind structural adjustment policies (Dasgupta 1997).

8. To offer a representative statement: "The current system of land rights in Thailand developed in response to the increased benefits of defining property rights in land induced by the commercialization of agriculture and appreciation in the agricultural terms of trade" (Feder and Feeny 1991).

9. This argument parallels similar earlier sociological arguments by Barrington Moore (1993 [1966]) and Theda Skocpol (1979).

10. The World Bank's oral history interview material documents Krueger's intolerance of staff members contradicting her views (see also Stein 2008, 37); see the recollections of John Lewis and Devesh Kapur (Yudelman 1991).

11. More generally, work on the reception of Ester Boserup's theories at the World Bank mentions the names of authors involved in landmark publications (Turner and Fischer-Kowalski 2010).

12. According to the bank's oral history interview with Binswanger (Binswanger 1991).

13. Bazbauers (2018, 77) calls this the "fusion" between poverty alleviation and neoliberalism.

14. Krueger's perception explains, according to the interview with Uma Lele (2005), why Krueger read Lele's work as criticism of Yudelman's policy preferences and promoted her.

Parts of this chapter have appeared in a modified form in Mihai Varga, 2020, "Poverty Reduction through Land Transfers? The World Bank's Titling Reforms and the Making of 'Subsistence' Agriculture," *World Development* 135 (November 2020), article 105058.

Chapter 2

1. From a neoliberal perspective, the advice for post-communist countries would have been to privatize their state-owned farms; this is exactly what several countries, mostly in East Central Europe, did (Swinnen and Rozelle 2006). However, in most post-Soviet countries the World Bank supported throughout its landmark publications the far more ambitious proposal of breaking up the former collective farms entirely and pursuing an egalitarian land reform that would turn rural dwellers who worked on collective farms into property-owning farmers.

2. Michael Lipton, Scott Rozelle, and Johan Swinnen worked only briefly at the World Bank (Swinnen as lead economist) but participated in authoring some of the bank's reports. Scott Rozelle is the co-author of one of the best-known World Bank reports on poverty reduction in China (Nyberg and Rozelle 1999).

3. Other publications with stocktaking ambitions, written not by lead economists or advisors but by World Bank consultants, are also taken into account if they deal with land reform in communist and post-communist countries—for example, the work of anthropologist Nora Dudwick (Dudwick, Fock, and Sedik 2007). The central stocktaking document is the bank's *World Development Report* (WDR) *2008*, the second WDR devoted to agriculture over a period of twenty-five years (World Bank 1982, 2007). Many of these documents are authored by some of the World Bank's most important experts on poverty and agricultural economics,

including such economists behind "landmark" publications as Klaus Deininger (lead economist), and Johan Swinnen, Csaba Csáki, and Zvi Lerman. Csáki and Lerman served as long-time World Bank advisors; Swinnen had only a brief stint at the Bank. Stocktaking publications include the following: Abele and Frohberg 2003b; Dudwick, Fock, and Sedik 2007; Lerman 2017; Lerman and Schreinemachers 2005; Lerman and Sutton 2008; Satana, Törhönen, and Adlington 2014; World Bank 2004a; Möllers et al. 2016.

4. The World Bank's involvement in both countries peaked between 2007 and 2009. Throughout those years, the Bank assisted Romania in drafting the legislation to help it meet the requirements of the EU's Common Agricultural Policy (World Bank 2008) by "improving the security of land property rights and the functioning of rural land markets." In 2009, it successfully "pressured," together with the IMF, the Republic of Tajikistan to pass a presidential decree ensuring the transferability of land titles (Lerman 2017). The incident is detailed also in the cables of the US embassy in Dushanbe, available from WikiLeaks and stating that "the draft decree appears to have been prepared in its entirety by [World Bank consultant] Saavalainen" ("Agricultural Reforms in Tajikistan: More Manure?," telegram, WikiLeaks, July 15, 2009, https://wikileaks.org/plusd/cables/09DUSHANBE846_a.html).

5. For criticism, see Clarke et al. (2000) and Southworth (2006).

6. See Csaki and Lerman (1997); for contrasting conclusions on subsistence to the extent it does not support collective farms, see Lipton (2009, 217).

7. All structural adjustment documentation available from the World Bank for the late 1990s and early 2000s initially praises Tajikistan for its reforms: 1998 and 2001 documentation praises the country's privatizing reforms at length, especially the new Land Code, which allows the "unrestricted transfer and inheritability of land access rights" (World Bank 1998, 5). The 2004 report, however, claims that the country is struggling with implementation issues and notices that privatization hardly works in raising the incomes of agricultural workers (World Bank 2004b).

As for Moldova, the 2001 report for a structural adjustment loan positively recommends the loan after noting: "Agriculture: Required number of farms were restructured, and Government established legal basis for land tradability. Most state and collective farms have entered privatization process and the process has been completed through land titles distribution for over 40% of agricultural land in Moldova. In preparation for SAC [Structural Adjustment Credit], large agro-processing SOEs [state-owned enterprises] were included in the privatization plan. Adequate legal framework to implement land reform was established in 1999. However, the number of registered post-privatization land transactions remains very low. Privatization of large agro-processors was behind schedule, but majority of restructured firms were finally sold. Privatization: Progress was made in accelerating sale of businesses and land plots, although many transactions occurred later than envisioned. Interest from foreign investors has been very low, mainly due to unattractive properties and failure by the government to establish a positive environment for investment" (World Bank 2000a, 1).

8. This is a common finding in sociological, anthropological, and political economy literature on post-communist agricultural transitions (Allina-Pisano 2004, Rona-Tas 1994, Verdery 2003).

9. In an analysis of three post-Soviet countries that achieved relatively fast individualization and abolishment of collective farms (Armenia, Azerbaijan, and Georgia), Zvi Lerman equates agricultural growth with higher incomes for rural populations and argues that smallholders in these countries are better off than smallholders in Russia, Ukraine, and Kazakhstan as they achieve higher commercialization rates. Yet while commercialization rates (percentages of households that sell production) are higher in these countries (60–87 percent) than in Ukraine (60 percent), only in Ukraine do commercial households reach 50 percent sales of their production (Lerman 2006, 120). As in other World Bank reports and papers, here too the argument is that since commercialization increases with farm size, proper pro-poor policies need not end with land transfers, but need to "overcome land fragmentation and smallness" (Lerman 2006, 120; for a cautious note about "consolidation," see Lipton 2009, 242).

Parts of this chapter appeared in a modified form in Mihai Varga, 2020, "Poverty Reduction through Land Transfers? The World Bank's Titling Reforms and the Making of 'Subsistence' Agriculture," *World Development* 135 (November 2020), article 105058.

Chapter 3

1. Data from Swinnen and Rozelle (2006, 20).

2. Thus, in presenting Poland as a successful case from which Moldova can learn, the World Bank document equates the decreases in small-scale farm numbers with the "professionalization of the sector," without, however, presenting data on whether Polish small-scale farms indeed "professionalized" (Möllers et al. 2016, 43) and without discussing the limited generalizability of the Polish case given that communist Poland's attempt at collectivizing agriculture failed. The Polish study cited in the document explains the decrease in small-scale farming as "due to the halving of the number of small farms with up to 1 hectare UAA [utilized agricultural area] withdrawing from production" (Potori, Chmieliński, and Karwat-Wózniak 2014, 12). What Potori et al. argue is that in Poland there were 14–18 percent increases in the numbers of farms with 30 to 50 hectares and over 50 hectares between 2002 and 2010, or farms that by no means qualify as "small-scale." If the

Polish case has a story to tell, then it is one of expanding or consolidating large and middle-sized farms and of small-scale farms disappearing rather than entering the commercial sector.

3. Furthermore, subsuming millions of smallholders under the term *subsistence* and reducing the diversity of their life situations to one particular trait is reminiscent of the discourse on "peasants," criticized long ago for failing to admit "complexity" and the "degrees of ambivalence" involved in peasant livelihoods (Shanin 1982).

Chapter 4

1. Pierre Souchon (2014) documents this argument. In Romania, state authorities actively pursue a policy of excluding small farms from various payments in order to reduce their number (Knowles 2011).

2. This latter formulation is indebted to the sustainable livelihoods approach (De Haan 2012, 347).

3. There were, however, enormous production decreases if one compares the 2010s to the late 1980s. Even in 2017 production stood at only 52 percent of the 1990 figure (Ukrstat 2018, 40).

4. Agro-holdings are very large corporate actors achieving the vertical integration of various supply chain elements, from former collective farms to processing and exporting facilities. Although not the case of Mriya and Svarog, Ukraine's largest agro-holdings even include retailing facilities.

5. As a confirmation of this figure, the state authority administering EU agricultural subventions registered 50,537 requests for subventions, the highest in the country (State 2015). The total figure of farms was far larger, as not all farms qualify for subventions; some fall below the EU requirements regarding economic size, while some—and most of those included in this study—shun the controls entailed by registration. In fact, at the time of fieldwork some 71 percent of small farms in Romania (3 million holdings) were excluded from subventions as they were too small (Knowles 2011; Tudor 2015).

6. With the exception of the Sums'ka and Chernihivs'ka regions (and leaving out the two war-torn regions in the east), all other regions saw increases in household production numbers as compared to 1990 and 2000.

Parts of this chapter appeared in Mihai Varga, 2016, "Small Farms' Survival and Growth: Making Investments Despite Credit Constraints." *Sociologia Ruralis* 57 (S1):641–60; and Mihai Varga, 2017, "Cash Rather Than Contract: The Re-emergence of Traditional Agrifood Chains in Post-Communist Europe," *Journal of Rural Studies* 53:58–67.

Chapter 5

1. This aspect is a key element of Szelényi's (1988) theory of socialist entrepreneurship; future rural entrepreneurs would "park" in such jobs, "waiting" for market conditions to be ripe for entrepreneurial activity but also for entrepreneurial knowledge to build up.

2. See the work of Marie-France Garcia Parpet (2008) for a description of this process in France; one possible exception is Italy (D'Amico 2015).

3. For a similar discussion distinguishing between traders of various sizes and how fragmentation affects the power of traders, see Jonge (1993).

4. For the importance of knowledge for local traders in Southeast Asia, see Jonge (1993); Scott (1972, 97–98).

Parts of this chapter appeared as Mihai Varga, 2019, "Resistant to Change? Smallholder Response to World Bank-Sponsored 'Commercialisation' in Romania and Ukraine," *Canadian Journal of Development Studies/Revue canadienne d'études du développement* 40 (4):528–45.

Chapter 6

1. These documents are also issued in English, enabling linguistic comparisons. In Romanian, a cognate of the English *subsistence* (*subzistenţă*) is used, while in Ukrainian, *subsistence* translates as "production predominantly for one's own use" (*produktsiya perevazhno dlya vlasnoho spozhyvannya*).

2. Lerman and Sedik (2014) acknowledge the problem of double taxation and so do national strategy documents, promising to address this problem, but the communist psychological legacy receives most explanatory power in these accounts.

3. This qualifies as what James C. Scott (1998) described as a "high modernist" perspective, devaluing local knowledge as unscientific and therefore illegitimate.

Conclusions

1. These would continue with Vladimir Lenin's and Eugen Varga's preoccupation with the peaceful "conversion" of peasants (Mitrany, 1951, 25, 209) and the forceful approaches called for by Leon Trotsky and Josef Stalin (Viola et al. 2005, 14).

2. In the words of David Mitrany (1951, 102), writing about post-WWI reforms: "Yet none of the governments concerned, though one might except that of Czechoslovakia, took steps to make the best of the new division of the land. They displayed an astonishing neglect of agriculture and its workers. The new peasant proprietors, except for a small minority, had not the means to acquire animals or implements or fertilizers; they were given neither credits nor guidance to replace the earlier compulsion."

3. Communists would later use arbitrary definitions for identifying "kulaks" (Kligman and Verdery 2011, Viola 1987).

References

Abele, Steffen, and Klaus Frohberg. 2003a. "Introduction." In *Subsistence Agriculture in Central and Eastern Europe: How to Break the Vicious Circle?*, edited by Steffen Abele and Klaus Frohberg, i–vii. Halle (Saale): Leibniz Institute of Agricultural Development in Transition Economies.

———, eds. 2003b. *Subsistence Agriculture in Central and Eastern Europe: How to Break the Vicious Circle?* Halle (Saale): Leibniz Institute of Agricultural Development in Transition Economies.

Abrahams, Ray, ed. 1996. *After Socialism: Land Reform and Social Change in Eastern Europe.* Providence, RI, and Oxford, UK: Berghahn Books.

Agarwal, Bina, Krisztina Melinda Dobay, and Rachel Sabates-Wheeler. 2021. "Revisiting Group Farming in a Post-socialist Economy: The Case of Romania." *Journal of Rural Studies* 81:148–58.

Aistara, Guntra A. 2009. "Maps from Space: Latvian Organic Farmers Negotiate Their Place in the European Union." *Sociologia Ruralis* 49 (2):132–50.

Akerlof, George A., and Dennis J. Snower. 2016. "Bread and Bullets." *Journal of Economic Behavior & Organization* 126:58–71.

Akram-Lodhi, A. Haroon. 2008. "(Re)imagining Agrarian Relations? The World Development Report 2008: Agriculture for Development." *Development and Change* 39 (6):1145–61.

Akram-Lodhi, A. Haroon, and Cristobal Kay. 2010. "Surveying the Agrarian Question (Part 1): Unearthing Foundations, Exploring Diversity." *Journal of Peasant Studies* 37 (1):177–202.

Allina-Pisano, Jessica. 2004. "Land Reform and the Social Origins of Private Farmers in Russia and Ukraine." *Journal of Peasant Studies* 31 (3–4):489–514.

———. 2008. *The Post-Soviet Potemkin Village: Politics and Property Rights in the Black Earth.* Cambridge: Cambridge University Press.

Amelina, Maria. 2000. "Why Russian Peasants Remain in Collective Farms: A Household Perspective on Agricultural Restructuring." *Post-Soviet Geography and Economics* 41 (7):483–511.

Amsden, Alice. 1989. *Asia's Next Giant. South Korea and Late Industrialization.* Oxford: Oxford University Press.

———. 1994. "Why Isn't the Whole World Experimenting with the East Asian Model to Develop?: Review of the East Asian Miracle." *World Development* 22 (4):627–33.

Ang, Yuen Yuen. 2016. *How China Escaped the Poverty Trap.* Ithaca, NY: Cornell University Press.

Aoki, Masahiko. 1997. "Unintended Fit: Organizational Evolution and Government Design of Institutions in Japan." In *The Role of Government in East Asian Economic Development: Comparative Institutional Analysis*, edited by Masahiko Aoki, Hyung-Ki Kim, and Masahiro Okuno-Fujiwara, 233–53. New York: Clarendon Press.

Appel, Hilary, and Mitchell Orenstein. 2018. *From Triumph to Crisis: Neoliberal Economic Reform in Postcommunist Countries.* Cambridge: Cambridge University Press.

Applbaum, Kalman. 2005. "The Anthropology of Markets." In *A Handbook of Economic Anthropology*, edited by James G. Carrier, 275–89. Cheltenham, UK, and Northampton, MA: Edward Elgar.

Ashley, Caroline, and Simon Maxwell. 2001. "Rethinking Rural Development." *Development Policy Review* 19 (4):395–425.

Babb, Sarah L., and Alexander E. Kentikelenis. 2018. "International Financial Institutions as Agents of Neoliberalism." In *The SAGE Handbook of Neoliberalism*, edited by Damien Cahill, Melinda Cooper, Martijn Konings and David Primrose, 16–27. London: SAGE.

Bailey, Alastair, and Cornelia Suta. 2014. "Small Farming across the EU-27." *EuroChoices* 13 (1):26–27.

Banerjee, Abhijit V., Angus Deaton, Nora Lustig, Kenneth Rogoff, and Edward Hsu. 2006. *An Evaluation of World Bank Research, 1998–2005.* SSRN 2950327. Written September 24, 2006; posted April 12, 2017. https://dx.doi.org/10.2139/ssrn.2950327.

Barnett, Michael N., and Martha Finnemore. 1999. "The Politics, Power, and Pathologies of International Organizations." *International Organization* 53 (4):699–732.

————. 2004. *Rules for the World: International Organizations in World Politics.* Ithaca, NY: Cornell University Press.

Barros, Arthur do Nascimento Ferreira, Raimundo Nonato Rodrigues, and Luiz Panhoca. 2019. "Information on the Fight against Corruption and Corporate Governance Practices: Evidence of Organized Hypocrisy." *International Journal of Disclosure and Governance* 16 (2–3):145–60.

Bauer, Péter Tamás. 1976. *Dissent on Development.* Cambridge, MA: Harvard University Press.

————. 1981. *Equality, the Third World, and Economic Delusion.* Cambridge, MA: Harvard University Press.

Bazbauers, Adrian Robert. 2018. *The World Bank and Transferring Development.* Cham, CH: Springer.

Béland, Daniel, and Mitchell A. Orenstein. 2013. "International Organizations as Policy Actors: An Ideational Approach." *Global Social Policy* 13 (2):125–43.

Binswanger, Hans P. 1991. "Transcript of Interview with Hans Binswanger." In *World Bank History Project,* interviewers John Lewis, Richard Webb, and Devesh Kapur. Washington, DC: World Bank. https://oralhistory.worldbank .org/transcripts/transcript-oral-history-interview-hans-binswanger-held -october-17-1991.

Binswanger, Hans P., and Klaus Deininger. 1993. "South African Land Policy: The Legacy of History and Current Options." *World Development* 21 (9):1451–75.

Binswanger, Hans P., Klaus Deininger, and Gershon Feder. 1993. "Agricultural Land Relations in the Developing World." *American Journal of Agricultural Economics* 75 (5):1242–48.

————. 1995. "Power, Distortions, Revolt and Reform in Agricultural Land Relations." In *Handbook of Development Economics,* edited by Jere Behrman and T. N. Srinivasan, 2659–772. Amsterdam: Elsevier.

Binswanger, Hans P., and John McIntire. 1987. "Behavioral and Material Determinants of Production Relations in Land-Abundant Tropical Agriculture." *Economic Development and Cultural Change* 36 (1):73–99.

Binswanger, Hans P., and Mark R. Rosenzweig. 1986. "Behavioural and Material Determinants of Production Relations in Agriculture." *Journal of Development Studies* 22 (3):503–39.

Bíró Boróka, Júlia. 2015. *Locul și rolul fermelor mici în ruralul românesc și evoluția acestora sub impactul politicii agricole comune* (The place and role of small farms in Romania's rural landscape and their evolution in light of the Common Agricultural Policy). Bucharest: Editura ASE.

Bøås, Morten, and Desmond McNeill. 2003. *Multilateral Institutions: A Critical Introduction.* London: Pluto Press.

Bockman, Johanna. 2011. *Markets in the Name of Socialism*. Stanford, CA: Stanford University Press.

Bockman, Johanna, and Gil Eyal. 2002. "Eastern Europe as a Laboratory for Economic Knowledge: The Transnational Roots of Neoliberalism." *American Journal of Sociology* 108 (2):310–52. doi: 10.1086/344411.

Bogdan, Maria. 2017. "Suceava și Bacău, în topul celor mai mari crescători de bovine și păsări" (Suceava and Bacău rank highest among the largest growers of cattle and poultry). *Lumea satului*, August 16, 2017, 32–33. https://www.lumeasatului.ro/articole-revista/cresterea-animalelor/4052-suceava-si-bacau-in-topul-celor-mai-mari-crescatori-de-bovine-si-pasari.html.

Borras, Saturnino M. 2003. "Questioning Market-Led Agrarian Reform: Experiences from Brazil, Colombia and South Africa." *Journal of Agrarian Change* 3 (3):367–94.

Borras, Saturnino M., Jr., A. Haroon Akram-Lodhi, and Cristóbal Kay. 2007. "Agrarian Reform and Rural Development: Historical Overview and Current Issues." In *Land, Poverty and Livelihoods in an Era of Globalization. Perspectives from Developing and Transition Countries*, edited by A. Haroon Akram-Lodhi, Saturnino M. Borras Jr., and Cristóbal Kay, 1–40. London and New York: Routledge.

Bosc, Pierre-Marie, Julio A. Berdegué, M. Goïta, Jan Douwe van der Ploeg, Kae Sekine, and Linxiu Zhang. 2013. *Investing in Smallholder Agriculture for Food Security: A Report by the High Level Panel of Experts on Food Security and Nutrition*. Rome: FAO.

Bourdieu, Pierre. 2005. *The Social Structures of the Economy*. Cambridge: Polity.

Boyer, Robert. 2018. "Expectations, Narratives, and Socio-economic Regimes." In *Uncertain Futures: Imaginaries, Narratives, and Calculation in the Economy*, edited by Jens Beckert and Richard Bronk, 39–61. New York: Oxford University Press.

Brenner, Robert. 1976. "Agrarian Class Structure and Economic Development in Pre-industrial Europe." *Past & Present* 70 (1):30–75.

———. 1977. "The Origins of Capitalist Development: A Critique of Neo-Smithian Marxism." *New Left Review* 104:25.

Broad, Robin. 2006. "Research, Knowledge, and the Art of 'Paradigm Maintenance': The World Bank's Development Economics Vice-Presidency (DEC)." *Review of International Political Economy* 13 (3):387–419.

Brooks, Karen, and Mieke Meurs. 1994. "Romanian Land Reform: 1991–1993." *Comparative Economic Studies* 36 (2):17–32.

Broome, André, and Joel Quirk. 2015. "Governing the World at a Distance: The Practice of Global Benchmarking." *Review of International Studies* 41 (5):819–41.

Brunsson, Nils. 1993. "The Necessary Hypocrisy." *International Executive* 35 (1):1–9.

Buchowski, Michał. 2006. "The Specter of Orientalism in Europe: From Exotic Other to Stigmatized Brother." Social Thought & Commentary. *Anthropological Quarterly* 79 (3):463–82.

Burkitbayeva, Saule, and Johan Swinnen. 2018. "Smallholder Agriculture in Transition Economies." *Journal of Agrarian Change* 18 (4):882–92.

Burns, Sarah L., and Lukas Giessen. 2016. "Dismantling Comprehensive Forest Bureaucracies: Direct Access, the World Bank, Agricultural Interests, and Neoliberal Administrative Reform of Forest Policy in Argentina." *Society & Natural Resources* 29 (4):493–508.

Cammack, Paul. 2004. "What the World Bank Means by Poverty Reduction, and Why It Matters." *New Political Economy* 9 (2):189–211.

Centeno, Miguel Angel, and Alejandro Portes. 2006. "The Informal Economy in the Shadow of the State." In *Out of the Shadows: Political Action and the Informal Economy in Latin America*, edited by P. Fernández-Kelly and J. Shefner, 23–48. University Park: Pennsylvania State University Press.

Chayanov, Alexander V. 1966. *Peasant Farm Organization: The Theory of Peasant Economy*. Madison: University of Wisconsin Press.

Chen, Kevin Z., and Kostas G. Stamoulis. 2008. "The Changing Nature and Structure of Agri-Food Systems in Developing Countries: Beyond the Farm Gate." In *The Transformation of Agri-Food Systems*, edited by E. B. McCullough, P. I. Pingali, and K. G. Stamoulis, 167–82. London: Routledge.

Chen, Zhuo, Wallace E. Huffman, and Scott Rozelle. 2011. "Inverse Relationship between Productivity and Farm Size: The Case of China." *Contemporary Economic Policy* 29 (4):580–92.

Chenery, H., and M. Syrquin. 1975. *Patterns of Development, 1950–1970*. London: Oxford University Press.

Chenery, Hollis, Montek S. Ahluwalia, John H. Duloy, C. L. G. Bell, and Richard Jolly. 1974. *Redistribution with Growth; Policies to Improve Income Distribution in Developing Countries in the Context of Economic Growth*. Oxford: Oxford University Press.

Christoffersen, Leif. 2016. "Transcript of Oral History Interview with Leif Christoffersen." In *World Bank Group Archives*, Interviews on the McNamara Years (1968–1981), interviewed by John Heath. Washington, DC: World Bank. https://oralhistory.worldbank.org/transcripts/transcript-oral-history-interview-leif-christoffersen-held-october-12-2016.

Ciaian, Pavel, Jan Fałkowski, and K. d'Artis. 2012. "Access to Credit, Factor Allocation and Farm Productivity: Evidence from the CEE Transition Economies." *Agricultural Finance Review* 72 (1):22–47.

Clarke, Simon, Lena Varshavskaya, Sergei Alasheev, and Marina Karelina. 2000. "The Myth of the Urban Peasant." *Work, Employment and Society* 14 (3):481–99.

Cohn, Avery S., Peter Newton, Juliana D. B. Gil, Laura Kuhl, Leah Samberg, Vincent Ricciardi, Jessica R. Manly, and Sarah Northrop. 2017. "Smallholder Agriculture and Climate Change." *Annual Review of Environment and Resources* 42:347–75.

Connell, Raewyn, and Nour Dados. 2014. "Where in the World Does Neoliberalism Come From?" *Theory and Society* 43 (2):117–38.

Coulson, Andrew. 2014. "The Agrarian Question: The Scholarship of David Mitrany Revisited." *Journal of Peasant Studies* 41 (3):405–19.

Creed, Gerald W. 1998. *Domesticating Revolution: From Socialist Reform to Ambivalent Transition in a Bulgarian Village.* University Park: Penn State University Press.

Csaki, Csaba, and Zvi Lerman. 1993. "Land Reform and the Future Role of Cooperatives in Agriculture in the Former Socialist Countries in Europe." *Romania—revue trimestrielle consacrée à l'étude des langues et des littératures romanes* 41 (4):1–13.

———. 1997. *Land Reform in Ukraine: The First Five Years.* Washington, DC: World Bank.

Csaki, Csaba, Zvi Lerman, and Gershon Feder. 2002. *Land Policies and Evolving Farm Structures in Transition Countries.* Washington, DC: World Bank.

Curtis, Bruce, and Cate Curtis. 2011. *Social Research: A Practical Introduction.* London: Sage.

D'Amico, Simona. 2015. "Alternative Food Networks (AFNs) in Calabria: A Sociological Exploration of Interaction Dynamics." PhD diss., Wageningen University.

Darity, William A., Jr. 1980. "The Boserup Theory of Agricultural Growth: A Model for Anthropological Economics." *Journal of Development Economics* 7 (2):137–57.

Dasgupta, Biplab. 1997. "The New Political Economy: A Critical Analysis." *Economic and Political Weekly* 32 (4):PE13–26.

De Haan, Leo J. 2012. "The Livelihood Approach: A Critical Exploration." *Erdkunde* 66 (4):345–57.

De Janvry, Alain, and Elisabeth Sadoulet. 1989. "A Study in Resistance to Institutional Change: The Lost Game of Latin American Land Reform." *World Development* 17 (9):1397–407.

———. 2010. "Agricultural Growth and Poverty Reduction: Additional Evidence." *World Bank Research Observer* 25 (1):1–20.

De Soto, Hernando. 1989. *The Other Path.* New York: Harper & Row.

Deininger, Klaus W. 2003. *Land Policies for Growth and Poverty Reduction.* World Bank Policy Research Report. Oxford: Oxford University Press; Washington, DC: World Bank.

———. 2018. "For Billions without Formal Land Rights, the Tech Revolution Offers New Grounds for Hope." *Let's Talk Development*, March 15, 2018. http:// blogs.worldbank.org/developmenttalk/billions-without-formal-land-rights -tech-revolution-offers-new-grounds-hope.

Deininger, Klaus, and Hans P. Binswanger. 1999. "The Evolution of the World Bank's Land Policy: Principles, Experience, and Future Challenges." *World Bank Research Observer* 14 (2):247–76.

Deininger, Klaus, and Derek Byerlee. 2011. *Rising Global Interest in Farmland: Can It Yield Sustainable and Equitable Benefits?* Washington, DC: World Bank.

Deininger, Klaus, and Denys Nizalov. 2016. "26 Years of Land Reform: The Glass Is Half-Empty or Half-Full." *Vox Ukraine*, October 7, 2016. https://voxukraine .org/en/26-years-of-land-reform-en/.

Deininger, Klaus, Denys Nizalov, and Sudhir K. Singh. 2013. "Are Mega-farms the Future of Global Agriculture? Exploring the Farm Size-Productivity Relationship." World Bank Policy Research Working Paper no. 6544. Washington, DC: World Bank.

Demsetz, Harold. 1974 [1967]. "Toward a Theory of Property Rights." In *Classic Papers in Natural Resource Economics*, edited by Chennat Gopalakrishnan, 163–177. London: Palgrave Macmillan.

Díaz, Alejandro, Jorge A. Lacayo, and Luis Salcedo. 2007. "Selling to 'Mom-and-Pop' Stores in Emerging Markets." *McKinsey Quarterly* 2 (1):71–81.

Diaz, Ramon P. 1986. "Capitalism and Freedom in Latin America." Paper presented at International Symposium on Economic, Political, and Civil Freedom, Napa Valley, CA.

Dobrincu, Dorin. 2009. "Persuasion, Delay and Coercion. Late Collectivization in Northern Moldova: The Case of Darabani (Suceava Region)." In *Transforming Peasants, Property and Power: The Collectivization of Agriculture in Romania, 1949–1962*, edited by Constantin Iordachi and Dorin Dobrincu, 275–303. Budapest: Central European University Press.

Dollar, David. 2007. "Poverty, Inequality, and Social Disparities during China's Economic Reform." World Bank Working Paper. Washington, DC: World Bank.

———. 2008. "Lessons from China for Africa." World Bank Policy Research Working Paper. Washington, DC: World Bank.

Dorondel, Ştefan. 2016. *Disrupted Landscapes: State, Peasants and the Politics of Land in Postsocialist Romania*. New York and Oxford: Berghahn Books.

Dorondel, Ştefan, and S. Serban. 2014. "A Missing Link: The Agrarian Question in Southeast Europe." *Martor* 17 (2):288–307.

Dudwick, Nora, Karin Fock, and David J. Sedik. 2007. *Land Reform and Farm Restructuring in Transition Countries: The Experience of Bulgaria, Moldova, Azerbaijan, and Kazakhstan*. Washington, DC: World Bank.

Easterly, William. 2006. "Freedom versus Collectivism in Foreign Aid." In *Economic Freedom of the World: 2006 Annual Report*, by James D. Gwartney and Robert Lawson, 29–41. Vancouver, BC: Fraser Institute.

Eccles, Stephen D. 1994. "Transcript of Oral History Interview with Stephen Eccles Held on March 23, 1994." *World Bank Group Archives*, interviewed by Jochen Kraske. Washington, DC: World Bank. https://oralhistory.worldbank .org/transcripts/transcript-oral-history-interview-stephen-d-eccles-held-april -5-11-18-and-25-1995.

Edelman, Marc. 2013. "What Is a Peasant? What Are Peasantries? A Briefing Paper on Issues of Definition." Intergovernmental Working Group on a United Nations Declaration on the Rights of Peasants and Other People Working in Rural Areas, Geneva, July 15–19, 2013.

Ernst and Young. 2014. *Retail Market in Ukraine: Industry Trends.* https:// vibdoc.com/industry-trends-ey-5f0c2e9d9d7cb.html.

Escobar, Arturo. 1984. "Discourse and Power in Development: Michel Foucault and the Relevance of His Work to the Third World." *Alternatives* 10 (3):377–400.

———. 1995. *Encountering Development: The Making and Unmaking of the Third World.* Princeton, NJ: Princeton University Press.

European Commission. 2014. *The Economic Impact of Modern Retail on Choice and Innovation in the EU Food Sector.* Brussels: Publications Office of the European Union.

Eurostat. 2016. Farm Structure Survey. Database. https://ec.europa.eu/eurostat/ web/microdata/farm-structure-survey.

Feder, Gershon. 1985. "The Relation between Farm Size and Farm Productivity: The Role of Family Labor, Supervision and Credit Constraints." *Journal of Development Economics* 18 (2–3):297–313.

———. 1987. "Land Ownership Security and Farm Productivity: Evidence from Thailand." *Journal of Development Studies* 24 (1):16–30.

———. 1988. *Land Policies and Farm Productivity in Thailand.* Baltimore, MD: Johns Hopkins University Press.

Feder, Gershon, and David Feeny. 1991. "Land Tenure and Property Rights: Theory and Implications for Development Policy." *World Bank Economic Review* 5 (1):135–53.

Feder, Gershon, and Raymond Noronha. 1987. "Land Rights Systems and Agricultural Development in sub-Saharan Africa." *World Bank Research Observer* 2 (2):143–69.

Feeny, David H. 1984. "The Development of Property Rights in Land: A Comparative Study." Discussion paper. https://elischolar.library.yale.edu/egcenter -discussion-paper-series/467.

Feldbrugge, Ferdinand J. M. 1984. "Government and Shadow Economy in the Soviet Union." *Soviet Studies* 36 (4):528–43.

Ferguson, James. 1990. *The Anti-Politics Machine: "Development," Depoliticization and Bureaucratic Power in Lesotho.* Cambridge: Cambridge University Press.

Fligstein, Neil. 2001. *The Architecture of Markets: An Economic Sociology of Twenty-First-Century Capitalist Societies.* Princeton, NJ: Princeton University Press.

Fligstein, Neil, and Iona Mara-Drita. 1996. "How to Make a Market: Reflections on the Attempt to Create a Single Market in the European Union." *American Journal of Sociology* 102 (1):1–32.

Forrester, J., and F. Fischer. 1993. *The Argumentative Turn in Policy Analysis.* Durham, NC: Duke University Press.

Fox, Katy. 2011. *Peasants into European Farmers?: EU Integration in the Carpathian Mountains of Romania.* Münster: LIT Verlag.

Gaddy, Clifford G., and Barry William Ickes. 2002. *Russia's Virtual Economy.* Washington, DC: Brookings Institution Press.

Garcia-Parpet, Marie-France. 2008. "The Social Construction of a Perfect Market: The Strawberry Auction at Fontaines-en-Sologne." In *Do Economists Make Markets?*, edited by Donald MacKenzie, Fabian Muniesa and Lucia Siu, 20–53. Princeton, NJ: Princeton University Press.

Gardner, Bruce, and Zvi Lerman. 2006. "Agricultural Cooperative Enterprise in the Transition from Socialist Collective Farming." *Journal of Rural Cooperation* 34 (1):1–17.

Goldman, Michael. 2005. *Imperial Nature: The World Bank and Struggles for Social Justice in the Age of Globalization.* New Haven, CT: Yale University Press.

———. 2007. "How "Water for All!" Policy Became Hegemonic: The Power of the World Bank and Its Transnational Policy Networks." *Geoforum* 38 (5):786–800.

Griffin, Keith. 1979. *The Political Economy of Agrarian Change: An Essay on the Green Revolution.* London and Basingstoke: MacMillan.

Griffin, Keith, Azizur Rahman Khan, and Amy Ickowitz. 2004. "In Defence of Neo-classical Neo-populism." *Journal of Agrarian Change* 4 (3):361–86.

Grigg, David. 1979. "Ester Boserup's Theory of Agrarian Change: A Critical Review." *Progress in Human Geography* 3 (1):64–84.

Gulhati, Ravi. 1991. "Transcript of Oral History Interview with Ravi Gulhati Held on July 9, 1991." In *World Bank Oral History Program,* interviewed by Richard Webb and Devesh Kapur. Washington, DC: World Bank. https://oralhistory .worldbank.org/transcripts/transcript-oral-history-interview-ravi-gulhati -held-july-9-1991.

Güven, Ali Burak. 2012. "The IMF, the World Bank, and the Global Economic Crisis: Exploring Paradigm Continuity." *Development and Change* 43 (4):869–98.

Hagedorn, Konrad. 2014. "Post-Socialist Farmers' Cooperatives in Central and Eastern Europe." *Annals of Public and Cooperative Economics* 85 (4):555–77.

Hall, Peter A., and Michèle Lamont. 2013. *Social Resilience in the Neoliberal Era.* Cambridge: Cambridge University Press.

Hann, Chris M. 1993. "From Production to Property: Decollectivization and the Family-Land Relationship in Contemporary Hungary." *Man* 28 (2):299–320.

———. 2005. "Postsocialist Societies." In *A Handbook of Economic Anthropology,* edited by James G. Carrier, 547–58. Cheltenham, UK, and Northampton, MA: Edward Elgar.

Harberger, Arnold C. 1970. "Economic Policy Problems in Latin America: A Review." *Journal of Political Economy* 78 (4):1007–16.

Hart, Keith. 2006. "Bureaucratic Form and the Informal Economy." In *Linking the Formal and Informal Economy: Concepts and Policies,* edited by Basudeb Guha-Khasnobis, Ravi Kanbur, and Elinor Ostrom, 21–35. Oxford: Oxford University Press.

Hatos, Adrian. 2006. *Colectivism după colectivism? Forme asociative de organizare în agricultura românească de tranziție: 1990–2002* (Collectivism after collectivism: Associative organizational forms in Romanian transition agriculture: 1990-2002). Iași: Editura Lumen.

Heidhues, Franz, and Michael Brüntrup. 2003. "Subsistence Agriculture in Development: Its Role in Processes of Structural Change." In *Subsistence Agriculture in Central and Eastern Europe: How to Break the Vicious Circle?*, edited by Steffen Abele and Klaus Frohberg, 1–17. Halle (Saale): Leibniz-Institut für Agrarentwicklung in Mittel- und Osteuropa (IAMO).

Helfand, Steven M., and Matthew P. H. Taylor. 2020. "The Inverse Relationship between Farm Size and Productivity: Refocusing the Debate." *Food Policy* 99:101977.

Ho, Peter. 2014. "The 'Credibility Thesis' and Its Application to Property Rights: (In)Secure Land Tenure, Conflict and Social Welfare in China." *Land Use Policy,* 40:13–27.

Holovne upravlinnya statystyky u Chernivets′kiy oblasti. 2015. *Sil′s′ke hospodarstvo Chernivets′koi oblasti u 2015 rotsi* (Agriculture in the Chernivets′ka region in 2015). Chernivtsi: Holovne upravlinnya statystyky u Chernivets′kiy oblasti.

Homolar, Alexandra, and Pablo A. Rodríguez-Merino. 2019. "Making Sense of Terrorism: A Narrative Approach to the Study of Violent Events." *Critical Studies on Terrorism* 12 (4):561–81.

Hu, Angang, Linlin Hu, and Zhixiao Chang. 2005. "China's Economic Growth and Poverty Reduction (1978–2002)." In *India's and China's Recent Experience with Reform and Growth,* edited by Wanda Tseng and David Cowen, 59–90. London: Palgrave Macmillan.

Huang, Yasheng. 2012. "How Did China Take Off?" *Journal of Economic Perspectives* 26 (4):147–70.

Humphrey, Caroline. 1998. *Marx Went Away—But Karl Stayed Behind*. Ann Arbor: University of Michigan Press.

Iancu, Gheorghe. 2001. "Aspecte din procesul colectivizării în România (1949–1960)" (Aspects of the collectivisation process in Romania [1949–1960]). *Yearbook of "G. Barițiu" Institute of History* 15:205–30.

Jehlička, Petr, and Joe Smith. 2011. "An Unsustainable State: Contrasting Food Practices and State Policies in the Czech Republic." *Geoforum* 42 (3):362–72.

Johnson, Chalmers. 1999. "The Developmental State: Odyssey of a Concept." In *The Developmental State*, edited by Meredith Woo-Cumings, 32–60. Ithaca, NY: Cornell University Press.

Jones, Michael D., and Mark K. McBeth. 2010. "A Narrative Policy Framework: Clear Enough to Be Wrong?" *Policy Studies Journal* 38 (2):329–53.

Jonge, Huub de. 1993. "Credit, Trust and Knowledge: Middlemen and Commercialization on the Island of Madura." In *Commercialization and Market Formation in Developing Societies*, edited by Huub de Jonge and Willem Wolters, 116–39. Saarbrücken, DE: Breitenbach.

Kaplinsky, Raphael, and Mike Morris. 2000. *A Handbook for Value Chain Research*. Vol. 113. Sussex: University of Sussex, Institute of Development Studies.

Kapur, Devesh, John P. Lewis, and Richard C. Webb. 1997. *The World Bank: Its First Half Century*. Vol. 1. Washington, DC: Brookings Institution Press.

Keyzer, Michiel A., Max D. Merbis, Alex N. Halsema, Valeriy Heyets, Olena Borodina, and Ihor Prokopa. 2017. "Unlocking Ukraine's Production Potential." In *The Eurasian Wheat Belt and Food Security*, edited by Sergio Gomez y Paloma, Sébastien Mary, Stephen Langrell, and Pavel Ciaian, 141–54. Cham, CH: Springer.

Kideckel, David A. 1982. "The Socialist Transformation of Agriculture in a Romanian Commune, 1945–62." *American Ethnologist* 9 (2):320–40.

———. 1993. *The Solitude of Collectivism: Romanian Villagers to the Revolution and Beyond*. Ithaca, NY: Cornell University Press.

Kligman, Gail, and Katherine Verdery. 2011. *Peasants under Siege: The Collectivization of Romanian Agriculture, 1949–1962*. Princeton, NJ: Princeton University Press.

Knowles, Barbara. 2011. *Mountain Hay Meadows: The Romanian Context and the Effects of Policy on High Nature Value Farming*. London: Society of Biology.

Koester, Ulrich, and Ludwig Striewe. 1999. "Huge Potential, Huge Losses—The Search for Ways Out of the Dilemma of Ukrainian Agriculture." In *Ukraine at the Crossroads: Economic Reforms in International Perspective*, edited by Axel Siedenberg and Lutz Hoffman, 259–70. Heidelberg: Physica-Verlag.

Kostov, Philip, and John Lingard. 2002. "Subsistence Farming in Transitional Economies: Lessons from Bulgaria." *Journal of Rural Studies* 18 (1):83–94.

Krueger, Anne O. 1986. "Aid in the Development Process." *World Bank Research Observer* 1 (1):57–78.

Kuns, Brian. 2017. "Beyond Coping: Smallholder Intensification in Southern Ukraine." *Sociologia Ruralis* 57 (4):481–506.

Kurakin, A., A. Nikulin, and O. Visser. 2019. "Smallholders, Large Farm Enterprises and the State in Rural Russia: From Symbiosis to Corporate Social Responsibility?" *Canadian Journal of Development Studies* 40 (4):580–99.

Lahiff, Edward, Saturnino M Borras Jr., and Cristóbal Kay. 2007. "Market-Led Agrarian Reform: Policies, Performance and Prospects." *Third World Quarterly* 28 (8):1417–36.

Lardy, Nicholas R. 1983. *Agriculture in China's Modern Economic Development.* Cambridge: Cambridge University Press.

Lee, Joonkoo, Gary Gereffi, and Janet Beauvais. 2012. "Global Value Chains and Agrifood Standards: Challenges and Possibilities for Smallholders in Developing Countries." *Proceedings of the National Academy of Sciences* 109 (31):12326–31.

Lele, Uma. 2005. "Transcript of Oral History Interview with Uma Lele held on October 25 and 26, 2005." In *World Bank Group Archives*, interviewed by Marie T. Zenni. Washington, DC: World Bank. https://oralhistory.worldbank .org/transcripts/transcript-oral-history-interview-uma-lele-held-october-25 -and-26-2005.

Lerman, Zvi. 1998. "Does Land Reform Matter? Some Experiences from the Former Soviet Union." *European Review of Agricultural Economics* 25 (3): 307–30.

———. 2004. "Policies and Institutions for Commercialization of Subsistence Farms in Transition Countries." *Journal of Asian Economics* 15 (3):461–79.

———. 2006. "The Impact of Land Reform on Rural Household Incomes in Transcaucasia." *Eurasian Geography and Economics* 47 (1):112–23.

———. 2012. "Rural Livelihoods in Tajikistan: What Factors and Policies Influence the Income and Well-Being of Rural Families?" In *Rangeland Stewardship in Central Asia*, edited by Victor R. Squires, 165–87. Dordrecht: Springer.

———. 2017. "Privatisation and Changing Farm Structure in the Commonwealth of Independent States." In *The Eurasian Wheat Belt and Food Security*, edited by S. Gomez y Paloma, S. Mary, S. Langrell, and P. Ciaian, 15–32. Cham, CH: Springer.

Lerman, Zvi, and Dragoş Cimpoieş. 2006. "Land Consolidation as a Factor for Rural Development in Moldova." *Europe-Asia Studies* 58 (3):439–55.

Lerman, Zvi, and Pepijn Schreinemachers. 2005. "Individual Farming as a Labour Sink: Evidence from Poland and Russia." *Comparative Economic Studies* 47 (4):675–95.

Lerman, Zvi, and David Sedik. 2008. "The Economic Effects of Land Reform in Tajikistan." In *Policy Studies on Rural Transition*. Budapest: FAO Regional Office for Europe and Central Asia.

———. 2009. "Agrarian Reform in Kyrgyzstan: Achievements and the Unfinished Agenda." In *Policy Studies on Rural Transition*, no. 2009-1. Budapest: FAO Regional Office for Europe and Central Asia.

———. 2014. "Agricultural Cooperatives in Eurasia." Discussion paper. Jerusalem: Hebrew University of Jerusalem.

Lerman, Zvi, David Sedik, Nikolai Pugachov, and Aleksandr Goncharuk. 2007. *Rethinking Agricultural Reform in Ukraine*. Halle (Saale): Leibniz-Institut für Agrarentwicklung in Mittel- und Osteuropa (IAMO).

Lerman, Zvi, and William R. Sutton. 2008. "Productivity and Efficiency of Small and Large Farms in Transition: Evidence from Moldova." *Post-Soviet Affairs* 24 (2):97–120.

Li, Tania Murray. 2007. *The Will to Improve: Governmentality, Development, and the Practice of Politics*. Durham, NC: Duke University Press.

———. 2014. "Fixing Non-market Subjects: Governing Land and Population in the Global South." *Foucault Studies* (18):34–48.

Lin, Justin Yifu. 1988. "The Household Responsibility System in China's Agricultural Reform: A Theoretical and Empirical Study." *Economic Development and Cultural Change* 36 (S3):S199–224.

———. 1992. "Rural Reforms and Agricultural Growth in China." *American Economic Review* 82 (1):34–51.

Lipton, Michael. 1977. *Why Poor People Stay Poor: A Study of Urban Bias in World Development*. Canberra: Australian National University Press.

———. 1988. "Land Assets and Rural Poverty." In *World Bank Staff Working Papers*. Washington, DC: World Bank.

———. 2009. *Land Reform in Developing Countries: Property Rights and Property Wrongs*. New York and Abingdon: Routledge.

MacDonald, James M., Penni Korb, and Robert A. Hoppe. 2013. *Farm Size and the Organization of US Crop Farming*. Economic Research Report no. 152. Washington, DC: US Department of Agriculture. www.ers.usda.gov/publications/err-economic-research-report/err152.aspx.

Maloney, William F. 2003. "Informal Self-Employment: Poverty Trap or Decent Alternative?" In *Pathways Out of Poverty*, edited by G. Fields and G. Pfeffermann, 65–82. Dordrecht: Kluwer.

Mamonova, Natalia. 2015. "Resistance or Adaptation? Ukrainian Peasants' Responses to Large-Scale Land Acquisitions." *Journal of Peasant Studies* 42 (3–4):607–34.

Mayer, Frederick W. 2014. *Narrative Politics: Stories and Collective Action*. New York: Oxford University Press.

McCullough, Ellen B., Prabhu I. Pingali, and Kostas G. Stamoulis. 2010. "Small Farms and the Transformation of Food Systems: An Overview." In *Looking East, Looking West. Organic and Quality Food Marketing in Asia and Europe* edited by R. Haas, M. Canavari, B. Slee, C. Tong, and B. Anurugsa, 47–83. Wageningen: Wageningen Academic Publishers.

McMillan, John. 1994. *China's Nonconformist Reforms*. IGCC Policy Paper no. 11. San Diego: University of California Institute on Global Conflict and Cooperation. https://ideas.repec.org/p/cdl/globco/qt9cn9b13c.html.

Mikulcak, Friederike, Jamila L. Haider, David J. Abson, Jens Newig, and Joern Fischer. 2015. "Applying a Capitals Approach to Understand Rural Development Traps: A Case Study from Post-Socialist Romania." *Land Use Policy* 43:248–58.

Mincyte, Diana. 2011. "Subsistence and Sustainability in Post-Industrial Europe: The Politics of Small-Scale Farming in Europeanising Lithuania." *Sociologia Ruralis* 51 (2):101–18.

Ministry of Agrarian Policy and Food of Ukraine. 2007. *Derzhavna tsil'ova prohrama rozvitku ukrainskoho sela na period do 2015 roku* (Comprehensive state program for the development of the Ukrainian village until 2015). Kyiv: Ministry of Agrarian Policy and Food of Ukraine.

———. 2015. *Single and Comprehensive Strategy and Action Plan for Agriculture and Rural Development in Ukraine for 2015–2020*. Kyiv: Ministry of Agrarian Policy and Food of Ukraine.

Mitchell, Timothy. 2005. "The Work of Economics: How a Discipline Makes Its World." *European Journal of Sociology/Archives Européennes de Sociologie* 46 (2):297–320.

———. 2007. "The Properties of Markets." In *Do Economists Make Markets? On the Performativity of Economics*, edited by Donald MacKenzie, Fabian Muniesa, and Lucia Siu, 244–75. Princeton, NJ: Princeton University Press.

Mitrany, David. 1951. *Marx against the Peasant*. Chapel Hill: University of North Carolina Press.

Möllers, Judith, Thomas Herzfeld, Simone Piras, and Axel Wolz. 2016. "Structural Transformation of Moldovan Smallholder Agriculture: Implications for Poverty and Shared Prosperity." In *Moldova Poverty Assessment*, edited by World Bank Group. Washington, DC: World Bank Group.

Moore, Barrington. 1993 [1966]. *Social Origins of Dictatorship and Democracy: Lord and Peasant in the Making of the Modern World*. Boston: Beacon Press.

Mosher, Arthur T. 1969. "The Development of Subsistence Farmers: A Preliminary Review." In *Subsistence Agriculture: Concepts and Scope*, edited by Clifton R. Wharton, 6–11. Chicago: Aldine.

Mundy, Karen, and Francine Menashy. 2014. "The World Bank and Private Provision of Schooling: A Look through the Lens of Sociological Theories of Organizational Hypocrisy." *Comparative Education Review* 58 (3):401–27.

Nagayets, O. 2005. "Small Farms: Current Status and Key Trends. Information Brief Prepared for the Future of Small Farms Conference." The Future of Small Farms Conference, Wye College, Ashford, UK, June 26–29, 2005.

Naughton, Barry. 1995. *Growing Out of the Plan: Chinese Economic Reform, 1978–1993*. Cambridge: Cambridge University Press.

Nikulin, Alexander M. 2011. "From Post-Kolkhoz to Oligarkhoz." *RUDN Journal of Sociology* 11 (1):56–68.

———. 2012. "Rural Informal Economy in Post-Soviet Russia." *Economic Sociology: The European Electronic Newsletter* 13 (2):46–49.

Nivievskyi, Oleg. 2018. "Agroholdings Can Be Considered the Outcome of the Moratorium on Land Sales in Ukraine." Large Scale Agriculture. Leibniz Institute of Agricultural Development in Transition Economies (IAMO). https://www.largescaleagriculture.com/home/news-details/oleg-nivievskyi -agroholdings-can-be-considered-the-outcome-of-the-moratorium-on-land -sales-in-ukrai/.

North, Douglass C. 1989. "Institutions and Economic Growth: An Historical Introduction." *World Development* 17 (9):1319–32.

———. 1990. *Institutions, Institutional Change and Economic Performance*. Cambridge: Cambridge University Press.

North, Douglass C., and Robert Paul Thomas. 1973. *The Rise of the Western World: A New Economic History*. Cambridge: Cambridge University Press.

Nyberg, Albert, and Scott Rozelle. 1999. *Accelerating China's Rural Transformation*. Washington, DC: World Bank.

Organization for Economic Co-operation and Development. 2012. *Competitiveness and Private Sector Development: Ukraine 2011; Sector Competitiveness Strategy*. Paris: OECD.

Ost, David. 2005. *The Defeat of Solidarity: Anger and Politics in Postcommunist Europe*. Ithaca, NY: Cornell University Press.

Paiu, Florin. 2018. "Scădere dramatică a numărului de vaci crescute în județul Suceava" (Dramatic fall in cattle numbers in the Suceava County). *Monitorul de Suceava*, February 14, 2018. https://www.monitorulsv.ro/Local/2018-02 -14/Scadere-dramatica-a-numarului-de-vaci-crescute-in-judetul-Suceava.

Pallot, Judith, and T. G. Nefedova. 2007. *Russia's Unknown Agriculture: Household Production in Post-Communist Russia*. Oxford Geographical and Environmental Studies Series. Oxford; New York: Oxford University Press.

Pasieka, Agnieszka. 2012. "Resurrected Pigs, Dyed Foxes and Beloved Cows: Religious Diversity and Nostalgia for Socialism in Rural Poland." *Journal of Rural Studies* 28 (2):72–80.

Patrichi, Vasile. 2013. "Asociaţia Crescătorilor de Bovine pentru Carne" (The Association of Beef Cattle Growers). *Profitul agricol.* http://www.agrinet.ro/content.jsp?page=1181&language=1.

Peck, Jamie. 2010. *Constructions of Neoliberal Reason.* Oxford; New York: Oxford University Press.

Peet, Richard. 2009. *Unholy Trinity: The IMF, World Bank and WTO.* London: Zed Books.

Plank, Christina. 2013. "Land Grabs in the Black Earth: Ukrainian Oligarchs and International Investors." In *Land Concentration, Land Grabbing and People's Struggles in Europe,* edited by Jennifer Franco and Saturnino M. Borras Jr., ch. 12, 184–90. Amsterdam: Transnational Institute for European Coordination Via Campesina and Hands Off the Land Network. https://www.tni.org/files/download/land_in_europe_0.pdf#page=184.

Platteau, Jean-Philippe. 1996. "The Evolutionary Theory of Land Rights as Applied to Sub-Saharan Africa: A Critical Assessment." *Development and Change* 27 (1):29–86.

Plehwe, Dieter. 2007. "A Global Knowledge Bank? The World Bank and Bottom-Up Efforts to Reinforce Neoliberal Development Perspectives in the Post-Washington Consensus Era." *Globalizations* 4 (4):514–28.

———. 2015. "The Origins of the Neoliberal Economic Development Discourse." In *The Road from Mont Pelerin: The Making of the Neoliberal Thought Collective,* edited by Philip Mirowski and Dieter Plehwe, 238–79. Cambridge, MA: Harvard University Press.

Podolny, Joel M. 1993. "A Status-Based Model of Market Competition." *American Journal of Sociology* 98 (4):829–72.

Portes, Alejandro, and Richard Schauffler. 1993. "Competing Perspectives on the Latin American Informal Sector." *Population and Development Review* 19 (1):33–60.

Potori, Norbert, Paweł Chmieliński, and Bożena Karwat-Wózniak. 2014. "A Comparison of the Agro-Food Sectors in Poland and Hungary from a Macro Perspective." In *Structural Changes in Polish and Hungarian Agriculture since EU Accession: Lessons Learned and Implications for the Design of Future Agricultural Policies,* edited by Norbert Potori, Paweł Chmieliński, and Andrew Fieldsend, 9–33. Budapest: Research Institute of Agricultural Economics.

Presidential Commission for Agricultural Development Policies. 2013. *Cadrul naţional strategic pentru dezvoltarea durabilă a sectorului agroalimentar şi a spațiului rural în perioada 2014-2020-2030* (National strategy framework for the sustainable development of the agrifood sector and of rural areas for 2014-2020-2030). Bucharest: The Romanian Academy.

Provost, Claire, and Matt Kennard. 2015. "Lidl Has Received Almost $1bn in Public Development Funding." *Guardian*, July 2, 2015. https://www.theguardian .com/business/2015/jul/02/lidl-1bn-public-development-funding -supermarket-world-bank-eastern-europe.

Putterman, Louis G. 1993. *Continuity and Change in China's Rural Development: Collective and Reform Eras in Perspective.* Oxford: Oxford University Press on Demand.

Rapsomanikis, George. 2015. *The Economic Lives of Smallholder Farmers: An Analysis Based on Household Data from Nine Countries.* Rome: Food and Agriculture Organization of the United Nations.

Ravallion, Martin. 2009. "Are There Lessons for Africa from China's Success against Poverty?" *World Development* 37 (2):303–13.

———. 2011. "A Comparative Perspective on Poverty Reduction in Brazil, China, and India." *World Bank Research Observer* 26 (1):71–104.

Ravallion, Martin, and Shaohua Chen. 2004. "China's (Uneven) Progress against Poverty." Policy Research Working Paper no. 3408. Washington, DC: World Bank. https://openknowledge.worldbank.org/handle/10986/14241/.

Ravallion, Martin, and Dominique Van De Walle. 2008. "Land and Poverty in Reforming East Asia." *Finance and Development* 45 (3):38–41.

Reardon, Thomas, Christopher B. Barrett, Julio A Berdegué, and Johan F. M. Swinnen. 2009. "Agrifood Industry Transformation and Small Farmers in Developing Countries." *World Development* 37 (11):1717–27.

Reardon, Thomas, C. Peter Timmer, Christopher B. Barrett, and Julio Berdegué. 2003. "The Rise of Supermarkets in Africa, Asia, and Latin America." *American Journal of Agricultural Economics* 85 (5):1140–46.

Reutlinger, Shlomo. 1987. "Poverty and Malnutrition Consequences of Structural Adjustment: World Bank Policy." *Food and Nutrition Bulletin* 9 (1):1–4.

Rich, Bruce. 1994. *Mortgaging the Earth: World Bank, Environmental Impoverishment and the Crisis of Development.* London: Routledge.

Ries, Nancy. 2009. "Potato Ontology: Surviving Postsocialism in Russia." *Cultural Anthropology* 24 (2):181–212.

Rodrik, Dani. 2008. "Second-Best Institutions." *American Economic Review* 98 (2):100–104.

Roger, Antoine. 2014. "'Romanian Peasants' into 'European Farmers'? Using Statistics to Standardize Agriculture." *Development and Change* 45 (4):732–52.

———. 2016. "Power in the Field: Explaining the Legitimisation of Large-Scale Farming in Romania." *Sociologia Ruralis* 56 (2):311–28.

Romanian Ministry of Agriculture and Rural Development. 2008. *National Rural Development Programme 2007–2013*. Bucharest: Ministry of Agriculture and Rural Development.

———. 2014. *Programul naţional de dezvoltare rurală* (National Rural Development Program 2014–2020). Bucharest: Ministry of Agriculture and Rural Development.

Romanian National Statistics Institute. 2011. *Laptele reprezintă o problemă socială în România* (Milk represents a social problem in Romania). Bucharest: National Statistics Institute.

Rona-Tas, Akos. 1994. "The First Shall Be Last? Entrepreneurship and Communist Cadres in the Transition from Socialism." *American Journal of Sociology* 100 (1):40.

Sabates-Wheeler, Rachel. 2002. "Farm Strategy, Self-Selection and Productivity: Can Small Farming Groups Offer Production Benefits to Farmers in Post-Socialist Romania?" *World Development* 30 (10):1737–53.

Sachs, Jeffrey, and Wing Thye Woo. 2001. "Understanding China's Economic Performance." *Journal of Policy Reform* 4 (1):1–50. doi: 10.1080/13841280008523412.

Samberg, Leah H., James S. Gerber, Navin Ramankutty, Mario Herrero, and Paul C. West. 2016. "Subnational Distribution of Average Farm Size and Smallholder Contributions to Global Food Production." *Environmental Research Letters* 11 (12):124010.

Sarna, Arkadiusz. 2014. "The Transformation of Agriculture in Ukraine: From Collective Farms to Agro-Holdings." OSW Commentary, Centre for Eastern Studies, July 2, 2014. https://www.osw.waw.pl/en/publikacje/osw-commentary/2014-02-07/transformation-agriculture-ukraine-collective-farms-to.

Sarris, Alexander H, Tomas Doucha, and Erik Mathijs. 1999. "Agricultural Restructuring in Central and Eastern Europe: Implications for Competitiveness and Rural Development." *European Review of Agricultural Economics* 26 (3):305–29.

Satana, Suha, Mika-Petteri Törhönen, and Gavin Adlington. 2014. "Economic Impact of 20 Years of ECA Land Registration Projects." Annual World Bank Conference on Land and Poverty, Washington DC.

Sato, Hiroshi. 2003. *The Growth of Market Relations in Post-Reform Rural China: A Micro-analysis of Peasants, Migrants and Peasant Entrepreneurs*. London and New York: Routledge.

Schultz, Theodore William. 1964. *Transforming Traditional Agriculture*. New Haven, CT: Yale University Press.

Scott, James C. 1972. "Patron-Client Politics and Political Change in Southeast Asia." *American Political Science Review* 66 (1):91–113.

———. 1977. *The Moral Economy of the Peasant: Rebellion and Subsistence in Southeast Asia.* New Haven, CT: Yale University Press.

———. 1998. *Seeing Like a State: How Certain Schemes to Improve the Human Condition Have Failed.* New Haven, CT: Yale University Press.

———. 2015. *How Grains Domesticated Us.* London: SOAS Food Studies Centre.

Selbin, Eric. 2013. *Revolution, Rebellion, Resistance: The Power of Story.* London: Zed Books.

Şerban, Adela, and Alina Juravle. 2012. "The Romanian Rural Areas in the Context of European Development Strategies." *Revista Română de Sociologie* 23 (3–4):265–81.

Shandra, John M, Heidi Rademacher, and Carolyn Coburn. 2016. "The World Bank and Organized Hypocrisy? A Cross-National Analysis of Structural Adjustment and Forest Loss." *Environmental Sociology* 2 (2):192–207.

Shanin, Teodor. 1966. "The Peasantry as a Political Factor." *Sociological Review* 14 (1):5–27.

———. 1982. "Defining Peasants: Conceptualisations and De-conceptualisations: Old and New in a Marxist Debate." *Sociological Review* 30 (3):407–32.

Shleifer, Andrei. 2009. "Peter Bauer and the Failure of Foreign Aid." *Cato Journal* 29 (3):379–90.

Sicular, Terry. 1988. "Plan and Market in China's Agricultural Commerce." *Journal of Political Economy* 96 (2):283–307.

———. 1995. "Redefining State, Plan and Market: China's Reforms in Agricultural Commerce." *China Quarterly* 144:1020–46.

Skinner, G. William. 1985. "Rural Marketing in China: Repression and Revival." *China Quarterly* 103 (September 1985):393–413.

Skocpol, Theda. 1979. *States and Social Revolutions: A Comparative Analysis of France, Russia, and China.* Cambridge and New York: Cambridge University Press.

Slobodian, Quinn 2019. "Democracy Doesn't Matter to the Defenders of 'Economic Freedom.'" *Guardian*, November 11, 2019. https://www.theguardian.com/commentisfree/2019/nov/11/democracy-defenders-economic-freedom-neoliberalism.

Smith, Adrian, and Alena Rochovská. 2007. "Domesticating Neo-Liberalism: Everyday Lives and the Geographies of Post-Socialist Transformations." *Geoforum* 38 (6):1163–78.

Smith, Joe, and Petr Jehlička. 2013. "Quiet Sustainability: Fertile Lessons from Europe's Productive Gardeners." *Journal of Rural Studies* 32:148–57.

Smith, Joe, Tomáš Kostelecký, and Petr Jehlička. 2015. "Quietly Does It: Questioning Assumptions about Class, Sustainability and Consumption." *Geoforum* 67:223–32.

Somers, Margaret R., and Fred Block. 2005. "From Poverty to Perversity: Ideas, Markets, and Institutions over 200 Years of Welfare Debate." *American Sociological Review* 70 (2):260–87.

Souchon, Pierre. 2014. "Back to the Land in Romania." *Le Monde Diplomatique*, February 2014. https://mondediplo.com/2014/02/09romania.

Soulsby, Anna, and Ed Clark. 2007. "Organization Theory and the Post-Socialist Transformation: Contributions to Organizational Knowledge." *Human Relations* 60 (10):1419–42.

Southworth, Caleb. 2006. "The Dacha Debate: Household Agriculture and Labor Markets in Post-Socialist Russia." *Rural Sociology* 71 (3):451–78.

Spoor, Max, and Oane Visser. 2001. "The State of Agrarian Reform in the Former Soviet Union." *Europe-Asia Studies* 53 (6):885–901.

State, D. 2015. "Câți fermieri vor primi subvenții în acest an" (How many farmers will receives subventions this year). *Capital Online*, July 15, 2015. http://www.capital.ro/cati-fermieri-vor-primi-subventii-in-acest-an.html.

Stein, Howard. 2008. *Beyond the World Bank Agenda: An Institutional Approach to Development.* Chicago: University of Chicago Press.

Stern, Ernest. 1995. "Transcript of Oral History Interview with Ernest Stern Held on December 16 and 29, 1994, and January 5, 1995: Third Interview Session." In *World Bank Group Historian's Office*, interviewed by Jochen Kraske, Louis Galambos, and David Milobsky. Washington, DC: World Bank. https://oralhistory.worldbank.org/transcripts/transcript-oral-history-interview-ernest-stern-held-december-16-and-29-1994-and-january.

Stone, Deborah A. 2002. *Policy Paradox: The Art of Political Decision Making.* 3rd ed. New York: W. W. Norton.

Stone, Diane. 2012. "'Shades of Grey': The World Bank, Knowledge Networks and Linked Ecologies of Academic Engagement." *Global Networks* 13 (2):241–60.

Stone, Randall W. 2002. *Lending Credibility: The International Monetary Fund and the Post-Communist Transition.* Princeton, NJ: Princeton University Press.

Strassmann, W Paul. 1976. "Development Economics from a Chicago Perspective." *Journal of Economic Issues* 10 (1):63–80.

Swain, N. 2013. *Green Barons, Force-of-Circumstance Entrepreneurs, Impotent Mayors: Rural Change in the Early Years of Post-Socialist Capitalist Democracy.* Budapest: Central University Press.

Swinnen, Johan F. M. 1999. "The Political Economy of Land Reform Choices in Central and Eastern Europe." *Economics of Transition* 7 (3):637–64.

———. 2005. "Agricultural Transformation: Lessons from Experience: Simon Brand Memorial Lecture." *Agrekon* 44 (1):17–36.

Swinnen, Johan F. M., and Hamish R. Gow. 1999. "Agricultural Credit Problems and Policies during the Transition to a Market Economy in Central and Eastern Europe." *Food Policy* 24 (1):21–47.

Swinnen, Johan F. M., and Scott Rozelle. 2006. *From Marx and Mao to the Market: The Economics and Politics of Agricultural Transition*. Oxford: Oxford University Press.

Swinnen, Johan F. M., Anneleen Vandeplas, and Miet Maertens. 2010. "Liberalization, Endogenous Institutions, and Growth: A Comparative Analysis of Agricultural Reforms in Africa, Asia, and Europe." *World Bank Economic Review* 24 (3):412–45.

Szelenyi, Ivan. 1988. *Socialist Entrepreneurs: Embourgeoisement in Rural Hungary*. Madison: University of Wisconsin Press.

———, ed. 2002. *Privatizing the Land: Rural Political Economy in Post-Communist and Socialist Societies*. London: Routledge.

Thompson, Sarahelen. 1993. "Agrarian Reform in Eastern Europe following World War I: Motives and Outcomes." *American Journal of Agricultural Economics* 75 (3):840–44.

Tudor, Monica Mihaela. 2015. "Small Scale Agriculture as a Resilient System in Rural Romania." *Studies in Agricultural Economics* 117 (1):27–34.

Turner, Benjamin L., and Marina Fischer-Kowalski. 2010. "Ester Boserup: An Interdisciplinary Visionary Relevant for Sustainability." *Proceedings of the National Academy of Sciences* 107 (51):21963–65.

Ukrstat. 2018. *Agriculture of Ukraine. Statistical Yearbook*. Kyiv: State Statistics Office of Ukraine.

———. 2021. *2020—Agriculture of Ukraine. Statistical Publication*. Kyiv: State Statistics Service of Ukraine.

van der Ploeg, Jan Douwe. 2008. *The New Peasantries: Struggles for Autonomy and Sustainability in an Era of Empire and Globalization*. London: Earthscan.

———. 2010. "The Peasantries of the Twenty-First Century: The Commoditisation Debate Revisited." *Journal of Peasant Studies* 37 (1):1–30.

Van Meurs, Wim. 1999. "Land Reform in Romania—A Never-Ending Story." *SEER (South-east Europe Review) for Labour and Social Affairs* (02):109–22.

Varga, Mihai. 2011. "An Anatomy of 'Collective Anti-Collectivism': Labor Sociology in Ukraine and Romania." *Global Labour Journal* 2 (1):43–63.

———. 2015. "Value Chains or Social Capital? Producer Organizations in the Citrus Fruit Sector." *International Journal of Sociology of Agriculture and Food* 22 (2):85–103.

———. 2016. "Small Farms' Survival and Growth: Making Investments Despite Credit Constraints." *Sociologia Ruralis* 57 (S1):641–60.

———. 2017. "Cash Rather Than Contract: The Re-emergence of Traditional Agrifood Chains in Post-Communist Europe." *Journal of Rural Studies* 53:58–67.

———. 2018. "'Subsistence' Readings: World Bank and State Approaches to Commercialising Agriculture in Post-Communist Eurasia." *Journal of Development Studies* 55 (6):1253–1266.

———. 2019. "Resistant to Change? Smallholder Response to World Bank-Sponsored 'Commercialisation' in Romania and Ukraine." *Canadian Journal of Development Studies/Revue canadienne d'études du développement* 40 (4):528–45.

———. 2020. "Poverty Reduction through Land Transfers? The World Bank's Titling Reforms and the Making of 'Subsistence' Agriculture." *World Development* 135 (November 2020), article 105058. doi: 10.1016/j.worlddev.2020 .105058.

Verdery, Katherine. 2003. *The Vanishing Hectare: Property and Value in Postsocialist Transylvania, Culture and Society after Socialism*. Ithaca, NY: Cornell University Press.

Viola, Lynne. 1987. *The Best Sons of the Fatherland: Workers in the Vanguard of Soviet Collectivization*. New York: Oxford University Press.

Viola, Lynne, V. P. Danilov, N. A. Ivnitskii, and Denis Kozlov, eds. 2005. *The War against the Peasantry, 1927–1930: The Tragedy of the Soviet Countryside*. New Haven, CT: Yale University Press.

Visser, Oane. 2009. "Household Plots and Their Symbiosis with Large Farms Enterprises in Russia." In *The Political Economy of Rural Livelihoods in Transition Economies*, edited by Max Spoor, 76–98. London and New York: Routledge.

Visser, Oane, Natalia Mamonova, Max Spoor, and Alexander Nikulin. 2015. "'Quiet Food Sovereignty' as Food Sovereignty without a Movement? Insights from Post-Socialist Russia." *Globalizations* 12 (4):513–28.

Vitenko, Mykola. 2013. "Zavershal'nyi etap ta osnovni naslidky kolektivizatsii na teritorii zakhidnykh oblastey URSR (1948–1953 rr.)" (The final stage and the main consequences of collectivization in the Western regions of the Ukrainian SSR, [1948–1953]). *Visnyk Prykarpats'koho Universytetu* (23–24):125–30.

von Braun, Joachim, and Daniela Lohlein. 2003. "Policy Options to Overcome Subsistence Agriculture in the CEECs." In *Subsistence Agriculture in Central and Eastern Europe: How to Break the Vicious Circle*, edited by Steffen Abele and Klaus Frohberg, 46–70. Halle (Saale): IAMO.

von Braun, Joachim, and Alisher Mirzabaev. 2015. "Small Farms: Changing Structures and Roles in Economic Development." October 1, 2015. https://ssrn .com/abstract=2672900.

von Cramon-Taubadel, Stephan, and Sergiy Zorya. 2001. "Agricultural Policy Reform in Ukraine. Sequencing and Results." In *Policies and Agricultural Development in Ukraine*, edited by Stephan von Cramon-Taubadel, Sergiy Zorya and Ludwig Striewe, 20–31. Aachen: Shaker.

Vorley, Bill. 2007. "Supermarkets and Agri-Food Supply Chains in Europe: Partnership and Protest." In *Supermarkets and Agri-Food Supply Chains: Transformations in the Production and Consumption of Foods*, edited by D. Burch and G. Lawrence, 243–67. Cheltenham: Edward Elgar.

Wade, Robert Hunter. 1996. "Japan, the World Bank, and the Art of Paradigm Maintenance: The East Asian Miracle in Political Perspective." *New Left Review* 217 (1):3–37.

———. 2002. "US Hegemony and the World Bank: The Fight over People and Ideas." *Review of International Political Economy* 9 (2):215–43.

Wädekin, Karl Eugen. 1973. *The Private Sector in Soviet Agriculture*. Berkeley: University of California Press.

Walker, Michael A., ed. 1988. *Freedom, Democracy and Economic Welfare*. Vancouver: The Fraser Institute.

Wapenhans, Willi. 1991. "Transcript of Oral History Interview with Willi Wapenhans Held on September 6, 1991." In *World Bank History Project*, interviewed by John Lewis, Richard Webb and Devesh Kapur. Washington, DC: World Bank. https://oralhistory.worldbank.org/transcripts/transcript-oral-history -interview-willi-wapenhans-held-september-6-1991.

Weaver, Catherine. 2007. "The World's Bank and the Bank's World." *Global Governance*:493–512.

———. 2008. *Hypocrisy Trap: The World Bank and the Poverty of Reform*. Princeton, NJ: Princeton University Press.

Weber, Isabella. 2020. "Origins of China's Contested Relation with Neoliberalism: Economics, the World Bank, and Milton Friedman at the Dawn of Reform." *Global Perspectives* 1 (1):12271.

Wegren, Stephen. 1998. *Land Reform in the Former Soviet Union and Eastern Europe*. London and New York: Routledge.

———. 2005. *The Moral Economy Reconsidered: Russia's Search for Agrarian Capitalism*. New York: Palgrave Macmillan.

White, Harrison C. 1981. "Where Do Markets Come From?" *American Journal of Sociology* 87 (3):517–47.

———. 2002. *Markets from Networks: Socioeconomic Models of Production*. Princeton, NJ: Princeton University Press.

Wolf, Martin. 2019. "Ernest Stern, Economist, 1933–2019." *Financial Times*, June 27, 2019. https://www.ft.com/content/5b0c17f6-975d-11e9-9573-ee5cbb 98ed36.

Wolford, Wendy. 2016. "State-Society Dynamics in Contemporary Brazilian Land Reform." *Latin American Perspectives* 43 (2):77–95.

Woods, Ngaire. 2006. *The Globalizers: The IMF, the World Bank, and Their Borrowers*. Ithaca, NY: Cornell University Press.

Working Group on Poverty Reduction—Tajikistan. 2000. *Interim Poverty Reduction Strategy Paper*. Dushanbe: Government of the Republic of Tajikistan and the World Bank.

World Bank. 1975. *Land Reform*. Sector Policy Paper. Washington, DC: World Bank.

———. 1982. *World Development Report 1982*. New York: Oxford University Press.

———. 1994. *Romania—Agricultural Projects*. Washington, DC: World Bank.

———. 1996. *Ukraine—Country Assistance Strategy*. Washington, DC: World Bank.

———. 1998. *Proposed Structural Adjustment Credit to the Republic of Tajikistan*. Washington, DC: World Bank.

———. 1999. *Moldova—Poverty Assessment*. A World Bank Country Study. Washington, DC: World Bank.

———. 2000a. *Second Structural Adjustment Loan to the Republic of Moldova*. Washington, DC: World Bank.

———. 2000b. *Tajikistan—Poverty Assessment*. Washington, DC: World Bank.

———. 2003a. *Romania—Poverty Assessment*. Washington, DC: World Bank.

———. 2003b. *Ukraine—Country Assistance Strategy*. Washington, DC: World Bank.

———. 2004a. *Achieving Ukraine's Agricultural Potential. Stimulating Agricultural Growth and Improving Rural Life*. Washington, DC: World Bank.

———. 2004b. *Implementation Completion Report for a Structural Adjustment Credit to the Republic of Tajikistan*. Washington, DC: World Bank.

———. 2005. *Ukraine—Poverty Assessment: Poverty and Inequality in a Growing Economy*. Washington, DC: World Bank.

———. 2006. *Romania—Farm Restructuring Project*. Washington, DC: World Bank.

———. 2007. *World Development Report 2008: Agriculture for Development*. New York: Oxford University Press.

———. 2008. "Romanian Food and Agriculture from a European Perspective." In *SDN ESW Results Story*, edited by World Bank. Washington, DC: World Bank.

———. 2012. *Agricultural Competitiveness Report—Moldova*. Washington, DC: World Bank.

———. 2014. *Tajikistan—Agriculture Commercialization Project*. Washington, DC: World Bank.

———. 2015. *Increasing Access to Finance for Ukrainian Farmers*. Washington, DC: World Bank.

Xenos, Nicholas. 1987. "IV. Liberalism and the Postulate of Scarcity." *Political Theory* 15 (2):225–43.

Yefimov, Vladimir. 2003. "Agrarian Reform and Subsistence Agriculture in Russia." In *Subsistence Agriculture in Central and Eastern Europe: How to Break the Vicious Circle?*, edited by Steffen Abele and Klaus Frohberg, 161–78. Halle (Saale): Leibniz Institute of Agricultural Development in Transition Economies.

Yudelman, Montague. 1986. "Transcript of Oral History Interview with Montague Yudelman," July 18, 1986. In *World Bank Archives*, interviewed by Robert Oliver. Washington, DC: World Bank. https://oralhistory.worldbank.org/transcripts/transcript-oral-history-interview-montague-yudelman-held-july-18-1986.

———. 1991. "Transcript of Oral History Interview with Montague Yudelman Held on September 12, 1991." In *World Bank History Project*, interviewed by John Lewis and Devesh Kapur. Washington, DC: World Bank. https://oralhistory.worldbank.org/transcripts/transcript-oral-history-interview-montague-yudelman-held-september-12-1991.

Žižek, Slavoj. 1991. "The Totalitarian Invitation to Enjoyment." *Qui Parle* 5 (1):73–100.

Zorya, Sergiy. 2003. "Interdependencies between Agriculture and Macroeconomics in Ukraine." PhD diss., Georg-August-University of Göttingen.

Index

Printed and bound by CPI Group (UK) Ltd, Croydon, CR0 4YY

16/04/2025

14658399-0002